Madness or Knowing the Unbearable Truth

Madness or Knowing the Unbearable Truth offers readers a narrative of the relationship between a therapist and her patient who desperately wants to discover her past. With no memory and no way of knowing what was real, her long therapeutic journey was to last 26 years, half her lifetime. Her only reality was the life she lived in the presence of her therapist. The narrative unfolds to reveal a story of horrific events that must be hidden, yet can no longer be kept secret. It sheds light on how chronic long-term traumatisation within a closed family circle can create madness in a vulnerable and lonely child, and helps the reader gain an understanding of the enigmatic phenomena of Dissociated Identity Disorder.

Having been terrorized into silence, destroying her ability to use language in a house of secrets and lies, the therapy reveals how this patient struggles to come out of her autistic-like state in search of ways to find her past, her "self" and her voice. In this struggle, the reader becomes an audience exposed to the birth of dissociative personae who come forth to tell her story. As language slowly unfolds, she begins to share a first-hand account, albeit in written form, of the most complex psychological forces involved in a victim of incest who simultaneously loves, hates and is terrorized by her lover–father.

Through live vignettes, it demonstrates how external violence can create inner violence that threatens to annihilate the soul, leaving only a body to survive. The book provides an original contribution to our understanding of the complex psychological forces involved in incest, featuring the patient's own, coherent written texts, mediated by her therapist. The former's remarkable insights represent essential reading for all readers involved in policy development for the protection of children at high risk of suffering abuse.

Tova Zaltz is a clinical psychologist and a psychoanalyst, member of the Tel Aviv Institute of Contemporary Psychoanalysis, with a private practice near Jerusalem, where she works with people of all ages. She has treated and supervised individuals, groups and staff in private and public institutions, including children with learning difficulties, high-risk families, as well as bereaved families. Tova has extensive experience in the development of psychoanalytic thinking within educational systems.

"This is a most striking account where different phases and happenings are recorded not in the mind but in bodily formations. For any therapist working with bizarre forms of psychosis this is an inspiring book."
—**Neville Symington**, author, *Narcissism: A New Theory, The Making of a Psychotherapist, Becoming a Person through Psycho-Analysis* and co-author of *The Clinical Thinking of Wilfred Bion* (Routledge)

"This stunning book is destined to become a classic. The story of this patient's journey is gripping, touching and overwhelming as it probes various depths of the most profound suffering in the face of ultimate human cruelty, the patient's brilliantly creative – bordering on and including deranged – psychological strategies of survival, and the exquisite sensitivity of the therapist to unconscious processes along with deep caring and respect for her patient."
—**Israel W. Charny**, PhD, author, *Psychotherapy for a Democratic Mind: Treatment of Intimacy, Tragedy, Violence and Evil*

"What a wonderful book Tova Zaltz has written. A detailed portrayal of a twenty year journey in therapy engaging madness within and madness without. Profound engagement with psychic reality opened doors of violent abuse in childhood mirrored by the patient's aggression turned against herself. This book is packed with rich psychological themes expressed in moment to moment interaction. One comes through, with Tova and her patient, challenges of working together and the need to grow."
—**Michael Eigen**, PhD, author, *Faith, Contact with the Depths,* and *The Challenge of Being Human*

"This is a rare book – I am not aware of any other that provides a detailed and respectful clinical account of a twenty-six year psychoanalytic treatment of a woman with Dissociative Identity Disorder. This is written by a brave and significant newcomer to the field with lyrical and painful openness and rigour who has honed her understanding through the encounter and fulfils the wish of the patient to be remembered."
—**Valerie Sinason**, PhD, MACP, MInstPsychoanal, Founder Director Clinic for Dissociative Studies, 2016 ISSTD Lifetime Achievement Award

Madness or Knowing the Unbearable Truth

A Psychoanalytic Journey in Search of Sanity

Tova Zaltz

LONDON AND NEW YORK

First published 2019
by Routledge
2 Park Square, Milton Park, Abingdon, Oxon OX14 4RN

and by Routledge
52 Vanderbilt Avenue, New York, NY 10017

Routledge is an imprint of the Taylor & Francis Group, an informa business

© 2019 Tova Zaltz

The right of Tova Zaltz to be identified as author of this work has been asserted by her in accordance with sections 77 and 78 of the Copyright, Designs and Patents Act 1988.

All rights reserved. No part of this book may be reprinted or reproduced or utilised in any form or by any electronic, mechanical, or other means, now known or hereafter invented, including photocopying and recording, or in any information storage or retrieval system, without permission in writing from the publishers.

Trademark notice: Product or corporate names may be trademarks or registered trademarks, and are used only for identification and explanation without intent to infringe.

British Library Cataloguing in Publication Data
A catalogue record for this book is available from the British Library

Library of Congress Cataloging in Publication Data
Names: Zaltz, Tova, author.
Title: Madness or knowing the unbearable truth : a psychoanalytic journey in search of sanity / Tova Zaltz.
Description: Abingdon, Oxon ; New York, NY : Routledge, 2018. | Includes bibliographical references.
Identifiers: LCCN 2018022710 (print) | LCCN 2018031480 (ebook) | ISBN 9780429449338 (Master eBook) | ISBN 9781138327283 | ISBN 9781138327283 (hardback) | ISBN 9781138327290(paperback) | ISBN 9780429449338(ebk)
Subjects: LCSH: Multiple personality--Patients--Biography.
Classification: LCC RC569.5.M8 (ebook) | LCC RC569.5.M8 Z35 2018 (print) | DDC 616.85/236--dc23
LC record available at https://lccn.loc.gov/2018022710

ISBN: 9781138327283 (hbk)
ISBN: 9781138327290 (pbk)
ISBN: 9780429449338 (ebk)

Typeset in Times New Roman
by Taylor & Francis Books

Printed and bound in Great Britain by
TJ International Ltd, Padstow, Cornwall

For 'Caroline'
one of the speechless victims of a world without mercy,
who trusted me enough to be able to tell her story.

Contents

Acknowledgements ix

Introduction 1

PART I
Creating a safe place inside 5

1 In the beginning – a stone 7
2 Separating inside from outside 19
3 Take out the badness, I want to be loved 33
4 From dead ends to DID 49
5 An alternative way to communicate: Written language 62
6 How can I know that we are real? 79
7 The story of incest: Keeping it all in the family 89
8 The danger of the good object 98
9 On incest, blindness and paranoia 108
10 The hospital dream: A place to bring the madness 119
11 The silence is not to be battled – but understood 124
12 The death of Dad: Loneliness 131
13 On pimps and prostitution 139
14 When trauma has no witness 150

PART II
Living the past in the present: dying, to get somewhere 155

15 Enactment instead of memory 157

16 From "hanging the doll" to "death by hanging" 175

17 The cult dream 185

18 Alice in Horrorland 196

19 The mysterious garden 203

PART III
From inside to outside: choosing life 209

20 Thou shalt not tell 211

21 From pregnancy to birth 219

Epilogue 235
Bibliography 246
Index 250

Acknowledgements

Each of my supervisors contributed immeasurably with their experience and wisdom to my development as a psychoanalyst. I know that I often presented them with challenges they had not previously confronted. Each, in her and his special way, met these challenges in a way that gave me confidence, trust and a strong belief that where two thinking hearts meet a way can be found. My deep gratitude goes to them – in chronological order: Bat Sheva Adler, Neville Symington, and Hanni Biran.

To my friends and colleagues Dr Shlomit Cohen and Nezer Dai who were always there to challenge my thinking and help me find my own voice, I am most appreciative. I am most grateful and feel lucky to have such good collegial friends who read the text with love, fruitful input and much encouragement: Ahuva Schul, Judy Katz-Charny, and Sara Haramati. Rhona Strauss, in addition to her psychological insights, was of immense help in the language editing of the final version of this book. Hannah Groumi made the preparation for publication of all the technical editing aspects feel doable in a way I did not imagine possible.

A source of invaluable support throughout the years was my own analyst, Tirza Sandbank. Without her understandings I would not have been able to survive all the madness projected into me by my psychotic patient. Her belief in me and in my ability to write this book made it into a reality. Tirza was always there for me: in moments of fear, in moments of doubt in my ability to treat Caroline and at times depression threatened to overwhelm me for fear I had taken on something I could not do. Knowing she was there with desire to read the text and give live feedback was having that "special someone to write to" in moments of extreme loneliness.

Most of all, I am indebted to my husband, Yossi Zaltz, who supported me throughout the years while I treated Caroline in a way that at times put strain on our relationship. Without his love and devotion to myself and our three children – Yuval, Amit, and Yifat – our family would not have become the strong unit that it is.

Especially, I thank my brave, courageous patient for allowing me into her mind where I learnt so much about the vicissitudes and complexity of human nature. At the same time, by taking me on this journey in search of sanity she reinforced and renewed my appreciation for the irreplaceable power of the written word. Her insistence that I *write* this book, which allowed for the inclusion of her brilliant and amazing texts that I thought needed to be revealed to the world, were the main motivating force that made this happen.

Introduction

> Bernardo: How now Horatio! You tremble and look pale:
> Is not this something more than fantasy? What think you on't?
> Horatio: Before my God, I might not this believe
> Without the sensible and true avouch
> Of mine own eyes. ...
> Let us impart what we have seen to-night
> Unto young Hamlet; for upon mine life this spirit
> Dumb to us will speak to him.
> W. Shakespeare: *Hamlet*: Act I, scene I

This book is about recovery.

The dictionary defines **recovery** as:

1 the regaining of or possibility of regaining something lost or taken away.
2 the process of becoming well again after an injury or illness.

The need to write this book is to allow my recovery after having spent 26 years together in one room, sharing one small physical space in therapy with a patient who was often psychotic. Caroline, the name I will give my patient, came to therapy to recover her memory. She claimed to have no memories. We called it psychotherapy and so it was. But nothing I had studied in my psychoanalytic training nor experienced with other difficult patients had prepared me for what I was to experience with Caroline. The book describes her expressed reason for coming, what she suffered from and how this therapy evolved and how we suddenly had to end our meetings quite abruptly so that what was actually uncovered (recovered – found) in the therapy would not lead to her death but would allow her to live. Yes, I became convinced that there was *real danger*, were we to continue to meet. While for most of the time everything that happened in the therapy was subjected to doubt about its reality, what was uncovered in the analysis and the consequent repercussions in her encounter with reality, put Caroline in real danger.

This book is also about **believing**, believing one's patient. Can someone who is outside the experience believe that what has happened is true rather than "not something more than fantasy"? Shakespeare, in the above quote, lets us feel through Horatio's experience, that now that the ghost of Hamlet's father had been seen by his own eyes, he could be convincing enough to share this with Hamlet. He also knew that the ghost would only speak to the heart of Hamlet. It took years of therapy before Caroline could feel trust in my listening heart. As will be described, her psyche developed the rare defensive mechanism of Dissociative Identity Disorder (DID) and "lived with" a persona that forbade her to speak. Only when conditions were made safe for the entry of another Persona – a little girl in the same body of Caroline, could language be used to speak of the past horrors. My experiences with Caroline were often so overwhelming and felt "unbelievable" that I actually introduced a camera into the therapy so as to have "proof" at times of the horrors revealed. I, too, would experience the concern that I might not be believed.

On the stage, Hamlet can see and speak with the ghost of his dead father who tells him about the hidden crimes of the past. In the art of fiction – a ghost can be portrayed in various artistic ways and a well written narrative can arouse a strong sense of conviction about the truth of historic events. But in fiction there is no need to deal with the question, "Did it really happen?" But when the patient comes to therapy with a need to find her truth – how does this happen? How is one to convince the therapist that a crime has been committed and needs to be acknowledged? In her most unusual way Caroline "created" a ghost that would talk to her therapist, myself, and even convince me of her truth. One of the endeavours of this book is to try and share this uncanny experience.

Shakespeare knew how to write the dialogue between Hamlet and the ghost. I had never thought of myself as a play writer but when I *met* "the ghosts of the past", in vivo, as it were – I found myself, of necessity playing parts in a drama and needing to invent spontaneously "appropriate" dialogue I had had no training for. This "technique" of working with dissociated selves that appear "unexpectedly" in therapy, born spontaneously from my experience, may be helpful to others dealing with this unusual phenomena of DID. I have given extensive vignettes so as to share this unusual experience.

Hamlet's father's ghost's last words to Hamlet are: "Hamlet, *remember me*" (Act I, V). The murdered king's ghost will not rest until the hidden crime is dealt with. Caroline thought it might be important to remember her past so as to make sense of her present. There was an internal drive that awoke in her after having been dormant most of her life. With this request she came to therapy – to search for her truth, to know who she was and from whence she came.

Perhaps there is some deep unconscious need to have the truth known about atrocities that have been witnessed yet hidden. Dori Laub, a psychoanalyst and Holocaust survivor, writes about his experiences with holocaust survivors in the chapter titled: The Imperative to Tell:[1]

> The survivors did not only need to survive so that they could tell their story; they also needed to tell their story in order to survive. There is, in each survivor, an imperative need to tell and thus to come to know one's story, unimpeded by ghosts from the past against which one has to protect oneself. One has to know one's buried truth in order to be able to live one's life.

Hamlet took the command to *remember* his father to mean a search for justice via the action of revenge resulting in a tragic end. Fortunately, Caroline turned to therapy in her need to remember. But this road was not devoid of violence. For the violence of the past had to be revived in the present for it to be known and believed.

When I agreed to join Caroline in her search I had no idea, in her words, "what I was getting into". I found myself walking on dangerous ground and looked for those who could help. Sometimes, I found support in books, and the knowledge that I had a supervisor who would listen to my anguish was an invaluable source of learning and support always. But most of the time, as in most therapies, the struggle to survive and to find meaning in the chaos, was something to be done alone, just by my patient and me. But this was often too lonely a road. In a search for deeper understanding and a containing environment, I joined the psychoanalytic institute[2] where I could be in a milieu where understanding the strange workings of the mind was a primary concern.

When Caroline first appeared in my clinic I was a relatively novice therapist and in the 26-year journey in which I joined her search for sanity I often found myself falling down the hole into chaos and darkness with her. I am sure I often blundered, causing both of us much pain and confusion. I am sure if I were to treat her today, with all the knowledge acquired over the years, including much through the recent literature on the phenomenon of DID, some things I would do differently but I doubt we would have suffered less pain. I do believe that part of the healing process was due to my allowing her to "use me" therapeutically for her needs. It is this complex process that I will try and share in this book.

In this respect, this book describes the way it was – the way one particular therapist did psychoanalysis inside her clinic with one particular patient. It is not necessarily a recommendation about *how* things should be done, but rather the sharing of how it was.

What contributed to my ability to share such intimate and exact texts from inside the privacy of the clinic was the fact that Caroline very much wanted everything written down so as to have a concrete record of our work together and her last, but often repeated, request of me was that I should write her story. Perhaps this is her way of saying: "Remember me!"

This book is our story. But Caroline also wanted to find her voice to sound the cry for many who cannot speak, living in homes where violence reigns behind closed doors.

Notes to reader

1 Since Caroline spoke in a very unusual way, with gaps and breaks between her words, I have designated this in the written text by separating some of the words with dots: …
2 This way of speaking was relatively consistent throughout the therapy but so as not to burden the reader with this disquieting visual effect I have only written in this form on occasion.
3 Caroline often brought me texts to read. When these texts were her own writing, the beginning and end will be denoted by the sign ~ and the text will be in a different font.
4 Since there is a lot of dialogue in this book and it is difficult to transmit changes in tone of voice in a purely visual way, I have chosen to emphasis certain words by use of italics to stress a point.
5 The words "therapy" and "analysis" were used interchangeably in the text meaning: "treatment". When I began the treatment I was a novice therapist and became a psychoanalyst in the process. I do not go into the differences in meaning allocated to these terms.
6 In Chapter 2 poems written by the patient are quoted. All the misspelled words are intentional, representing puns and play on words.

Notes

1 Felman, S. & Laub, D., (1992). *Testimony: Crisis of Witnessing in Literature, Psychoanalysis and History.* London: Taylor & Francis.
2 In 2007 I joined the Tel Aviv Institute of Contemporary Psychoanalysis (TAICP) as a candidate.

Part 1

Creating a safe place inside

Chapter 1

In the beginning – a stone

> I knock at the stone's front door.
> "It's only me, let me come in.
> My world is worth returning to.
> I'll enter and exit empty-handed.
> And my proof I was there
> Will be only words,
> Which no one will believe".
> I knock at the stone's front door.
> "It's only me, let me come in".
> "I don't have a door," says the stone.
> From *Conversation with a Stone* by Wislawa Symborska

Timeline: the first 11 years

There was actually nothing very unusual about the way she looked. A little on the thin side, dressed casually in slacks and a buttoned shirt, that unisex dress that was quite fashionable at the time, her features being on the delicate side. If I would have passed her on the street I would not have taken notice of her since there was nothing to notice. Actually, there was nothing in her appearance or in her general manner at the time of our first meeting that gave me any sense that I would spend the next 26 years with Caroline, often five times a week. The room would become the stage for madness, enactments of atrocities and appearance of dissociated personae.

For the purposes of this book, and to preserve her anonymity, I have called my patient Caroline. Other details have been changed to protect her identity. Since I now know that for most of this period, Caroline, then in her late twenties, was to be in a psychotic transference, saying almost nothing and being as immobile as a sphinx, I will relate here in detail the information I received from her in these first sessions. Because all too soon she would fall silent, saying nothing that would resemble normal language.

Deciding to start therapy

Caroline came to therapy when she was in her late twenties, after having had what was, for her, an unusual experience. She had had an emotional outburst at work. This happened after a man came to visit a colleague at work with whom she shared her office. She became very upset, ran home, cried and would not come back to work for a long time, even after her colleague and boss tried to persuade her to do so. This emotional outburst was very unusual for Caroline. She had never behaved like this and she was unable to make sense of it. Her friend gave her a book about childhood abuse and as she read it, Caroline had a thought that perhaps she had suffered some form of abuse in childhood, although she had no memory of such a thing. She hoped therapy might help her find out.

The only reason Caroline thought that she might have been abused was that she realized that her response to the incident at work was way out of proportion but it was the first time she felt her feelings were *real*. I understood that that meant that most of the time Caroline behaved in a very rational, unemotional way and that this emotional outburst had been quite out of character for her and very distressing. When I tried to understand what she meant by things not feeling real, she quoted the line from the Simon and Garfunkel song: "I am a stone – a stone feels no pain". She reported that while reading the book on sexual abuse she felt some anxiety and distress, and she said this was also unusual for her. She was worried that she might believe the fantasy that she had been abused by her father.

The sentences just written sound quite clear and coherent. However, over the years I would come to realize that most of the time Caroline does not "feel" at all and not feeling contributed to her overall sense of unrealness. To me, as I assume for most people, to feel real most of the time seems so obvious that to realize that for Caroline this was a constant uncertainty took me years to understand experientially, to think of and eventually to conceptualize. I think, at first, I probably wasn't quite sure if I believed her. It was only after many years of therapy that Caroline would reveal to me that most of the time the reality of the therapy itself was in doubt for her. At the time she revealed it, she already knew that I believed her.

Background

Caroline was born into a Christian family in an English-speaking country. She is the second of four children. All her siblings seem to have problems in interpersonal relationships, living lonely lives, although all are very well educated and highly intelligent, and have high-status professional jobs. Caroline herself also holds degrees in higher education, and works in a very intellectually demanding profession where she has minimal contact with other people. When I first met her she was working on her doctoral thesis at a prestigious university. She was not sure if she would continue working on her thesis since she explained she disliked interacting with people and the dissertation would involve conducting interviews and discussing her work with others. She lived alone and said she preferred it this way, saying she disliked being observed by others. When she first came, she said that until now she had been a relatively happy person, never feeling anything. She had a way of turning emotional pain into something she "brushed off" and thus any hurt was quickly made insignificant. She said she kept her mind closed and did not allow herself to think. She led me to believe that, for her, thinking itself was not really desirable. If it hadn't been for the incident of her unexplained emotional outburst it is doubtful that she would have sought therapeutic help.

Caroline said she really had very few memories she could tell me, only two that she could think of that she "knew to be real". They were of events in childhood when she had been physically hurt by accidents – once when she hit herself with a sports bat in school and another time when she had fallen off a wall. These events seemed particularly important to her because of the accompanying thought she had: "Now Mom will pay attention to me" and then another thought: "Now she'll have to believe me." When I asked about the significance of this for her she said that usually her mother would "brush her off" and if Caroline asked her questions about what to do with things, or where to put them she would mock and humiliate her with comments such as "Go put it in the bath". About her father, she said that she hated him coming home and intruding on her togetherness with her mother. She seemed to insist on using the words Mom and Dad, and not father or mother and not being able to explain why she did this. She also said that when she was with her dad in the car she always wanted him to fall out of the car, but she could say nothing about why this was so. She did say that he spoke very little, often not even responding to questions he might be asked

Caroline grew up as a lonely child with no friends at all. Her only attachment was to her mother and it sounded quite complex. There were hints of sado-masochistic elements. Her mother used her as a confidante to complain about her misfortunes, mainly about her relationship with her non-communicative husband (Caroline's father) and various physical ailments of the rheumatic kind. Her family were active members of a devout Christian community. Caroline's relationship towards both her mother and religion were characterized by feelings of guilt. She said that she was not able to reveal the truth to her mother that she only pretended to take an interest in what her mother spoke about, whether religion or physical ailments. She also seemed disturbed by the fact that she pretended to take on board her mother's religious preaching.

When I had only known Caroline for a few months, her parents actually came to visit her in Israel and she very much wanted me to meet them. Although I met the three of them together only once this scene is as fresh in my mind as though it happened yesterday. Her mother was an attractive and very verbal, talkative woman who seemed very self-involved. She spoke the whole time, never pausing to get a response from her captive audience, while Caroline and her father did not say a single word. They sat next to each other in total *silence*, looking very much alike. I recall thinking that perhaps the father was schizophrenic and the mother's talking might be covering up for that. Her mother either seemed oblivious, or in denial, to any of Caroline's difficulties. She described her daughter's childhood and adolescent development as normal, a good student. She seemed totally unconcerned that Caroline had never had any friends. However, she did express a complaint that Caroline used to cling to her physically for many years, demanding physical contact such as hugs and kisses. I was quite shocked by her when she described to me that when her children asked about how babies were born, she indicated that she concretely showed them where babies come from! I was left speechless, fearing for a moment that she might demonstrate her actions to me! This memory of such a literal way to deal with complex issues and the mother's apparent taking this for granted that this was normal, remained with me.

Without yet knowing much about Caroline's background, this single meeting with her parents left me with the uneasy feeling that she had grown up in a house of madness where the concrete could be substituted for the symbolic and where both silence and, or, verbal flooding substituted for true communication.

In addition to the specific reason of the incident at work, one of the main reasons for Caroline's wanting therapy, was that she had recently, for the first time, found a friend. This was the colleague at work who had witnessed her emotional outburst. This aroused in her "a wish to be loved and be able to love in return". She added that now she felt she was "allowed to want that" and she sounded like she was quoting a sentence from a poem or song. She denied wishing for any physical contact with her friend; anything physical she experienced as abusive. I soon learnt that this was quite extreme, for example she would not answer the phone for fear of being penetrated – she experienced her ear as a hole by which unwanted things from the outside could enter her! The only way she would use the phone was if she had total control such as setting up specific calling times with her family. (This was in the pre-cell phone era where the only way to identify the caller was by answering.)

I was soon to learn that though Caroline outwardly seemed completely sexless and devoid of anything excitable, her inner experience was of sexualisation of every part of her body, her ear being just one example. It seemed that words themselves were experienced as concrete objects that could penetrate her rather than a means for human communication. At this early stage of our contact I did not experience her as psychotic yet wondered how I would reach her if words themselves felt unsafe.

Caroline's friend had complained to her that she did not make any decisions on her own but was very dependent on the initiative of others or did things only out of compliance, out of a wish to please the other and then would be offended if she was not appreciated. This led to Caroline often being somewhat dishonest in her behaviour, for example by agreeing to take on some responsibility at work and then actually avoiding doing what was required of her and thus showing herself to be irresponsible. She said of herself that she could not be honest about her feelings, especially if she disagreed with the other, so outwardly she would seem to comply. I did wonder here how this related to her relationship with her father.

I also expected that this passive behaviour and compliance would be a feature in the transference relationship. It was not only at work that she was passive. For example, one recent extreme example that infuriated her friend to the extent of threatening the friendship was the following: it was Caroline's birthday but she did not let her friend know in any way that she wished to celebrate. On the contrary, she had said *nothing* about it, but instead stood outside her friend's house, hoping she would come out and be seen and be invited in. I did not then have a clue that this way of her being motionless and saying nothing, was soon to be her main way of communicating. I only expressed some surprise about this. Her response to my comment was quite severe – she said that she did not think she deserved to live, that if anyone was to truly know her no one would want to have anything to do with her because deep down she felt she was a *bad person*. The way she reacted to my response, which she experienced as lacking in empathy, was later to show me how utterly vulnerable she was to any semblance of criticism, which immediately led her to self-derogatory accusations. She explained that her feeling of "badness" was because she did not wish to take responsibility for any decision, nor to make any effort and she said that she knew she would turn everything into meaningless nonsense. And then she said, "I have a feeling of not knowing who I am because I don't know what I feel or think".

Keeping secrets

Caroline told me how she had only recently confided in her friend that she had a secret. Her secret was that she had doubts about the belief in Jesus and in his goodness and felt she could not express this to her religious parents. This keeping of a secret seemed to be a cause of stress for Caroline since she did not accept her parents' belief system. She seemed both overwhelmed by a sense of betrayal and concerned that she was an imposter. It had been a relief to her to tell her new friend this truth yet after telling *me* she became a little suspicious as to what I might do with this information. At the time I thought that with time I might understand more about her relation to religion and was not too concerned with her suspiciousness. Only with time would I learn that the issue of keeping secrets had been part of much childhood traumatisation.

At the time I was impressed by the fact that for Caroline a friendship was something so new and unknown that being able to share a secret was a sign of intimacy she had not known before. Little did I realize that very soon her whole experience of life was to be one of bitter conflict between being secretive and being honest – thus making the ability to develop a real relationship an overwhelming challenge.

To choose therapy is to choose life

In our third session Caroline said that she was terrified because she both wanted to be honest with herself but feared this greatly. The fear seemed associated with her concern that she might find out that she had some responsibility for the sexual abuse. It seemed that Caroline, although having originally presented the idea of having been sexually abused in a hypothetical way, was here relating to it as a "known fact". I had no idea at this time that this seeming contradiction about what is "known" was a precedent to Caroline's existential question concerning how she could know anything at all. At this early stage I found myself unable to form an opinion about what I believed and allowed myself to "keep an open mind" about what might or might not have happened. Caroline told me that she might have been seductive "and if so I don't want to take responsibility for anything in life. Life is too much of a struggle. I don't want to participate in living, I want to be a spectator of life". When I indicated that therapy meant trying to become emotionally involved in life and not remaining a spectator she expressed doubt about commencing therapy. She feared the change it might bring about in her life.

When I said: "Not going to therapy is also a decision!" she seemed shocked. Here she blushed, laughed in what seemed like an anxious way, the first sign of having an emotion in my presence, and said she had never taken a decision in her life, always doing things "without any sense of choice". Although her turning to therapy had been her own decision, the only other decision she had made out of free choice had been her decision to come to live in Israel. When I asked what made her want this, she said that she had doubts about most things – about believing in her mother and in God and how her doubts were causing her stress in living a Christian life. She said she had had the thought, "The Jewish people exist so God must exist". This thought had precipitated her decision to come to Israel. So it was a search to believe in *something* that seemed to be at the core of Caroline's seeking help. The search had taken her away from her home.

She wanted me to see her parents. She needed for me to see them in the most concrete way so that I would see the mad world she had left. She seemed to lack words to describe them. I wondered if I would be able to help her. I did feel that she could benefit from therapy, being of especially high intelligence and appearing to be very honest – especially about her being dishonest and struggling with wanting to take responsibility for her life.

Caroline decided to start therapy, asking for two sessions a week, saying she realized she wanted to live in spite of the fact that she had made lists of all the reasons why she did not wish to live.

To choose therapy was to choose life.

Little did I know then that this would be a journey of 26 years that would end dramatically because the tables would be turned – when to remain in therapy would mean risking her life. How this happened will be unravelled in this book.

Becoming a sphynx

It is very soon after we commenced therapy that I realize that Caroline was behaving differently. At first, it was not so obvious but soon I found myself with someone who had stopped talking and stopped moving. Her only movement involved entering and leaving the clinic but apart from that she became absolutely still. It was as though a self created spell had fallen on her whenever she was in my presence. Or was I the witch who had cast the spell and turned her into a petrified statue? (At a later time she would bring me a book titled: *So the Witch Won't Eat Me* by Dora Bloch.)

Thinking back to try and catch the moment of this transformation – I think I can relate it to the first time her wish coincided with mine. It seemed at the time just a small incident. I had wanted to change one of the days we met; it so happened that this is precisely what she had wished for as well but had said nothing! Immediately after having appreciated my having unknowingly met her wish, her positive feeling changed and she felt *she* had done something bad. She had dared to want something from me. Maybe she had made me do it. Caroline felt threatened and guilty. How quickly a moment of enjoyment was ruined! How quickly a feeling of closeness – having had one of her wishes met – became a threat. She was anxious that she might have manipulated me into doing something against my will.

I try to understand this sudden change of mood. In broken language – with long breaks in between the words, she lets me know she felt she deserved to be punished, "because ... of the way ... I got it – by ... dishonest ... means".

It seems she believed that if a wish or desire is actualized, she must have done something wrong. I had not accused her of manipulating my mind, but in her mind she was a *dangerous*, bad person. Seeing her deep anxiety, I decided I must be open with her and tell her my reality, relieve her of her guilt. Actually – when I say "I decided" – I do not think it was an active decision on my part at this early time in therapy. Over time I would realize the deep importance of the need for transparency and honesty and it would be an activating factor in my treatment of her. But at the time it was more an intuitive act, instinctively wanting to calm her for her seemingly innocent wish. I said that I had not read her thoughts, but had remembered that when we had first set up our schedule the two meetings were very close in the week and I had said that with time I would change a day so that our meetings would be spread better over the week and that this was possible now.

Her response was absolute shock and amazement: how was it possible that I should both recall what I'd said *and* mean it? "People … aren't like … that – they … say … and never … mean it". *She could not understand why I would do such a thing for her when I get nothing out of it.* It is one of the few moments where she expressed a spontaneous emotion, yet speaking in this fragmented, almost unintelligible way.

I think I registered this moment as the first sign of hope that I might become a good object for her – just because I had taken her seriously and had kept my word. I thought to myself that it seemed this was not how she was accustomed to being treated. A saying I liked, by the well-known American psychiatrist Karl Menninger, came to my mind: "When in doubt, be human".

It is important for me to stress that at the time I was still very much at the start of my career. I had not yet started psychoanalytic training. I had had little experience with psychotic patients, except for my internship in a psychiatric hospital. Caroline was one of my first private patients. Nothing I had experienced had prepared me for this. Although I was in supervision I found myself needing to think on my feet, decide things on the spot as though there were only the two of us in this world, and I had to be the responsible adult. This is not different from any other therapist–patient situation, however in this case from the beginning I was exposed to "new" phenomena I had not met even in professional literature. But fortunately I did have an outside other – a third – my supervisor, so that I was not truly alone. This knowledge was to be for me a source of deep comfort and safety that helped me survive moments of Caroline's bursts of paranoia.

In retrospect, with more psychoanalytic language at my disposal, I can describe the above incident in the language of psychoanalysis: Caroline had the omnipotent fantasy that I was under her control and that she could make me think certain thoughts. In her undifferentiated developmental stage in her mind she and I were one and since she did not feel she had a separate mind of her own she easily projected onto me her own fears – that perhaps I did not have a mind of my own and I was influenced by her seductive wishes. After all, very likely, with her father, she being an oedipal daughter, she had dared to desire him and if sexual contact had occurred this could leave her believing in her omnipotent fantasies and thus feel responsible, guilty and bad. Her sense of being innately bad was already a prominent feature of her being. What oedipal children need is to be able to safely desire and have sexual fantasies. Experiencing that fantasies remain fantasies and are not realized contributes to the ability to have an internal life from which creativity develops. Abuse destroys this. Instead, vigilance and the reliance on what is concrete become defensive ways of surviving.

A stone does not talk

But back to Caroline. Although I have recorded her responses as whole sentences that one can make sense of, she actually began to speak in a most peculiar way that was to become the only way she spoke throughout the years. The following is a description I wrote of the way she spoke with me after several months with her:

> She spoke very slowly, weighing each word. The silences between words could be ten minutes long and often I would lose the meaning of the sentence because of this. With time I would write these words down as a means of holding onto them until she finished the sentence. It was obvious that she needed to have total control over everything and over every word. There is no room for any incorrect word, nor any spontaneity. No word that had a double meaning could be used. For example "to want" was not allowed, nor the word "to feel". Later I was to understand that since "to feel" could mean both "to touch" and "to have an emotion", and "to want" can imply "to desire" – both words were eroticized for her. Therefore she did not allow them to be used – not by her nor by me. If I happened to be forgetful and use a "forbidden" word she'd accuse me of deliberately trying to confuse her. With time she "taught me" to speak slowly and clearly, also using very few words, adapting myself to her capacity to listen to me, trying to attune myself to her (Stern, 1985). She was often inaudible and I needed to ask her to repeat her words several times in order for me to hear her. Needless to say, any interpretation of resistance in this behaviour "fell on deaf ears". Language itself got fragmented and I lost the ability to hold onto the continuity of the sentence while "waiting in the spaces" (Bion, 1959). Yet, the reverse side of this was that in the silences I had time to think, to listen to my feelings – to reverie (Bion, 1962a). I began to share my thoughts with her (since nothing else was being said anyhow). At times my words moved her and I would see silent tears rolling down her face. What a relief this was for me, often being the only sign that I was with an alive, feeling human being. It reinforced my, at times, shaky belief that we were doing something very meaningful and that I must be patient. It would take years to understand the meaning of this behaviour. Caroline would communicate with me in live speech in a way that was almost incomprehensible, requiring of me a constant effort to understand her. It was as though speech was being used as a weapon in the therapy, both creating in me hateful counter-transference feelings towards her while attracting me to her in my constant effort to try and make sense of things, my "raison d'être" to stay with her.

In retrospect, I came to realize that her bizarre way of communication was a way of letting me know: "**I will not use speech with you as a form of communication**" and this itself *was* the communication she needed me to understand.

***

Caroline's inner wisdom must have guided her to help me be able with time to arrive at such an understanding. Because several months after the beginning of therapy she asked to increase the sessions to three times a week. This intensity would continue for the next 20 years, until her father died. (She then would ask for a fourth meeting per week, and for good reasons to be elaborated later). The additional third session allowed me to contain her in a way much more adaptive to her needs. Only in retrospect I realized that until then, I had obsessively written down at the end of each session her last three words. Without this concrete act I had no way of remembering anything from the sessions that had been mostly fragmented non-verbal communication. She opened each session using those three words as though no time had elapsed since we last met. It was her attempt to establish continuity. Without those three words, I could not keep her in my mind in any way. When we started to meet three times a week I found I could remember her. I experienced some calmness that allowed me to let go of this ritual of holding onto those three little words. Three times a week became sufficient to create a holding environment replacing a clinging to three concrete words.

***

To return to our early meetings where this behaviour was just appearing and I had not yet known how extreme and interminable it would become. At the time I was still getting a response to my questioning as to the inaudibility and slowness of speech. She said that her mother had no patience for her slow way of talking: "When I couldn't get my words out, took a long time, she didn't have the patience to listen". In this way, Caroline was forcing me to become "a different mother" who would have to have patience for her. I became totally subjected to her control. I could know nothing unless it was her way. The only alternative was to "abort" her and part of this story is the struggle, lived out in our relationship, between just that – being with her in a way that often led me to such extreme exasperation that I on occasion would have murderous fantasies towards her, which quite shocked me. I at times found myself wanting to give up on her yet "hanging in there", constantly trying to make sense of things, wondering why she needed to be this way, what was she trying to tell me yet without actually telling me? Was she manipulating me or was this unconscious behaviour that she had no control over and did she need my help to decipher, understand, interpret?

Yet, with all the exasperation, most of the time I was quite patient, waiting in the silence for her to feel ready or safe enough to give voice to her almost inaudible words. I sensed that deep down my patience was a way of showing my caring for this wounded, fragile being. But after suffering through several years of this enigmatic way of talking, which seemed entirely within her control, I would allow myself to lose my patience more frequently at needing to make such an effort to just hear her. It was only after 12 years of therapy, both of us having survived my expressions of anger, that Caroline would reveal to me, *in writing*, some of the meaning of this way of communication.

A stone does not move

Caroline's strange behaviour was not limited to the way she talked. Accompanying the verbal strangeness was the way she moved, or rather the way she did not move. Again, after several months together the following is a description I wrote about this. As with the way of talking, this too would be persistent until the end, but in my presence only:

> She walks into the room in slow motion, with eyes closed as though not seeing will make her invisible, yet she is of course most conspicuous because of this. If anything is "not as it should be" in the clinic she "freezes" until I fix it, for example if a piece of furniture had been moved. During the sessions she never moves at all, but always sits in the same position: legs wide open with one leg crossed over the other. There is something inappropriate, sexual, about this posture but I dare say nothing about this. Her hands hold tight to a plastic coated paper clip. An example of the extremeness of "no movement": if her nose happened to run from crying she would just let it drip, even though I was nauseated at the sight and asked her to wipe it. I, at such times, would turn away to prevent vomiting and feel quite helpless and at times angry.

The issue of *non-movement* was to be repeatedly "analysed" over the years but it never changed. It is a behaviour that I believe exists only in the therapy. Outside she runs, rides a bike and to all outward appearances appears "normal". But if I happened to see her in movement, as I did once by accident outside the clinic, riding her bike and our eyes met, she immediately froze on the spot and was *almost killed* by a car in the process. This moment was so dramatic that I insisted that she try and tell me what about my seeing her in motion was so threatening to her that she risked her life just so that I would not see her move. She said nothing but did at a later time introduce a special "dictionary" for my benefit (see Chapter 2).

Under the word Movement was written:

> Hiding by not being seen or heard.
> Slowness: to try and know what's happening – to find time to know; don't do anything fast – maybe you want to hide something.

From this written communication from Caroline it was clear that not to move in my presence was an active conscious decision.

Here is another extreme example of not being able to move in my presence: on one occasion Caroline asked me to leave the room for a few minutes. A strange request – yet I must have picked up a sense of urgency so I agreed. On my return I saw that she had changed the position of her hand to a "comfortable" place but her hand was purple. At the time (about ten years into therapy) she had been lying immobile under a low coffee table in a foetal position. I then understood that she had made this unprecedented request because she felt numbness in her hand because the flow of blood was getting cut off. She could not move her hand in my presence! I had no language for this phenomenon. Was there an unconscious meaning to this conscious act, or non-action? Did she know why I must not see her move but had to hide the meaning from me? Was I to guess on my own – because she could only "show me things" but explain nothing?

These kind of questions began to exist in my mind, making me feel on very unsteady ground. I soon realized that I was not able to know if I believed her. Was she sincere, or was I a pawn being played with by a manipulative patient? Yet, there remained the question why: why would she do such a thing? It was a question that gave me no rest. Was she hiding something? After all, from the first session she had told me of her suspicion that her father had abused her sexually so there was no secret to hide from me, from herself. Or was there?

The "hiding" I soon observed, seemed to be more generalized. Actually, even the sentence: "I observed" needs to be de-constructed. It would be more accurate to say "my eyes saw but the process of perceiving and giving some meaning to it" took years in itself. One could say: the meaning itself was being hidden from me in an active way by Caroline. I am describing the phenomenon that I will call "separating inside from outside". At times, meaning would be separated from the word and words would be separated from each other by time.

Chapter 2

Separating inside from outside

Timeline: still the first 11 years

In the first years, as I was to only notice retrospectively, nothing, other than a paper clip, is brought into the clinic from the outside world. It, too, is hidden in her closed hands. But the clip gets manipulated and "held onto" through the sessions in the first years. It serves the function of an "autistic object" (Tustin, 1980) as though keeping her concretely "held together". One day, I saw she had a new paper clip – a red one instead of the blue one she always held. Daring to ask her about it, she replied: "I left it in Auschwitz." I was left baffled; in her "absence" there was no one to elaborate. I knew her Christian family could not have had a Holocaust history, so why or when had she been to Auschwitz? Years later she would tell me – that she had been to Poland on a tour with the choir in which she participated while I had been on vacation. At the time her secretiveness was so extreme that I knew nothing of her life outside the clinic, including the fact that she participated in a choir. It would take another *20 years* before she revealed the reason for this action.

I first noticed this phenomenon of bringing nothing (no-thing) into the clinic – neither things nor information – when there was an extreme instance: a particularly cold day when the rain was pouring down. Caroline came in, as always, without an overcoat or an umbrella, yet she was dry. I was puzzled by this. I knew she rode a bike. When I asked her about it, as expected, I received no reply. It would take many years before Caroline would be able to tell me that she left all her things hidden outside the clinic, the reason being "so that nothing from the outside would be brought to the inside".

As with all her unusual behaviour, this needing to separate inside from outside had multiple meanings to be slowly unravelled over the years. Her needing to separate objects in this bizarre way I thought represented a psychotic fear of the loss of bodily boundaries, as though any overlap or contact would cause her to be contaminated or spill out and be annihilated. I therefore accepted and respected this need without trying to "interpret it away".

Nine years into therapy, Caroline began to want me to read material (see Chapter 5). So she now *had* to bring in something "from the outside to inside". She did this in a most enigmatic way. The text would "appear" on my table as though by magic. She developed a way to do this by somehow hiding the text while walking in front of me and put what she wished to show me on the table before I noticed her doing so. The reading material was to become one of her primary ways of communication with me. Some of the meanings of the need to hide that anything came from outside the room, was revealed with time inside the texts themselves. For example, it was her way of making believe it wasn't from the outside and thus "not contaminated". Another meaning: in this way Caroline was trying to be as close as possible to not existing and if she didn't exist "she didn't do it"; and if she didn't exist it wasn't real.

Another meaning was her wish to deny the existence altogether of a world outside my room. This bizarre behaviour was to remain an enigma for a very long time.

Poetry or the ravings of a lunatic

The first time Caroline brought anything from the outside was in the fifth year of therapy. She brings me many sheets of paper, with poems typed on both sides. I am to read them after she goes. I read, then read again and yet again. Every word has a double meaning. The vocabulary is idiosyncratic, ingeniously original. I feel stupid, overwhelmed, confused. I feel my brain has been attacked. But I also "know" from these poems that she must have been a victim of incest; each poem has something vulgar about it, almost pornographic. How else could my innocent-looking patient know such language unless she has been exposed to perverted sexuality? I will give just a few examples from the 72 poems she left for me to read:

> **Schizophrenia**
> Enclothed within white lines
> – liars, all of them –
> sleeping between
> lying around,
> sheet by jowl:
> goaled in a ward where
> languaging imprisoned.
> Paper thinned out
> so that only its cracks show through;
> underlined and stated over
> and over my skimmed body:
> dead, in your words.
>
> **Abhortion**
> Tarted off on
> the wronged feet – us
> (whore is she –

her brothel's keeper?),
blown on their
own strumpets
(called a girl),
slutting her throat
bathed in bad blood;
foundered in
execruting the curse,
contemned to death
in being dis-a-proved:
incensed.

Aspirations
Breathing lessons: lessens
how to breathe
the last of yore
your last
breathe………d;
ex-hale, and heartily
(looking out for yourself:
in spire ringed by you're little I)
pried by a falling,
in and out,
of
temperament
tempted to,
at-tempting
espy-rales –
rations, of dispirited asps:
vipers arising as vespers in a
breath, freshly aired and
feted
fetid
fated
to
grasp, gasp, rasp: in pyres:
dying to get somewhere:
dying, to get somewhere.

These poems were brought to me over about a year, with several months separating between each batch. In later years she would again bring me her writings, but never again in poetry form.

I was overwhelmed by these poems. I have a B.A. degree in English literature and love poetry but never before had I read anything like this. I felt that language itself was being abused, not only when alive, in my presence, but now in writing as well. Was she writing in a code I was to decipher? Yet, I had no way I could do this without her help. Out of desperation at my ability to make a reasonable judgment as to the quality of these lines as poetry, I showed them to a friend who was a poet and writer and asked for his impression. His response was that they lacked a soul, as though there was not a human person behind the words! His words resonated well and received further surprising external confirmation when years later I came across the article titled "Soul murder reconsidered: did it really happen?" by Shengold (2000) describing the devastating effect of incest on its victims.

The unspoken promise

I would soon find out that she was readying me for the long, endless silences to come. To speak is to risk being dishonest and here in her therapy it was vital for her to be honest. Her search for truth was from the beginning her main concern. But here was the rub: how was this to come about in this "talking cure" – if language itself could not be trusted!

This sentence I just wrote: "...language itself cannot be trusted" already implies an understanding of the silences. It is in itself a simple statement. There is no way I can share what emotional states of agony, confusion, anger and frustration I was to undergo, to be put through by Caroline, before I could arrive at such understanding. Bion (1962b, introduction) verbalized this "impossible" experience in the following: "I have experience to record, but how to communicate this experience to others I am in doubt; ... it may be possible to give some idea of the world that is revealed by the attempt to understand our understanding".

In contrast to the poetry that was so incomprehensible to me, Caroline thankfully, also brought me a very readable book: *The Promise* by Chaim Potok. It was the first of many novels she would bring me over the years – other people's writings. As she said, and had demonstrated with her poetry – she could not describe her feelings, but if I read words written by others, she hoped, I might be able to understand and believe her to some extent. *The Promise* is about an emotionally disturbed boy who becomes "catatonic" refusing to speak to anyone until a young therapist is brought in to help him. The book is about the therapist's endeavours to communicate with this most difficult patient. The therapist himself tries everything possible, almost going mad himself, almost giving up – but eventually succeeds. At that time I was a young therapist. I thought to myself with foreboding: is this the promise that Caroline needs me to make?

Alternative communication

How did I learn about Caroline's experiences if language for her was almost unusable? Soon I was to discover how amazingly creative her determination and ingenuity were. The next chapters will describe her alternative ways of communication:

1 Written material, from others and with time her own words.
2 Body language.
3 Enactments.
4 "Other" personae arriving to show me what she could not tell.

Although I could make little sense of her first bit of writing, the fact that I was able to give it *that* sense – that she wanted me to experience *her* experience of the confusion of her mind – led her to dare to share more and more writings with me; more and more of other people's words. If she couldn't talk or tell me things – at least she was able to read, comprehend and chose texts to give me to read. True, at first she hoped I would intuitively know her thoughts, but when I told her that I did not have this talent and would need her participation – at times she would dare add something of her own.

An instance of this came early in our relationship. Caroline brought me an article from a book by Oliver Sacks: *The Last Hippie*. (In: *An Anthropologist on Mars*). It is an interesting case study of a young man who appeared detached and blissful, but after being hospitalized was found to have a brain tumour that had destroyed the memory system in the temporal lobe. Some memories of the pre-tumour period seemed intact. When I tried to question Caroline about what she wanted me to understand from the article she replied that she would like me to refer her to a neurologist. I could then express her thought that her "amnesia" was of neurological origins, perhaps like Greg's in Oliver Sack's article. She agreed. I then told her that I did not think this was a good idea. That the fact that she was able to work on a doctorate that involved most complex intellectual brain activity was counter-indicative of brain injury and that I thought we should continue our psychological investigation to try and find other possible reasons for her very limited memory of the past.

It would be many years later that, after both Caroline and I had simultaneously read the best-selling novel *The Curious Incident of the Dog in the Night-Time* by Mark Haddon, that we thought that she might be suffering from Asperger's syndrome. At this later time (the sixteenth year of therapy) I did think it wise for her to have psycho-neurological testing and arranged it. How different this felt from her initial request when we had just met. Looking back, I do believe that at the time it was her way of trying to share with me her inner experience of feeling as *though a part of her brain was missing*.

A mental experience was experienced as a bodily handicap in this concrete way.

***

The impact of Caroline's determination and motivation to stay in therapy, in spite of my difficulty in understanding her, but perhaps because of my motivation to continue trying, brings Caroline to make an effort to communicate to me in words, knowing this was my medium of preference. One attempt is in her creating a personal dictionary for us. It occurred in the twelfth year.

A private dictionary

A small vignette: Caroline has left me a dictionary she has composed, interpreting some of her odd behaviour in the therapy room. The actual act of showing me her dictionary is an expression of her trust in me and an expression of the part of her that wants me to understand her. Today, I am able to say that she needed me to know that in spite of her often successful effort to make sure I did not understand her, she also wanted me to understand that this is what she needed me to understand: *that she cannot allow herself to want to be understood in an open way*. She manages to say that the first "showing" of her dictionary was equal to "not hiding". She conveyed that it was not by chance that the first word in this "Our Dictionary" is the definition:

> Hiding: In the corner: sorry that I'm here
> Noise: Hiding by not being heard

And Caroline, with my encouragement, elaborates:

C: When words ... lose ... their meaning I have ... to make you go through it (the feeling) so that ... I can be sure you know what I feel ... And the need ... is to ... have someone ... know what I feel.
T: There is a basic distrust of words – one cannot be sure they say what they mean.
C: That is why ... the description (in the dictionary) is only of ... actions, not feelings.
T: If there is a mistrust of the other's words there is probably a mistrust of the other in general.
C: That is ... why doing something fast ... arouses ... suspicion and ... fear that something bad ... is being ... done, and hidden ... in the fastness. If it is done slowly ... enough ... to have time ... to know ... what is happening ... some security ... can be felt.

***

In this way, through Caroline's dictionary and occasional conversing about it, I was able to get a clue as to one reason for her extremely slow movement, both of bodily limbs and in her way of using speech.

Soon after having received this dictionary, after a day where I became especially annoyed at her way of talking, she brought me a page *she had written* for our next meeting. This would be one of the first of many texts written by herself that Caroline would bring me over the years. But for several years Caroline writes pages where she uses "my voice". *She* writes as if it is *I*, the therapist, writing the text about *her, the client*. In a way, she "impersonates" me in her writing.

~A function of hiding – e.g., of information, words, Caroline's thoughts (which at times can be very clear and with deep understanding) – is to have the other experience what Caroline experiences often: confusion, disruption of thought processes, memory etc. Caroline often experiences this "confusion" when language is "poured on" to her in an inappropriate – what feels like an inconsiderate – way; e. g. too fast, ambiguously, "taken for granted as understood", assumed to have an "emotional content", etc. This experience of not comprehending what the other is saying leads to very intense negative feelings – e.g. frustration, fury, rage, "imbecility". This is the experience Caroline "created" in me by hiding information in our communication as described above.

For Caroline to tell me what happens when she experiences me as being "inconsiderate" feels too difficult. First of all, if it happens too fast she anyway cannot cope with it. To say anything needs time first to know what's happening and then to find a way to put it into words. The better way to convey it in any case is to make the other go through the same experience. In this case the hiding can also serve as a "punishment": the "aggression" comes out not in words but in "actions". This way, too, Caroline can avoid experiencing the negative feeling herself, albeit it at the expense of not knowing what is happening and not feeling real. Thus, it seems that "hiding" information can be a double –edged sword. Although its main aim is to protect Caroline from being touched if she reveals her inside, the fact that it creates "confusion", there is a state of "I don't understand what's going on" in the other, etc. If this happens often the result can be (as I felt in a specific incident) a feeling of exasperation at my impotence at being unable to make sense of anything. Such a state can lead to an abandoning of Caroline and of a feeling of being "of no use to her" (in my case as a therapist), and thus Caroline would again be left alone and abandoned and have only herself to resort to: a state of "autism", confusion, and its resultant symptoms of not knowing what is real, etc.~

What can I learn from this page, written by Caroline in my name after our session? Firstly I need to share that much of what she describes here is an outcome of what was spoken in the therapy itself, mainly by me. So in a way it is quite honest of her to use my name to take ownership of these ideas. But I do not feel it as quite so simple. In this most clear piece she has shown me that she has clearly understood everything I have said and that she agrees with it. It is next to impossible to separate my ideas about her from her experience. It is truly the result of a co-production but also has the feeling of a brilliant but an almost incestuous merger.

These were my thoughts from Caroline's written text:

1   She has assumed ownership of her aggression and described her understanding of the mechanism of acting out.
2   She describes her conscious use by her of making things feel unreal, a symptom she suffers greatly from.
3   She uses what resembles Projective Identification in a conscious, intentional way. She states that this is her preferred way of communication her experience and also serves to punish the other, in this case myself, for making her feel confused by talking in an inconsiderate way.
4   I find myself thinking – how mad can such a sane logical person be?

I understood that I needed to cultivate tolerance to experience the enigma of being with her, to remain with the *not* knowing and to survive her aggression (Bion, 1970; Winnicott, 1971). I also understood that Caroline realizes that her hiding leaves her very much *alone* and even if for no other reason, she needs me to stay patiently with her so as not to fall into unbearable loneliness or an irreversible autistic state.

As can be seen above, there were small moments of clarity soon to be lost again in the death-like, motionless silences. But these precious moments of clarity were very gratifying for me. It was as though, albeit for a second or two, she would give me a huge gift, an expression of gratitude she felt when I was able to understand her. Thus, several months after she had given me "Our Dictionary" she left me the following typed piece of paper on my desk:

> ~The importance of writing this dictionary piece together, rather than alone, is to make sure it's not a secret, open to the eyes of the world and thus not something to be ashamed of. When Caroline. writes on her own, alone – her need to keep everything hidden – feel safe, created a writing which is almost, but not quite, comprehensible to anyone outside of her head.~

***

I think at the time I did intuitively know that all of Caroline's strange behaviour was a way of trying to make therapy a safe place. To do that, I had to comply with her needs. It was not what I had learnt to do in my training: to try and interpret resistance; not agree to be controlled by one's patient, and so on. But to rely on my learning at that time was to no avail. I soon realized that I had to learn from my patient. It was only by following her lead that there was a chance that she would take us somewhere.

Paradoxically, it was I who had to trust her so that with time she would learn to trust me, somewhat. Fortunately, many years later, I was to read in Winnicott's (1965b, 132–133) words how he too, when treating a young traumatized child, also followed the patient's lead. He had been treating a young girl hospitalized in a paediatric unit where, unknown to the staff, a pervert had preyed upon the children. He writes:

> The patient reclined on the couch as usual, and talked very softly of this and that. I needed to be (as usual with her) very close in order to be able to hear. At these moments she is very sensitive to any changes in the room, and I do avoid upsetting her by not making careless changes. In many ways the patient needs to get me in her control and I must give full attention. I follow her needs by altering the heat of the fire exactly as she wants or by opening or closing the window, and perhaps supplying her with handkerchiefs or other objects she knows are available. Conditions being well-nigh perfect, she begins to want me to talk, but there is no material for me to use ... She curls up and withdraws, and she is inconsolable. She cries and is clearly deeply wounded. There is now a time element involved, so that I cannot stop until I know the phase is past; the phase must be allowed to come to a natural conclusion.
>
> I am helped by my theoretical understanding of what Dr. Margaret Little calls the delusional transference. I do not have to bring in anything gross such as the matter of this pervert and his invasion of the children's ward. All I need to do is to accept the role allotted to me. In this way, within the ambit of a powerful positive transference, the girl becomes wounded and reaches the distress and the crying which she cannot reach on her own.

***

Let us go back to the beginning phase of the therapeutic process. Without noticing it, I find myself immersed in a process that has very little content. The sessions involve dealing with the tiniest increments of a gesture here, a facial expression there, the length of the silences and the relentless staring into my eyes. I find myself making decisions about whether to hold her gaze or blink or close my eyes because I cannot bear this and trying to talk about it leads to more accusatory staring. I do not know if I am with a baby who needs concrete mirroring to know she exists in my eyes or with a sadistic woman who in her paranoid state wants to destroy me.

This agonizing movement between these two positions becomes our focus for several years. At first I don't notice that there is no relating to anything outside our interaction in the room. It is as though no outside world exists.

***

The following are some scant notes I wrote down three years into therapy:

C: Talking about a feeling makes it disappear. (We are both silent.)
C: Do you know the Beatles song: Nowhere Man "through thick and thin you'll always love me, stick around – Nowhere Man?"

My unspoken thoughts: How long will I be able to stick around? And who is Nowhere Man? And is "stick" a penis that is going to be stuck into her, echoing the double meanings used in her pornographic poems? Was Nowhere Man her father, probably schizophrenic, but the only one who showed love to her but mingling it with sex? And will I feel I'm getting nowhere if I am left with all these unanswered questions because of my silent patient?

***

And on another day, all Caroline says is, "A dream – a blank slate".
I offer an interpretation: this is her response to my incorrect understanding of something. Her rage and despair has made her eliminate all of herself. She then becomes a blank slate.

C: A miracle, not only are you here when I'm angry but the opposite too – you're here when something good happens – someone to share it with.

***

I often write notes to myself after a session like, "I didn't understand anything except that she came in grateful and left disappointed."

The first time I announce a forthcoming two-week holiday she bends down slowly to tighten her shoelace. I think: she feels she might spill out and disappear while I am away. The therapy has become a secondary skin that she needs to hold herself together. With time I will learn that she indeed felt her life depended on therapy continuing. For years this will be the only consistent continuous thread that could be stated with certainty: she *had* to come to therapy and *"be dead" in my presence*. As she wrote in one of her poems: *"Dying, to get somewhere."*

Paradoxically, if she could "play dead" in my presence she could stay alive.
Any cancellation or vacation gave rise to a fear of *annihilation* – both of her existence and of everything we had done in the years of therapy. She

feared being eradicated in my mind, since her existence depended on *my* memory alone. Having no memory of her past – she was in danger of disappearing. Her dependence on me felt very concrete. Years later she was to give words to it in this way: "The intervals between our meetings are spaces into which I fall – a black bottomless fall, an abyss."

In the ninth year into therapy, when I went away on a particularly long vacation she asked to be hospitalized. I arranged for her hospitalization in a psychiatric unit "for safe keeping" as it were. Over the years, as she developed, Caroline became capable of forming a real friendship. In the last years she has been living with a girlfriend so separations from therapy, in outer reality at least, became possible without endangering her, or needing hospitalization. But for years I used to feel very guilty about taking a vacation or cancelling a session. However, I would like to emphasize – in her experience the separation from me was different from other patients experiencing separation anxiety. For her, she conveyed that it was *literally* a fall, not *like* a fall. In later years the concreteness of this experience was enacted by her sitting on the floor in the corner of the room so as *not to fall* into the abyss when the past entered the therapeutic space. Winnicott (1963a) describes anguish as a primitive anxiety characterized by sensations such as not being held, falling for ever, there being no safe place to be able to be alive in. What had happened to Caroline that she suffered such anguish?

How do you know I'm telling the truth?

Here is an example of the kind of session we have six years into therapy (one may note that the content concerns the kind of movement in the room):

It is after the summer vacation. We had walked into the room in the ritualistic way that has developed: very slowly, she walking before me through the corridor, me keeping a "safe " distance behind her. Caroline is silent, staring into my eyes, then says:

C: You remembered! (I understand she is referring to the way we entered the room).
T: It means I care about you and respect your needs.
C: Yes ... How do you ... know I'm telling ... the truth?
T: A difficult question to answer. I don't *know*, but I do believe you. Why shouldn't I?
C: I have no choice ... only if ... I tell the truth... I can know...what is real.

Actually, she has not told me anything. What I know and believe through her past actions and non-verbal behaviour is that she needs this ritualistic kind of entry. But she is touching on a deeper issue of what contributes to the experience of believing one's patient. In my experience with Caroline our interaction has mostly been me being the dominant voice and she, the silent one. This often left me wondering if the things we "know" about her were only my creation, a figment of my imagination as it were. This in itself is a strange, unnerving feeling. If Caroline has no memories she will own, if she rarely confirms things, doesn't speak and it is only *myself* who is doing the thinking and talking – then how can I know that what I think is real for her, is actually so? This is an example of how *I* experienced the maddening effect of doubting my own thinking processes – itself an example of Projective Identification. Projective Identification is considered an unconscious mechanism yet Caroline has written that she intentionally needs for me to feel what she has gone through for lack of other ways to communicate her experiences to me. So am I a pawn in her game? And if so – perhaps I should surrender to the experience (Ghent, 1990) and in this way maybe I will understand her better. Perhaps this experience itself is expressing through me that she was "played with", never being sure when the game will end and real life will begin.

Hypnosis

In the seventh year of therapy, when frustration concerning the bareness of our futile search for memories was at one of its peaks, the idea of trying hypnosis as a means to finding repressed memories came up. I, with her permission and even encouragement, discussed this with a colleague, an expert in the field and begin planning this intervention. Caroline was willing but showed me an article from a newspaper her mother has sent her, after she had mentioned the idea to her. The article warns against *false memories* induced by psychologists through hypnosis. I wonder about the mother's motivation and check with Caroline if she is still interested. I am not quite sure myself about the status I give memories arising under hypnosis but am open to anything that might create movement in what has come to feel like a stalemate. There is also a felt sense that I think we both feel (though not articulated) that somewhere in her brain there is "a place" where the memories are hiding and we are both seeking ways to access this archaeological site that we feel must contain the clue to her illness and thus her potential health.

C: How will … I know if it's really… a memory?
T: I can't really answer this question – other than 'we shall see'. At times you feel things here are real, and then you feel trust. Maybe you will know from your *feelings*.

Feelings have been present in therapy for some time. At this stage, seven years into therapy, this is a "far cry" from the initial "stone age" As Bion (1976) says in his seminar "Evidence": "A feeling is one of the few things which analysts have the luxury of being able to regard as a fact".

C: If nothing ... comes up ... does it mean that ... nothing ... happened?
T: I don't see it necessarily meaning that. It is what it is. And I give her an example of a boy I treated who was being evaluated for autism and when tested did not speak at all, yet I knew him and knew he did have an inner world and could speak. So no single event is proof of anything.

C: So you have ... other means of knowing ... Not just ... from me?

She wants to know if I trust the hypnotist and wants me there – but hidden, since she can't move in my presence. "Can you be there and not be there at the same time?" (I arrange this: I will sit just outside the room, with the door open, seeing and hearing but out of her sight – seeing but not being seen, so that she will not feel alone with a strange man.)

Sometimes Caroline tells me a joke. On this occasion it was: "Do you know the definition of life? Life is a sexually transmitted disease." I wonder if her telling me a joke is a little present from her in appreciation for my agreeing to go with her to the hypnotist. She questions if I will not be ashamed to be seen with her in the outside world. I wonder if it has to do with her outer appearance, which she seems to have gradually made less attractive by shaving her hair and becoming even thinner.

The experience at the hypnotist's clinic is itself quite representative of Caroline's enigmatic way of being. Outwardly, she appears accepting and cooperative of the instructions given. She does as asked, closing her eyes and trying to imagine a safe place, as instructed. However, no memories are aroused. The hypnotist thinks she shows signs of being hypnotizable and a second appointment is made but she refuses to go. I am not able to understand the reason. With time I understand that Caroline was unable to cooperate because she could not imagine any safe place to go to in her mind as instructed by the hypnotist. Although she had said nothing to him, she had expected that her silence would be understood by him as indicating this. As I learnt from him, the opposite had occured: he had taken her quiet silence to indicate agreement and cooperation.

The episode with the hypnotist makes me think about how difficult it is to really know what the other is thinking, experiencing, if there is only silence and an inability to use language. I wonder about how much this is a repetition of her passive agreement to her father's desires, being compliant and outwardly cooperative. She also expresses bitter disappointment in me for not having known that this is what she experienced on the inside, that she could not imagine any safe place since she had no memories of any such place. Did she believe that I was able to see her inside, like a small child who is sure parents have omnipotent powers and can read his thoughts? After all, I had often succeeded when only the two of us were present. It makes me wonder if this could be a transference from how she experienced her mother – a passive bystander – yet knowing everything.

***

Four years after the experience of hypnosis, when Caroline is already using written texts freely to convey to me what she cannot tell me in live words, she brings me a page and on it was typed a text she had copied from an unspecified book:

> Hypnosis is the treatment which, of all treatments, most depends on the doctor's authority. If hypnosis is to be effective, the patient must accept the doctor's suggestions without question. Hypnosis puts the patient into the position of an obedient, compliant child who does what he is told because authority tells him. His is not to reason why … although there may still be a case for the use of hypnosis in a case of traumatic neurosis, in which the patient needs to recall and re-live painful experiences, it is a technique which is in principle opposed to psychotherapy based on the analytic method. The purpose of psycho-analytic psychotherapy is to help the patient to help himself; to facilitate his taking more responsibility for his actions; to aid his autonomy, not to undermine it.

Years will have to pass before Caroline will be able to talk to me about her experiences in her own words. But it seems that gradually a safe place was being created within the walls of the therapy itself, safe enough to be able to feel and to be able to tell me about her disappointment and anger at me for not knowing how it was for her with the hypnotist. Ogden (2016) in analysing Winnicott's concept of "use of the object" describes how the therapist, by enabling himself to be used as a real object, allowing herself to be "destroyed" and surviving the patient's destructive use of her, enhances the growth of a sense of reality in the patient.

I have described in these two chapters that cover approximately 11 years of therapy the various ways both Caroline and myself survived. This enabled the gradual formation of an internal life in Caroline. Evidence of this came when she reported, in actual spoken verbal language, her first dream.

Chapter 3

Take out the badness, I want to be loved

Timeline: 11 years into therapy

A dream of being called a four-letter word

Caroline's feeling of inner badness is physical, based in her body. In one of the earliest dreams that Caroline brought to me she tells me: "I was ... naked and ... my name ... was changed ... to a four-letter ... word."

At first, she is enigmatic, brings no associations. We can make no sense of it. However, she mentions it again a week later around something I say, thus inviting me to continue. I say: "You were touched and distorted and given a *dirty name*. You felt *you* were *made bad*, rather than something bad was done to you."

She says: "I'm sorry ... I didn't mean to".

I do not understand. She asks for an extra appointment, indicating some urgency. I comply, although it means my coming in especially to the clinic, thinking something has happened. She has never asked for an extra session before. Eventually, she tells me that her distress was because she felt she had contaminated me – through touch. Apparently, I had, unawares, left the door to my room closed. Thus, I had created the situation where, on exiting, she had to *touch* the door to open it, and she felt her inner physical badness had been imparted to me. So that is what the apology was about when she told me that she was sorry. But what a relief that she was able to tell me. A year ago she would have remained silent and I would have remained in lonely oblivion of her experience. Now I dare to put her psychotic thought into words and I say to her: "I know you do not have leprosy. Our work here is to help you heal. The feeling of badness is because of the illness." It shocks me that I have used such an extreme word as leprosy. Was it in her dictionary? I check. No – but under the word Objects is written:

> Won't touch anything: anything that belongs to you (part of the trouble in sitting in the chair again) makes things contaminated. You can't hold things that come from me, either: You might get infected. It's too close to touching me.

The struggle over a womb

She tells me with complete seriousness that she wants to have a hysterectomy and repeats her dream of being named a four-letter word. I echo: "You feel so bad that you want your insides physically taken out, to be emptied of the badness."

Caroline: "There are only two things I really know: that I want it taken out, and that it's the only way to rectify having been born!"

She starts relating in an obsessive way to her wish to have a hysterectomy, trying to enlist my help. I don't know how to deal with it. If I forbid it will she listen? I feel we need time to understand it better. I think I *don't quite believe* that her thinking can be so concrete and psychotic, and it frightens me. She seems so determined and it is such an insane idea. She is in her late thirties and this act would mean she might never give birth to a child. As it turns out, my fear is well founded. Many years later I will read in a book on DID about a patient who, when she was one of her personas, had irreversible eye surgery, which was quite detrimental to her vision when she was her "host" self (Brenner, 2014).

A concrete enactment of the four-letter word

The sense of despair in the wake of Caroline's dream of being called a four-letter word has brought us to an impasse. Convinced I cannot allow her to have a hysterectomy in reality, I suggest: "If you were a little girl I'd let you do this (have a hysterectomy) in play with a doll."

Caroline arrives at the next session, sees that there isn't a doll and hurls an accusation at me: "You didn't bring it so you didn't mean it." To her, simply my mentioning the possibility of using a substitute toy had become a promise in her mind. "We will need a doll," I say. Suddenly, my stomach contracts in fear: what if my new suggestion makes her lose contact with reality? After all, she wasn't a child and might not relate to it as play. I tell her my fears. I also speculate if she can play at all when she has been lying under a low table, curled up in the foetal position with me sitting on the floor next to her for over a year. So how will she be able to play with dolls, which would involve moving? She has even refused my suggesting she draw in the past because it would involve mobility.

The assaulted doll

Little did I know then what "plans" she had for us! At the next session I found a plastic bag hanging from the handle of my front door, containing a little blue-haired doll, made out of soft white material. With it is a note from Caroline: "I'll do it." In this session she does not take up her usual place under the table but sits on the floor near it. I sit in my usual place on the floor near her. As though out of nowhere a Japanese knife has appeared on the table. Somehow she gets me to cut off the doll's hair and when I cannot do so with this knife, she orders me to use scissors that she sighted on my desk. She then says very assertively, quite unlike her usual hesitant speech, that I am to write "FUCK" all over the doll's body. "She has to be punished," she says. She urges me to speak while I am cutting off the blue hair. The four-letter word of the dream has been spoken out loud!

As if under her spell, I do this. Spontaneously, I assume the "father" role, saying to the little doll: "You think you can go on looking like a cute little girl, with your cute fair hair!? No way! You'll look like a boy from now on and don't you dare grow your hair."

So, in this session I find myself simultaneously giving voice to both the adult Caroline and the child one, drawing on what I saw that morning, that Caroline had had her already short hair shaven to a very unflattering, masculine crew-cut!

"Go on!" she demands, and I obey. "You'll look like a boy from now on. Girls are seductive, tempting, they make me do things I shouldn't. It's your fault. Why did you keep on cuddling up to me, wanting to be held, hugged, patted, kissed, sitting all over me? Look what happened and it's all your fault! What's the matter with you!"

And then in the father's voice I add a warning: "Don't tell anyone. They will think you're crazy and no one will believe you."

She then commands me: "**Stick things into her!**" I take a pencil and pretend to stick it into the little doll, in acting mode, still in the father role: "Look what you made me do – you think you can just cuddle and kiss and nothing happens. Well I'll show you what happens ..."

Emotional rape

In the midst of our role play with the doll, Caroline orders me to stick the pencil in between the doll's legs. I suddenly feel quite mad, not knowing if I am an abuser or I am being abused. I only know I am being made to do something I don't want to. I stop.

"Go on!" she orders me. "Don't stop!" I experience her both as sadistic and perhaps in the throes of an orgasm in her aggressive intensive command and I refuse to participate and say so. I cannot and will not stick that pencil into the doll's vagina. The element of pretence in this game has become too real. She angrily gets up, grabs the doll and thrusts the pencil deep between her legs and walks to the wastepaper basket and throws her into it! I cannot recall Caroline ever moving so quickly. It is the end of the hour. She proceeds to leave slowly, silently crying and I hear her whisper, "It hurts ..." Her walk has a strange, new gait to it – it is as though something is painfully stuck between her legs! She was totally identified with that little girl from the past; the doll had become that girl.

After some moments of shock, alone in the room, I take out the discarded doll from the bin and hug the poor abused thing. Only much later will I "see" that although she had written the words "I'll do it" on the note – in some way that I still cannot recollect, she had got *me* to do it. I was so shaken up from having been "made" into an abuser, it felt like an emotional rape.

In retrospect, I understood that I had become like an actor in a play, who had to identify with the part in order to play it convincingly. The fact that I was actually in the doing mode, *really* cutting the doll's hair, added to the feeling of us being in present time while living an inner reality of something that felt very real from her past. This was to be only the first of such moments.

A terrifying nightmare

After that session when I felt I had been "made" to cut the doll's hair, and resisted doing it further harm, I had a nightmare. It is not the first nightmare I have had while in therapy with Caroline but it is the first one where I awoke screaming. I dream that I am on a roof with one of my sons and see Caroline watching us. My son, instead of going down the ladder carefully, makes a wrong judgment, slips and falls to his death. My screams awaken me.

Completely shaken, terrified, my dream challenges me to ask myself: Am I making wrong judgments? The "watching us" in the dream is a replica of the way Caroline stands ominously outside my clinic, stalking me. It has always given me an uneasy feeling but I had not yet felt able to talk to her about it. This will happen only years later when it becomes unbearable. Is this nightmare a sign that my intense emotional involvement with Caroline may be affecting my attentiveness to my own children? And how am I dealing with *my* guilt feelings – unconsciously wanting to blame the "careless child" for the consequences? And the rooftop – what dangerous "high" ground does it represent? I wonder if I am being drawn into some omnipotent phantasy that I can take on this challenge that is too high for me.

Petrified immobility

Caroline opens the next session with: "It hurts" and I find myself again, spontaneously joining her in the enactment, speaking what I think represents her past experience with her sadistic, abusive father:

> It hurts does it – well you deserve it, after what you've done, carrying on like that, seducing me, sitting on my lap. I'm glad it hurts you now. It will make you remember never to do it again, not to move, not to come near me.

Out of my pain at having been so sadistic – I then identify with the little girl, and in a whining child voice I say:

> I'm sorry, I didn't mean to. I didn't know that that's what would happen. I'm sorry, I promise never to do it again. I won't move. I'll be like a block of wood, like the furniture – so that you won't notice me – and you won't do it to me anymore. I won't exist!

Through verbalizing it, I have just understood that her petrified immobility is so as not to be seen, not "to be", so as not to be raped.

Caroline, listening intently, nods in agreement and cries silently. She then leaves with me the chopped off blue doll's hair from last time that she must have taken with her, and imperceptibly returned to the room today. I collected it into a small envelope, like a mother keeping the first curls of her baby.

Starved for love

When it is time for our next meeting Caroline stands outside the building and takes 25 minutes to enter. She wants to go on with the hurt. I speak in the little girl voice, through the doll:

> I didn't mean to. All I wanted was to be loved, to be held, to be cared about – I so much need that. I'm starved for love. So how did this happen? How did it become something bad, to be punished? I don't understand. It all happened so quickly. It's so confusing. I don't understand.

Caroline nods in agreement, that I am getting it right and that I am to continue this enactment. She repeats my words very slowly: "I ... don't understand ... it's so ... confusing."

I continue in the child voice:

> The hair, I'll keep it as a reminder of my punishment, not ever to do it again. But how did it happen? Why didn't you tell me, why didn't you warn me that if I move, or hug it can become so bad and hurtful?

Caroline cries silently until the end of the hour, gets up from under the table but then stands still as a statue near the door. Eventually, she lets me know nonverbally to throw the doll into the waste paper basket, as she had done on the previous day. I had been holding her in my arms until now. Reluctantly, I obey.

Giving words to the unspeakable

At the following session I insist she tells me how the session with the doll was for her. I refuse to continue with an enactment unless she does so. I have just done something I had never done before with an adult patient and I must know if I am not retraumatizing her. She answers by telling me that in the book *Trauma and Recovery* (Herman, 1992) it is written that there are no words where there is trauma because trauma is unspeakable. "You gave words to the unspeakable" is all she says. But these words are sufficient. I am so relieved. I needed this confirmation that I was not harming her. This was evidence that there was an observing ego developing in her and that she could separate inside from outside within her inner world. That her reality testing was developing. She was letting me know that she knew all this enactment was happening inside the safety of the therapeutic space. By these six words, "you gave words to the unspeakable", she signalled clearly that outside the therapy she was doing a lot of reading. It helped her know that this was therapy that we were doing together and not some madness I had been seduced to participate in.

With this in mind, I was able to share with her my association that I recently saw an interview with a Holocaust survivor on television who said he felt so estranged from people who had not been through the Holocaust because they could not really understand him. I share with her my thought that in order for me to be able to understand her, she needed me to go through (albeit in "play") some of the traumatisation that was hers. But I do not mention my traumatic dream where I am a mother who did not save her son. So, one might say, I too was feeling some deep aloneness which I could not share.

Enacting abortion

Caroline brings a brochure used in anti-abortion campaigning to the next session. It contains pictures and descriptions of abortions done in various ways such as vacuum, scraping and more.

She then gives me instructions that I am to tell the doll: 1. How she got here. 2. Why the abortion had to be carried out. She then resumes "the play".

Caroline (speaking the girl's role, protesting): "I don't want to!"

I now become the adult giving her child a little lecture on sexual education. I am sympathetic to her not wanting to have the abortion but in an "educative" way describe how terrible it will be for the unwanted baby were it to be born. What kind of life would she have? She might be ill-treated or need to be hidden so as not to shame the family. But I am unable to convince her. She refuses to comply. She doesn't want to abort. So I ask the simple question: Why not?

C: I'll be left empty.
T: Yes, being close to Dad you felt some fullness.

Since I am now getting some answers I ask Caroline why she needs to repeatedly end each session by throwing the doll into the bin.

C: Otherwise we won't know there was an abortion.

I think and say, that she identifies with this aborted foetus that no one wanted to live, who was not acknowledged and that at least now I can begin to understand how it was for her.

On the sense of conviction

What I understood from this interaction is, that though Caroline does not tell me her memories of these past traumas, she relates to these enactments as equivalent to memory. I find myself also relating thus to them. My emotions are so strong that I don't even seem to have doubts about them being real memories. My emotions – her memories? I wondered if this was the only way she had of letting me know what she had experienced. Is the body's felt sense to be the proof of her history? But as I write this, this argument feels so fragile – as though it could be torn to shreds at the slightest inclination. I find myself sympathizing with Caroline's sense of not being able to hold onto a sense of conviction for very long as to what really happened.

In and out of the madness

There were two of us in the room. So what was my function? I would at times feel that I was the witness, confirming what was real for Caroline, using my own experience based on what was real to me. This seems fair enough at moments when one feels that one is understanding the other; but how is a sense of conviction formed? One way is from receiving confirmation from the patient that what one thinks also feels true for her. This was just what was lacking in Caroline – a sense of conviction. Or, at best, it would be there for a moment and then evaporate like a cloud into wisps of invisible air. Then doubt would form in me as to the confidence with which I could rely on my own convictions that I understood her. Thus, I found that I was to experience in the countertransference what it felt like to be in danger of losing one's mind (Searles, 1959; Winnicott, 1965a). I was to allow myself to be an object "to be played with" by her while finding a way to survive as an "observing ego" by trying to understand all of this for her and for me. It felt that to the extent that I could do this I would be able to hold onto my own sanity. Thus, my function as her therapist, involved being able to shift positions: go inside the madness and experience it, and yet come out and be outside the madness, and differentiate between these different "places" and be able to keep some record of all this for use as a potential interpretative tool.

This tortuous process would be repeated over and over in our interaction. It took many years of re-experiencing it to be able to verbalize clearly what I just have in these last paragraphs. It seems that this experience of Projective Identification where Caroline was transferring to me her own tantalizing experiences was her main way of communicating her experiences to me. This process, of having pieces of her self- experiences returned to her through my mediation, was a driving force in Caroline's determination to continue this search for "the missing pieces" in the hope of being able to put them together into a unit whole.

The "Humpty Dumpty" metaphor

This phenomenon of putting the pieces together would be given the name "Humpty Dumpty" from popular children's rhyme: "Humpty Dumpty sat on a wall; Humpty Dumpty had a great fall; all the king's horses and all the kings men couldn't put Humpty together again." I recall that one of Caroline's two childhood memories was falling off a wall (Chapter 1).

The development of emotional thinking and the sense of reality

Winnicott and the lived experience

Winnicott was especially involved with the live experience as a central phenomenon to stimulate a sense of being alive in the patient and through this live experience transformation was made possible. Since "feeling alive" was one of the challenges in working with Caroline who was mostly silent and seemed to be dead in my presence, Winnicott's writings were often a helpful source of understanding. There is a connection between not feeling alive and a sense of de-realization. In the vignette described in Chapter 2 where he describes his treatment of a traumatised young girl, he writes: "At first she had not been believed and was thus not sure what was real". Continuing, he describes how the girl accessed her feelings of pain and was able to cry in his presence: "In this experience the patient had felt real because of the distress and the crying. She *always feels awful* but for a quarter of an hour she felt awful *about something*" (Winnicott, 1965b, 133)

For Winnicott, the girl's experience of feeling the pain in his presence enabled her to have it understood by someone outside herself who gave it meaning. It is worth noting how he connects *being believed* with a *sense of realness*. In this way the young girl was able to make sense of her experience. So too, Caroline, in the process of this long analysis, which had become three times a week from the first year, has experienced strong feelings very frequently, which often I was able to give sense to and find words for.

Emotional growth within the safety of therapy

In the safety of therapy feelings can be felt, named and given meaning, perhaps for the first time. This allows emotional growth and the development of emotional intelligence. When meanings are given, links in thought can be made and this hopefully will enable an expansion from concrete thinking to emotional thinking. But at this stage, this seems to happen only within the closed womb of the analysis. This developing capacity to contain feelings is very fragile and Caroline seems to allow herself to feel *only in my presence*.

***

Back to the clinic. In the session that followed the "education lesson to the pregnant child Caroline" via the doll, Caroline takes even longer to enter and then communicates in body language. Instead of going to her "usual place" under the table, she hides in a new place – under a very narrow desk. I can find no comfortable place to sit next to her. Eventually, she tells me that she is afraid to go to "where the operation was" (near the coffee table). At this point I "step out" of the transitional space of the enactment and introduce my own reality and physical limitations. I will not agree to sit where I am in physical discomfort. In this way I am conveying to her that we are not one body but two separate physical beings, each to be respected. I hope that this kind of unspoken message also reaches her internally to help her identify with me as someone who will not allow herself to be abused.

Concretely, I do agree to move the coffee table by a few centimetres so that she can return there, where I also have a place to sit. (We both know she is not ready to come out of hiding yet so it is not an option for her to sit in a chair or lie on the analytic coach.) And I add, speaking to the Caroline baby who I think is also identified with the aborted dead baby:

> Maybe you don't have to have this life killed. Maybe in this transitional space this baby can be given life. We can look after her, love her because she was not to blame for how she was created. Maybe what was the unspeakable doesn't have to happen again.

In this way, I am offering her the possibility of transforming the trauma to something new – life versus death with a new therapist as "alternative" mother figure.

After a very long silence, and staring intensely at me, Caroline asks, "Can you do it?"

T: "I think I can if you chose this alternative."

She cried throughout my talking.

***

To the following session she brings me a letter from a gynaecologist, addressed to her, stating that she will not agree to her request for a hysterectomy because "it is irrational and dangerous". The doctor's letter goes on to specify the dangers: she could suffer a stroke or die from the anaesthesia.

Caroline wants to convince me that it *is* rational for her to have the operation; that the doctor does not understand her. She wants my help to persuade her. Had she taken my offer to live as a promise to help her in this way? Here, I add my voice to the sane voice of the gynaecologist:

> To have the operation is irrational in its concreteness. You off-load your feeling of badness onto this body part, your womb, and want to think that if it is taken out the bad feelings will go away. But the badness you feel is as a whole person and there is no guarantee that if your womb is taken out you'll feel differently. And if you want to do it because you feel you may have sex again in the future without wanting to risk pregnancy – then that's for us to think about in therapy.

Caroline leaves very disheartened, taking both the doll and the letter with her. It is the first time she has taken the doll away since introducing her almost two months earlier.

Over the course of the coming sessions, Caroline tries to explain her logic. If she has her womb taken out it is evident that she wanted to prevent a pregnancy and thus an abortion. That she had no part in wanting to kill a foetus. This would ease her feeling of badness. I find myself immersed in her "logic", explaining that her action will not be understood like that. It will be thought that she had suffered from some physical illness and therefore had her womb removed, so even on these grounds it is irrational.

This argumentative mode only increases Caroline's despair and she angrily tells me a very lucid thought: "At least you understand that you cannot understand me!"

In the following session Caroline brought me Winnicott's article: "Fear of Breakdown" (1963a). It is the first psychological article she brought me. I had not mentioned to Caroline that I too was reading Winnicott and now it strikes me as remarkable that both of us, independently, should have been reading the same article at the same time.

Winnicott's understanding that the reality of the unknown past can only be recovered if it is relived in the transference situation was critical in my work with Caroline. If she could acknowledge what was real within the safety of therapy it could help her "know" her history.

Gradually, over time, I would realize that "Fear of Breakdown" provided me with the guideline as to how I should treat Caroline. Winnicott's brilliant insight that there had been a breakdown that had already happened but could not be known because it had happened before the capacity to know had developed, is an apt description of Caroline's trauma. Winnicott relates primarily to very early preverbal experiences, before mentalization has developed. However, a similar kind of experiencing that does not undergo mentalization (Fonagy, 2002) as such occurs when dissociation is activated. This can occur at any age and is a well-known phenomenon in victims of incest. The dissociation exists as a form of *absence*, which becomes a "no memory" – for how is one to have a memory of an absence? With time Caroline will find a way to become more conscious of this kind of ephemeral experience which contributes to the sense of unreality.

Winnicott's other important understanding that was so relevant here – was that for the trauma to become a memory it had to be *experienced* in the transference relationship. This I knew to be true. I knew her deadness in my presence was a re-experiencing of something. But how to know more specifically – a re-experiencing of *what*? She seemed to have created a re-experience of an abortion, using me to represent the abuser. Hopefully, we could now allow the working through process to develop. But Caroline had other plans for us.

A response to separation

On the day she brings me "Fear of Breakdown" Caroline says nothing, and lies motionless under the table. I hear three grunt-like sounds. With both verbal and bodily language not being of use she had left herself with only primitive vocalizations to resort to. I feel at a dead end again. My associations go to: is she showing me she has been left to die? Is she identified with the aborted foetus? I then recall that I have told her of a forthcoming holiday of a week, and also of an approaching month-long summer vacation I will be taking this year. Is she letting me know that it is *I* who is leaving her to die? She has always responded with dead-like long silences to any break that I initiate. When I leave she acts as though all memory of me as a good object gets annihilated inside her and she experiences a psychological death. Her response to separation is always extreme and devastating. Recall the time she asked to be hospitalized when I had taken a particular long vacation. In years to follow she will become capable of forming a real friendship and such severe measures will not be repeated.

Up to the month before my summer break we are still dealing with the abused doll, who, happily, is no longer being thrown into the dustbin. Caroline has brought her back and shortly before my trip I am surprised to see that she has put her *under* the carpet. She then asks if I am willing to take her with me. I had been holding her in my arms, like a loved baby in the past few sessions and understand that this doll is representative of the "newly reborn" Caroline baby, the one I had promised to try and help if she gave up on the idea of having a hysterectomy.

In asking me to take the doll, I interpret that Caroline thinks I will forget her unless I concretely take the Caroline doll with me. I counter that I will not need to take her and she will see for herself if I have been able to keep her held in my mind. And I add: "I cannot give to you what you should have had in the past and that is very painful. You fear that the doll under the carpet can be trodden on like a piece of shit, abused – done with whatever – when she is not being held and protected by her mother."

When Caroline leaves this session, this time leaving the doll with me, I find myself sitting with the doll cuddled in my lap, hoping she notices this visual image and that perhaps it will remain as a memory that will help her survive the month of separation. Maybe she will experience it somewhere between the concrete and symbolic – a representation of herself being "held in mind" even when we are concretely separated.

The importance of being honest

However, I decide *not* to take the doll with me on my long vacation. I had not actually been clear about telling her that but had left her request unanswered. On my return she meets me with:

C: You didn't take her?
T: No. I wanted a holiday. I didn't take anyone to look after.
C: You said you would. You wouldn't have told me the truth if I wouldn't have asked?
T: Probably not. I didn't have the courage to feel cruel to you. I knew you wanted me to take her. I didn't want to but I didn't want to disappoint you. I can understand you being angry about that.

I don't always think I have to be so openly honest with my patients. Sometimes it's more helpful to refrain from answering and thus allow space for projections; but as always, with Caroline I find that she will "see through me" if I do not answer her. In later years books will be published on therapy with victims of childhood incest where it is stressed that transparency in the patient–analyst relationship is essential so as not to repeat the pathological experiences of the family where the child was lied to so that the parent, rather than the victimized child would be protected.

Telling Caroline the truth first prompts her to wish to withdraw from me. But in spite of this she is able to share her experience. Perhaps because I was openly honest with her. She accuses me of humiliating her, making fun of her, leading her on to believe something that was not true. I again have doubts about what I did. Will she ever be able to separate me from her experience with her parents?

Still caring when apart

After ten years of working together I kept asking myself if anything positive had accumulated over time. I decided that this was an opportunity to "psycho educate" her about our separateness. After all, I could not truly maintain the illusion of symbiosis that she seemed to need or demand. When I say something to her in this light, she surprises me by taking it in – so much so that she asks me to write it down for her on paper so that she could take it with her. The following is what I said and gave to her written on a piece of paper:

> I cannot carry the concrete doll with me but that does not mean I forget you or do not care about you when we are apart. That is why we have symbols. Yet you need it to be concrete. You felt betrayed by me when I said I might take the doll with me and you heard I had not. You said that I led you to believe something that wasn't true. Like with your father – you believed he would hold you and hug you and he behaved differently.

When I mentioned her father, Dad, she started to cry. It was heartbreaking.

C: You've been laughing at me all this time?
T: No. But that's how it felt in the past – a double humiliation – abused and then lead to believe that it didn't happen; that you were imagining things ... That's why you always want to know exactly what's on the other's mind, so you won't misunderstand. That's why our language here is so under control. That's why the concreteness is so important to you.
C: If you take the doll concretely you don't have to worry about remembering her. Is that what you mean?
T: (impressed by her deep understanding) I think so – it has to do with trust. It's hard for you to believe that I remember you so you want me to take the doll concretely with me. Then you don't have to worry about that.

I think and interpret that Caroline is projecting onto me what happens to her – that she is unable to keep the memory of me inside her for long, as though there is no introject of me developing, and she thus always needs external proof from the outside that I exist. I wonder if "not keeping me inside her" is a defence against incest – wanting nothing of the incestuous father left inside her.

I then have a thought that I share with her, "As a little girl you had a huge hunger for physical contact – hugs, kisses from mother, but also guilt about hiding the relationship with father from her. Your need was insatiable because the moment the hug was over, you were left with your guilt. You could not tell her the truth out of fear of your mother's response."

Caroline asks seriously: "You're not laughing at me?" and she then asks me to write down what I have just said.

***

"I did the other one"

At the next session she does not arrive. I found her outside the clinic in the corridor sitting on the floor, her head between her knees. Eventually, I am able to encourage her to come inside. This is behaviour I am already familiar with. It happens often after something particularly painful has come up in the previous session.

Eventually Caroline says, "Do you know what it's like to have everything concrete?"

She talks about the badness: "It's inside – the badness. They didn't let me take it out."

She is under the table again, holding the little doll. "It's too much – both being it and talking about it."

T: I couldn't agree to the hysterectomy. You see it as a concrete taking out "the badness" but I believe in symbolization. It involves major surgery and you could die.
C: **But I did the other one!**

She informs me that she has had the sterilization operation. I am absolutely shocked. As far as I knew, it was the first time she had enacted her madness on the outside. I think I realized then: *she really is living the past in the present*. I insist she tells me the details, being reluctant to believe and needing "proof". (As has been the case in the past years, on my summer vacations she would go overseas to stay with the one sibling she was in positive contact with. This helped her survive our separations. This would continue until she develops a friendship with Anne and moves in to live with her around the eighteenth year of therapy.) She now tells how when she was overseas while I was on vacation she went to a private hospital where no questions were asked. She stayed overnight. No pain. No need to lie afterwards. Smiling a self-satisfied smile, Caroline says: "If I didn't do anything else at least I did that." And she added, seeing my look of total incomprehension: "So that it will never happen again!" as if that was a satisfactory explanation.

I am close to tears, the tears she can't feel, thinking – the blue-haired doll she has been carrying in and out of our place is the closest she will have to holding a baby. Is this the courage she needed to not repeat what she had experienced with her mother – feeling an unwanted baby who was emotionally aborted? I feel overcome by a deep sadness.

Caroline continues, "But the rest is still inside – the badness."

T: Yes, we'll have to find a way to transform concrete to symbolic.
C: Do you know what to do?

T: I'm not sure I do … we'll try together. You want me to do it rapidly like the sterilization. If I could wave a magic wand – just take out your inner feeling of badness. But I guess the physical, concrete is easier to do – go in and come out (of your body) – than dealing with the mind.
C: Yes.

Careful use of language

An explanation is needed concerning the above sentence. The words in brackets are *not said aloud*, the reason being that I have learnt that any reference to her body or body part is experienced concretely, as though I am *touching* her body. Thus I have learnt to be careful in my use of language with her.

***

Sterilization as turning point

It has been 11 years since the beginning of therapy. This coming out from under the table in order to "enact" the "rape scene" coincides with what could be called in retrospect the beginning of the second phase of the therapy where Caroline starts to become more coherent. She begins to bring written material to the sessions and there is now content to relate to, not just the creating of a safe place.

Retrospectively I conceptualize to myself that in this first period, of 11 years, Caroline has been intra-uterus: developing into a human baby in the safety of my protective womb, represented by the walls of my clinic. Under the table she lies in a foetus position immobile and silent. In the dictionary she had given to me, she had defined:

> Table: security; real/concrete.

Sterilization in the transference

The sterilization definitely was a turning point. It preceded the bringing of written texts which, as shall be seen, were a source of unimaginable information about Caroline's horrific ordeals. (see Chapter 5 and beyond) Retrospectively, I think that one of the reasons was that in the transference I represented both the abusive *and* desired loved father whom she both feared and wanted to seduce. The sterilization procedure enabled her to feel safe in the sense that she had done something to protect herself. She had acted to ensure that she could not get pregnant again, albeit from ME!

***

Immobility: mother's unconscious death wish

Thinking about Caroline's immobility, I often tried to interpret it over these years and new understandings continued to arise throughout our 26 years together. One of the first interpretations we gave to it was that it represented an identification with her mother's death wishes towards her. In order to not lose her mother's love she chooses to be as her mother had wanted – a dead, aborted thing. To confirm this interpretation she brought me a poem and underlined were the words: "I live inside someone who hates me."

So in my clinic she created a new womb in a therapist/mother who wanted her to live. She tested my ability to survive her for many years. The ability to love this silent non-communicative "thing" was not to be taken for granted. There were moments where I felt hate – hate for making me feel so frustrated, such a failure as a therapist, and hate for the attendant feelings of guilt. The guilt was often caused by the extreme response to any separation I caused. It was a hate that issued from my feelings of failure to give her *enough* life, not from a place that wanted her to die.

Deep down, I did believe that Caroline knew *I wanted her to live*. Her strong motivation to keep coming so persistently over all the years was based on the hope that through my wanting her to live she would be resuscitated. Yet, she seemed to constantly need to test me to see if I could survive her silent attacks and the silence was to remain.

Chapter 4

From dead ends to DID[1]

Time line: years 11–22

The following are some milestones on the therapeutic journey that led to the discovery of the Little Girl Caroline – a "separate" Persona, who suddenly came out of "hiding" after 22 years of therapy, appearing at my doorstep, as though for the first time.

Countertransference to the sterilization procedure

My reaction to Caroline's triumphant announcement about carrying out the sterilization was of extreme shock. At the time I did not yet know that this was only the first of many emotional shocks I was to receive. I feel it is important that I share with the reader what I experienced in response to her dramatic announcement and the concomitant understandings, even at the risk of some repetition.

To the extent that I was horrified – she was pleased. For her – she had done something positive with her life: she had taken control and ownership over her body in an active way. "So that it will never happen again!" she had said, with an air of satisfaction, and I had been completely speechless! As far as I knew she was celibate and phobic of men. Her seeking therapy was in response to her extreme reaction to being in the vicinity of a male who visited her office. Her action meant she was living the past and using action as a solution to her, in my mind, imagined difficulties. So she must be psychotic, I thought.

I realized my shock came from some unconscious belief, or a need to believe, that this was not so. Although much of her behaviour definitely was characterized by psychotic features, it seems, in my overall experience of her, I did not think of her as psychotic.

The fact that *only now*, after being with her in such a regressed way for 11 years, I had the thought: "She must be crazy for doing such a thing!" was rather mad in itself. Although I had no clear way to explain it to myself, my experience of her was incompatible with that of a mad person. I had related to her unusual behaviour as extreme regression and had contained it within the transference, without labelling it diagnostically. As far as I knew, in the real world, Caroline acted normally. How to reconcile these complex feelings in the countertransference? Theoretically, I could not really explain it. Although the concept of dissociation was known to me from textbooks – it was not a common diagnosis in those early years of therapy and, retrospectively, I can now understand that I had no idea what that syndrome was like. Without it being a conscious decision I had felt that what was important was that I try and understand her – without any form of categorization. I intuitively felt that any conscious attempt to diagnose her limited my capacity to keep myself open minded to whatever was to be. I think part of the shock I received was realizing that here *I understood nothing*. This act seemed to destroy my omnipotent belief that I was being of therapeutic help to her. Somehow, the fact that until then her bizarre behaviour was limited to the therapeutic space had kept me hopeful that with time we would understand something and that was of value in itself. Now this belief was shattered.

The action on her own body was irreversible and in my eyes, violent. It was physical. No interpretation, nor empathic understanding could undo this abusive action. At the time I was a mother of three young children and the fact that she had acted to prevent herself from ever becoming a mother was devastating to me. I think I did realize that she was totally identified with the abused child and any thought of becoming a mother was alien to her. Only many years later would I learn about the abusive experiences she suffered at the hands of her own mother. But at this time – nothing was yet "known". How much this act represented things she knew, even pre-consciously at the time, is an open question.

Caroline's action, to some extent, shook my belief in psychoanalysis itself. I believed then, naively, that a new relationship through psychotherapy could bring "new life" even to a very ill patient. For me, at that time, her act of making sure she herself could never give birth made me feel an incompetent mother in the countertransference. I had received a narcissistic blow. I lost belief in my relatively omnipotent belief at the time, that with care, hard work and learning, I could help anyone seeking help.

The immediate effect of her action, however, was to enhance my belief that she *had* been abused, become pregnant and had had an abortion. It's as though, having no language to tell me about it, she had to act to let me know, to let us both know. Her narrative had to be acted because it could not be "thought".

Yet, I feel the need to introduce another little thought that comes to me as I write. Perhaps there was an alternative explanation for my great shock response: perhaps I could not conceive of myself sitting with a fragmented person, three times a week, and feeling magnetized by her. Perhaps I feared it meant there was something wrong with me, so I needed to see her as healthier than she was? At the time I was too young in my career to know that this was a common countertransference response when working with psychotics. But, as I write this, no one answer feels quite right, just as no diagnosis quite fitted her. This way of thinking, often needing to contain the doubts, is just one example of the strain in the counter-transference I often experienced.

After the sterilization

The sessions were filled with silences that led nowhere. Here we were, frozen in space: she lying in a foetal position under the table, me sitting next to her on the floor, depleted. I think I was in mourning. I felt like a mother pregnant with a dead foetus. I was ready to abort her. She must have felt my despair. This mobilized something in her that made her more active to help us move out of this *dead end*, yet another of the many impasses that we came to. Had this not happened I think it would have been the end of therapy – a real dead end. Her activity, resuscitating us, was right on time. It helped remind me that we were in this struggle because it was her wish, and not some perverted curiosity on my part.

The Hanged Doll

She knew I also worked with children and after hearing a bit about play therapy from me she asked if I would agree to bring some things. Of course, I agreed. She made a list: scissors, string, red paint, a basin with water. On the day when I did bring everything, including a camera, which I added to the list, I found a little red-haired doll in a plastic bag waiting for me at the front door. In another plastic bag, hanging on my door handle, was a pile of fresh faeces!

In the session, which I photographed, she diligently went about cutting off all the doll's hair, then spread red paint all over the poor damaged thing, as well as all over her own bare arms, which were always exposed elbow high by having her sleeves rolled up, in all weather. She then tied this bleeding little bare haired doll to a string, which she strung up from the curtain rod on my window after climbing a chair.

Only later did I realize there had been unprecedented, live movement in the room. All this was enacted in total silence – almost in a trance state. So much vitality had been invested in creating a death scene! I took photographs. *Seeing is believing.*

I think I will never forget that incident. I wonder at times what it was that made this "act" feel so overwhelmingly devastating to me. After all, it was "only" a doll. The red paint was paint and not real blood. Thinking about it now – where at a distance I can find some words for the traumatic experience, I think what made it so difficult for me was the feeling of *realness* that was aroused. Caroline was not playing, the way children play, using the toys to express their imagination, fantasy, wishes and fears. Caroline was showing me something, re-living something she had to go through. She needed me to know something terrible. I am sure the faeces in the plastic bag, hanging on the door handle with the doll was a way to show me something of the physical panic, terror, she had experienced that arouses the loss of all bodily control, where one's insides spill out and there is a threat of falling apart.

At the time I could not say anything about the faeces except that I did not permit her to bring them to therapy. At the time, I was overwhelmed with disgust and fear. I thought of her as psychotic and myself with a task of representing "the rules of reality". At a conscious level, at the time I thought I was witnessing a re-enactment of an abortion she had experienced and had no way of putting into words. But unconsciously, my emotional reaction registered "something too terrible for words".

Some thoughts about the Hanged Doll enactment:

1 Being a child therapist, the use of play was familiar territory for me. But Caroline's "play" had a driven quality. It took on the quality of "putting on a play" for me to see. In my associations this took me to Shakespeare's use of a play within a play in *Hamlet*, where the prince wishes to reveal that he knows about the murder of his father, when this is too dangerous to speak about openly.
2 Why did I introduce a camera? It is not something I had ever done previously in therapy, either with her or anyone else. I believe I intuitively knew that one of my primary functions was to be a *witness* to something yet to be revealed. And a witness needs *evidence*. Also, the concreteness of a photograph seemed useful against the erasing of memory that Caroline activated.

A therapist's amnesia

About ten years later, towards the end of the therapy, the Hanged Doll incident came up again. She asked to see the evidence – the doll that I had kept in her box, as well as the chopped off hair and the photographs. (I had a box for her in which were kept her items, mainly texts she brought. I took this idea of a concrete box from my work with children in play therapy.)

What I found in the box was, to my shock, not the red-haired bleeding doll, but a blue-haired one, with her body covered with the word "fuck" written all over her. I had completely forgotten about the whole incident leading to that doll being put away in my box (see Chapter 3). It's true it had happened ten years earlier. However, the Hanged Doll incident I never forgot. So what had caused this massive repression concerning the Raped Doll that had happened only a few months before the Hanged Doll incident? Something in that enactment must have been "too much" for me. Perhaps it was specifically, *unbearable guilt*. (I had, after all "allowed" Caroline to abuse the little (girl) doll and had participated by carrying out her command and writing "fuck" all over her.) I think this incident confirmed for me the fact that quite massive amnesia can be caused by emotional trauma, especially when guilt feelings are involved. Caroline herself did remember all the details, and when I first could not recall *who* had written "fuck" all over her, *she* knew it had been me. I had repressed this "abusive behaviour" on my part to such an extent that until I checked my notes, which confirmed that she was right, I was not convinced.

Yet, it really had been me! The trauma of behaving so sadistically, even to a doll, had been erased in my memory. This incident helped me later empathize with Caroline's *needing not to know* about her own cruelty in the past. I had repressed the whole incident including my repugnant feelings at having agree to write "FUCK" all over this sweet little doll.

Later I was to wonder if perhaps my wish to introduce a camera to the Hanged Doll incident was directed by some unconscious "knowing" that I had repressed the earlier incident. Introducing the camera was a way of ensuring this would not be repeated. If I was to be a witness, at least my ability to remember the enacted traumas *in the analysis* should be guaranteed.

***

And now we must bury her in the *garden*

Now back to *"the hanging"*. The hanged dead doll was taken down from her noose. Caroline now wanted to actually *bury* the doll after we had taken her down. I found myself in a great dilemma. Somehow, having at times complied with concrete enacting in the therapy (reading the books she gave me, letting her be under the table and now bringing the items to do things to the doll) why not allow her to bury her? We started thinking of an "appropriate place" and came up with the backyard of my clinic. (At the time my clinic was in a rented apartment building). But suddenly I was overcome by dread. I envisioned Caroline coming to "mourn" the dead doll at all times of day and night, standing near the *grave* and thus unwittingly drawing danger to herself (I feared the neighbours would call the police). I suddenly realized that to comply with this wish of hers was to *enter into the madness* with her and thus to endanger her as well. I think I realized, after having agreed, that truly she could not use the doll as a symbol, but would relate to her as the thing in itself (Segal, 1957) as the dead baby aborted from her womb, whom she would wish to mourn concretely and I would then have encouraged her psychosis rather than acted as "the responsible adult/therapist" whose task is to help adjust to reality at the risk of disappointing and angering her.

So I told Caroline that I had changed my mind and that I could not allow her to actually bury her. She became furious and accused me of being unreliable and dishonest. She demanded an exact explanation. I thought she deserved one and described it in detail. Little did I know that some years hence I would find myself participating in an enactment of a "garden burial" with her.

From this crisis there was positive development. Caroline brought me a text describing her view of the events, which included *her being able to believe me* that my change of mind was only motivated by care for her. This was a completely new experience for her.

In time we shall see how important it was that I acted "as a real person", representing the boundaries of reality but also offering reality explanations for my behaviour and sharing my real thoughts and feelings with her – all of which proved growth enhancing for Caroline. This behaviour on my part showed her that I took her seriously and this in turn, contributed to her developing sense of feeling cared about as a separate person and *feeling real*.

"So therapy is a *real* space!"

The following is part of her amazing text in response to my change of mind about burying the doll:

> ~Having agreed that a grave might be a good idea, Tova then articulated her reservation that such a concrete object might simply externalize the problem: looking after the grave might become an obsession that would tie me to the past, just as much as holding onto the baby inside. It might pose an even greater problem than the latter, given that we can talk about the abortion/baby in therapy but she couldn't control how often I would go to the grave.
>
> In trying to find ways to get round this problem, we looked on the issue of consequences. Tova wanted to make sure that we didn't do anything that would be harmful to me – as happened with the abortion itself – as this time we had the option to look at all the implications and decide whether a particular course of action was good for me or not. What came out of that was that therapy constitutes a real space where I can be – where she endeavours to make sure my interests are served. This got through to me somehow – the fact that the therapy space is actually real ... I've created it – after a lot of checking and making sure that it's safe – and M/D (Mom/Dad) can't interfere or take it away. I've paid for it myself too. Somewhere deep down I've perhaps known that I needed such a space and not given up on finding it. It also made sense when Tova suggested that rather than making a grave – with all of the dangers implicit in such an act – we look at why I need a concrete object and can't be satisfied that she knows about the abortion and the baby and won't forget, which should be sufficient.~

What makes this text so remarkable for me is that it itself feels so "real" – written by a real normal person – normal in that she shows such capacity for coherent thinking. This, as mentioned before, is in absolute contrast to the "mad" Caroline I met in the room. You may have not noticed, as I didn't until writing this chapter, that in the text Caroline also "deciphers" why she has been sitting under the table for so long in her foetal position: she had been in this way obsessively *"holding onto the baby inside"*. (See lines four to five of her text above.) No wonder she wouldn't talk to me. She was "being a foetus" all that time! Also worthy of note is that in her *writing* she does not doubt having had an abortion. It is stated as a fact. How different from her tantalizing doubts when *talking* with me!

From mother's death to giving life

Seventeen years into therapy Caroline's mother died after a long illness. Caroline flew home to be at her mother's death bed and attended her funeral. On her return she was able to tell me that she had realized that all her life she had been afraid of her mother but only knew this now, since she recognized an *absence* of fear. This was a new experience for her. Another new experience was her actually sharing such thoughts and realizations with me, live, in present time, in the therapy room. She was sharing with me her ability to introspect and mentalize. Until now I only encountered this introspective Caroline through her writing. (At the time I myself was not aware of the newness of this experience so I did not think of mentioning it.)

Donation to a neonate unit

As a result of her mother's death Caroline received a large inheritance. By this time, as an outcome of her overall psychological development, Caroline had developed a close relationship with a colleague at work and they had actually become friends and now lived together. She was no longer totally alone with only me to rely on. After initially wanting to give all the inheritance away, her friend, who will be called "Anne" from now on, convinced her to do good deeds with it. Finally, after two years of our "preparation" in therapy – she donated a considerable amount for the purchase of new medical equipment for a neonatal unit in one of the large local hospitals. A plaque was put on the donors' wall in a ceremony that I attended. She actually related to me as the "guest of honour". It was a very exciting event for both of us. It was also the first time we met intentionally in outside reality. Photographs were taken of the event and this time it was she who asked my permission for this. Anne photographed the two of us standing on either side of the life-saving equipment, like two proud parents enjoying the fruit of their creation. Years later Caroline will tell me that she uses one of these pictures of us as the screen saver on her computer. Here is what she wrote to me shortly before the ceremony while debating what to write on the plaque:

~The whole point is to make the abortion – and the memory of it – concrete ... rather than the grave, that Tova had insisted wasn't a good idea ... Anne had suggested to donate something that would bring life instead of focusing on the death ... The first problem was the name. I don't want to use my family name – I don't want the baby to have to carry all that with her, to deal with it, to have to be a part of it. This is like a fresh start – a "newborn" baby who has a symbolic life even if she never had an actual one. I usually refer to her as "her" because to some degree I'm part of her.~

When Caroline cites *"that Tova had insisted wasn't a good idea"*. she is referring to the Hanged Doll incident of ten years previously. She relates to it as if oblivious of time, as though it were only yesterday that we had discussed making a grave for the hanged doll.

The sick rose

Eventually, Caroline decided not to write a name on the donor plaque but sign it with an engraving of a small rose. Only she and I knew that this was the rose from William Blake's poem: "The Sick Rose".

> Oh rose thou art sick. The invisible worm
> That flies in the night in the howling storm
> Has found out thy bed of crimson joy,
> His dark secret love
> Does thou life destroy.

We both felt that hospital donation to the neonatal unit represented a turning point in Caroline's life. The plaque on the hospital donation wall represented the outside world's recognition of her past traumas. As if to confirm this knowledge, the next day she brought me the photos in an envelope. I felt she was giving me a small gift, thanking me for my participation in her act of reparation. In the envelope was a note in her hand writing:

~Yesterday was a way of saying sorry for what had happened, acknowledging the existence of the baby that had never been acknowledged.~

Nothing changes

We both hoped and expected that now something would change and we would enter a new stage in our therapeutic endeavours. Perhaps a new Caroline could be born just as the donated equipment, made possible by the death of her mother, would allow new healthy babies to live. But, in spite of this development, as always, *nothing changed.* Caroline again reverted to her "familiar self" – of being immobile, not moving, with no proof that anything we "knew" was real. So it was another dead end. She again resorted to bringing me books to read. However, I noticed something different when she brought me the novel *Me & Emma* by Elizabeth Flock, When she came in with it, I thought I recognized some excitement or anticipation, quite uncharacteristic of her.

"Maybe I'm not the real one. I'm the imaginary person"

Caroline's giving me the book *Me & Emma* will be described in some detail because it was a significant milestone on the road to revealing a much hidden secret – the existence of the dissociated part of herself: Little Girl Caroline, who would soon "appear" in my clinic.

When Caroline gave me this book to read she made a special request – something she had never done in the past when giving me something to read. She asked that I tell her immediately when I finished reading it. This book took me completely by surprise. It is a fiction crime novel describing the ordeal of two sisters, one of which had witnessed *the murder* of her father and had since then become completely dumb, losing her ability to speak. She is the younger of the two sisters, and about five years old. Her name is Emma. The narrator is her older sister, Cathy[2] who is 12. Their mother remarries a very aggressive man who becomes sexually abusive to little Emma. He often takes her to his room and she obeys him in a trance-like state, emerging injured and dishevelled and yet *saying nothing*. The mother does not see what is happening, but stays "blind" to all this, being very dependent on her man. Eventually, with much struggle and anguish, to the great relief of the reader, Cathy manages to get hold of a gun and kills the stepfather, thus saving her little sister. The amazing ending is the surprising revelation to the reader at the close of the book, that *the two little girls are in fact one*, and the same girl. Emma was the externalization of the trauma of abuse suffered by the dissociated Cathy, the abused victim and the narrator – the book being written in the first person. It was the best work of fiction describing dissociation that I had ever come across.

When I finished the book, – I, too felt very excited and shared my emotional response to it with Caroline. It was as though Caroline, in her indefatigable search for books to describe her unbelievable experiences, had finally found something that came close to explaining to her the enigma of "not knowing anything" and being silent – made "dumb" like Emma.

The idea of her being in a dissociated state came into my mind more clearly as a possibility and I described this phenomenon to her, now having the book as a reference point. From the following text that Caroline gave to me after I told her excitedly that I had finished reading *Me & Emma* it is clear that Caroline herself understands and is becoming conscious of her "falling into" altered states of consciousness. She shares this with me in the following text, written four months before the new persona will make her unforeseen appearance in my clinic.

> ~Around a month ago, a neighbour was shouting and screaming when I arrived. It was clearly audible and I couldn't focus on anything else. When Tova asked me what it reminded me of, I said that either Mom was angry (with me) and /or that she'd found out. Tova thought that that was the middle of a sentence and that I was alluding to something I knew Mom had found out. When we started talking about that I lost touch with what was going on. About half an hour later (according to Tova) I came back to and realized that what we'd been talking about hadn't actually been there in the room – but it was a lived experience from the past. It was a very dramatic illustration of dissociation …~

For me, it was fascinating to read this, since in my actual presence, in real time, what I had seen was that Caroline "disappeared" after mentioning her association of her mom to the screaming noisy neighbour, and she was shocked that so much time had elapsed before she returned to consciousness. What made this feel such an immense moment was that this was the first time Caroline became aware of her dissociation and her "coming back" into the present space and time. It was the first time she was able to differentiate how the past intruded into the present rather than just enacting the past in the present. I was immensely relieved at this evidence of the development of mentalization.

She went on to give another example of a similar event where she dissociated in my presence:

> ~Today I'd wanted to talk about the pages I'd brought on Thursday to Tova. Tova said she'd put the sheets away, for safekeeping but couldn't locate them at that moment. I need to know because it's as though she'd hidden them. She said that it was like my never being sure whether anyone was telling the truth and having no one to check things with. But it was more than things being hidden: it was like me being hidden – so that I didn't exist; my existence was hidden because no one wanted to acknowledge it. I think part of the feeling came from the book *Me & Emma,* which I'd just given to Tova to read: the feeling that I'm not the real me, that I've invented myself so that I don't have to know what actually happened – what "I" experienced. With Cathy and Emma, Cathy externalized Emma so that she became an "outside reality", as it were. That way she could "know". I didn't do that, so all my knowledge got hidden, with no way to access it – or the person who experienced the events.
>
> Maybe I am not the real one. I'm the imaginary person: the "real" one, the one to whom everything happened – is dead. And I don't know anything more than imaginary things … what's here now is just a shadow –

living in the shadow of the past and knowing (as far as anyone imaginary can really "know" anything) somewhere that I'm not really real.~

On reading what Caroline has written, I again find myself filled with hope. Surely, if the "writing Caroline" whom I never meet, is capable of such insight and deep psychological understanding I will soon meet her in the clinic and "together" we will help her heal. But, as always, after this excitement around the book *Me & Emma*, again the familiar *deadness* returns and again a sense of "going nowhere" replaces the momentary liveliness we experienced together. This was so familiar by now – after the Raped Doll, the Hanged Doll, the Hospital Donation event – now *Me & Emma* would be added to the list of revealing events that seemed like dead leaves blown by the wind of the force of destruction. Caroline insisted, there were no real memories because she had no real experiences. Maybe she'd imagined it all and she was mad, and I was a fool for believing otherwise. Why was this? We had both read together about sexually abused patients, who were able to own their past in the form of memories and thus begin a healing process (Davies and Fawley, 1994). What was preventing this from happening here? I began to think that in her past much worse things must have happened than *merely* the trauma of incest and abortion. Something so dreadful must have taken place that it could not be known no matter how much she tried to find out – a "nameless dread" (Bion, 1970).

Immobility: being the dead aborted baby

Caroline's being "dead" now had an additional meaning – I saw her as being identified with the dead baby that I now thought may have been aborted as a live baby, that perhaps had died or been helped to die during birth. The idea of *a killing* came into my mind. It was a persistent reverie (Ogden, 2004b). I started having visual images of mass execution scenes I had seen in documentary films of the Holocaust. I was not hallucinating but something about her uncanny presence created my reverie and I had to attend to it. I found myself, daring, albeit very carefully, to ask if it could be that she had been involved in some way with seeing someone killed. This had been the trauma described in *Me & Emma* that had struck Emma dumb. Had she been involved in killings in some way? I raised this question very gently, fearing myself to receive confirmation. I related to it in the language of doubt – using non-committal words such as "perhaps" and "maybe". While maintaining silence she made an affirmative nod with her head, while *no word* was actually vocalized by her.

Amazingly, Caroline strengthened my suspicions by bringing me a book to read about mass slaughter. It was by Sebastian Barry and called *A Long Long Way*. It is about soldiers during the First World War witnessing and participating in mass slaughter in combat and in the trenches. There are very explicit horrific scenes describing slaughtered bodies, making it most difficult to read. The following is one of the paragraphs she underlined almost imperceptibly for me to read aloud:

> These were the bodies of creatures gone beyond their own humanity into a severe state that had no place in human doings and the human world.

Perhaps this explained her endless guilt and writing of herself as a "child killer".

The danger of suicide

Soon after the possibility of having killed a child was broached, Caroline begins to express thoughts of suicide. She fears that if we continue our search she might discover that she was *inhuman*. She wanted to end her life before this truth could become known to her, to us. The following is a vignette from this time:

> Anne, Caroline's close friend, calls me. She has never called before but she is very worried. Caroline had voiced suicidal thoughts to her. I arrange an emergency appointment with the psychiatrist. Caroline wants Anne and myself to attend with her. I am to be her voice. Perhaps Anne is her witness or protector. The psychiatrist prescribed a small dosage of anti-psychotic medication. I am in email contact with Caroline over the Passover vacation. Here is an email she wrote to me during my vacation:
>
> > I don't understand
> > I don't know what to do
> > I don't know where you are
> > I don't know how to reach you
> > I don't know how to go on
> > I don't know how to put a stop to things

When we met after my vacation Caroline was still contemplating suicide. She wanted to hear from me that if she did decide to end her life that I won't judge her, won't think badly of her. I told her that I cannot promise that. She cries and cries until the end of the hour.

***

In desperation Caroline again resorted to searching for herself in more books about victims of incest. Her search became obsessive – bringing chapter after chapter with underlined sentences; she wanted to know if the experience that other sexually abused victims described matched her experiences. So much was similar, so why wasn't she able to know? Why wasn't I helping her?

Perhaps I didn't know how? Perhaps. But what alternatives did we have? She wished to bring more articles for us to read. Perhaps the answer lay somewhere there. Finally, I felt and said: "No more! We cannot go on like this." I told her that I believed it was pointless to search for her memories in other people's words and that we had to stop using the books and return to our living relationship in the therapy to deepen our understanding.

My words struck her like lightning. Caroline did something she had never done before – she suddenly picked up her papers and walked out on me! Her first spontaneous movement in the 22 years I had known her! I was stunned and even more so when I found a note on the windshield of my car informing me that she would not be coming to her next appointment. But Caroline had never missed a session in our 22 years together. Could it be that she would not turn up for her hour? (In Chapter 15 of this book the narrative will continue from this point in time but first I must fill you, the reader in, with what had happened in these years in addition to the milestones just depicted.)

Notes

1 DID Dissociative Identity Disorder.
2 The narrator in *Me & Emma* is named Caroline. This is the origin of the pseudo name for my patient. In order to avoid confusion I have taken the liberty to change the name of the protagonist from the novel to Cathy, in this book.

Chapter 5

An alternative way to communicate
Written language

> Oh dear white children casual as birds, playing among the ruined languages, *So small besides their large confusing words.*
> from *Hymn to Saint Cecilia*, W.H. Auden

Timeline: years 11–22

This chapter will be devoted to describing Caroline's use of written texts as a means of communicating with me. Around the eighth year Caroline began to bring in an occasional article, and from the eleventh year onward she brought many texts.

When Caroline began to communicate in this way, at first she chose other people's words, some taken from books, poems or articles, even TV programs she had seen. The fact that she could choose such texts to let me know about her needs and experiences was reassuring since it allowed me to know that she was very intelligent, extremely well read and also at some deep level had an awareness of her traumas that she was trying to communicate to me, albeit, in this unusual way. For example, she had brought me a fascinating article by J. P Sartre describing Jean Genet's tragic existence together with an internet Wikipedia summary of his biography. The text describes Genet as an abandoned "motherless" child, a foundling.

This extreme contrast – between the Caroline in the outside world who reads Sartre and Winnicott and the one I encountered in my clinic, always left me with a sense of questioning – something I could not quite fathom – but engaged and curious about her. Why did she need to resort to such a severe split where no overlap between "inside" and "outside" was allowed? I could not put her into any neat slot, or categorize her in any clear diagnosis. Over the years, when I tried to on occasion, my "diagnosis" of her went from schizophrenia, to autism and then more specifically Asperger's syndrome, then post-trauma with psychotic manifestations, until finally, in the last four years, with the appearance of different personae I "settled" on DID. Reading up on this diagnosis (Sinason, 2002; van der Hart et al., 2006) I learnt that this is actually one of the characteristic experiences with those treating persons with DID – misdiagnosing their patients over many years until a persona appears.

In the twelfth year of therapy Caroline brought me the following text from Winnicott's *The Piggle* (1977, 170–171). The "Me" in the dialogue is Winnicott writing in the first person:

GABRIELLE: There. Mr. Winnicott I am going to stay a little bit longer than I usually do. I can play more if I have more time. I don't need to rush away.
ME: Sometimes you feel frightened about something, and then you feel you want to go suddenly.
GABRIELLE: Because it gets late ...
ME: Till you come next time. You feel that this gives you some hope of coming to me again.
GABRIELLE: For all time. (Then she looked at the portrait, mounted as it is in an oval mount, and said:) Look, she's in an egg.
ME: If she hadn't got a place to be she would be like Humpty Dumpty and go to pieces; but you have a place here where you can be.

***

I now had "Our Dictionary" and "The Piggle" to aid me. Humpty Dumpty had earlier become a metaphor in our work.

The above text, in a nutshell, contains all Caroline's wishes and needs: having a Person (Mr Winnicott) who provides a Place with Time where there is no need to rush, where there is a Someone who can put into words her feelings, who can hold onto her continuity, who understands that her fragile egg-self was shattered and she needs a Place to Be where the pieces can slowly be put together again. And I might add – a place to be able "to go to pieces" while holding on to hope that the pieces will be able to be put together.

In Hebrew the word "place" is "Makom". It is also used as one of the names for God. God first made a place and in that place, and only then, man was created. Once there is God /Place, a Human can be born. With time I discover that one of Caroline's deepest fears is that she is not human, that her inner "badness" is beyond the pale, beyond the bounds of the imaginable, beyond what can be forgivable. Caroline needed to create a new place – a womb within the walls of my clinic so as to have a safe place to be born into. Her foetal self needed time to grow. There was no way to rush her "birth", nor her speech. Winnicott (1960a) in one of his less known papers, describes that if a pregnant mother has negative fantasies about her foetus, if she sees him not as a whole human baby but as fragments of faeces or the like, this foetus may be dropped, aborted or even born distorted. Winnicott is relating to the pregnant mother as the patient when he describes possible reasons for spontaneous abortions: "It is as if she would be claiming what is false if she were to go through with the pregnancy and produce a whole baby" (p. 162).

My patient Caroline was that unwanted baby that though she was not physically aborted, seemed emotionally distorted from her very beginnings, a "false child" (see her quote from Sartre later in this chapter). Many years hence, she will find her own words to describe what contributes to her own sense of feeling a "false" person.

Because Caroline did not talk with me it was mostly the words of others she used. She added nothing to these written gifts so I could only speculate that she was identifying some part of herself in the writings. She was enacting the hope that I would understand something about her inner life without her needing to abandon that "foetal position" of being "dead" in my presence, curled up motionless under the table and silent.

The only sound heard was that of my voice reading aloud the texts she had brought for us. Although I did not know at the time if this was "the right thing" to do as a psychologist, I knew intuitively that I needed to accept her guidance. If I tried to insist on a less regressive way of communication, she would simply drop into total passivity and not cooperate, waiting for me to realize she had to have it this way.

A slight digression: Because Caroline was such an unusual case, I would at times take the opportunity to present her in supervision with guest experts from overseas who came for this purpose. On one occasion, (in a group supervision setting) when describing how I sat next to her on the floor, this supervisor was most critical of me, suggesting I was being controlled by her madness. On leaving the meeting, I was so distraught that I had a small car accident. I recall how devastating it was to feel so completely alone and misunderstood. Thankfully, I had support from my own supervisor who knew me and the case in a continuous way so I soon calmed down. I did, however, learn from this experience how traumatic it can be to be totally not understood. For a moment, I could identify with Caroline's unbearable pain and humiliation of having one's experiences scoffed at and devalued, yet having no outside third person to turn to for validation. It was to be years later that I come across Eigen's (2016) comforting words, quoting Bion:

> It is very important to be aware that you may never be satisfied with your analytic career if you feel that you are restricted to what is narrowly called a "scientific approach" … It is so important to dare to think or feel whatever you do think or feel, never mind how un-scientific it is.

Looking back, I think my reading aloud to Caroline the texts she brought me helped her to gather up her fragmented shards of self, mirroring them back to her in the hope that in the safety of this therapeutic womb a unitary self would evolve. I recall always speaking softly and gently as I read aloud her own words to her, a little like a mother singing a lullaby to her frightened child.

One of the first texts she brought me was by R. D. Laing from *Self and Others*. I will quote just a shortened version of what Caroline brought.

> There are many patients who are very sensitive to desertion, but are not sure of the reliability, much less validity, of their own sensitivity. They do not trust other people, and they cannot trust their own mistrust either ....

From this text I understood that Caroline wanted to share with me her sense of constant doubt about anything she thought and felt. I had been aware of this over the years and thought that this was a good example of what she had once expressed: her hope that if I read other people's words I might believe her. Since she lived in a constant doubt of knowing what to believe about her own experiences, her recurring fear was that I, too, would not believe her.

Caroline quoted several times from J. P. Sartre's essay (1952) on Jean Genet's life. His perversion is attributed to his difficult past, his mother having been a young prostitute. Sartre writes: "Having died in boyhood, Genet contains within him the dizziness of the irremediable, he wants to die again." In the extract Caroline brought, Sartre also writes:

> Innocent in general, he senses that he is suspect in particular. He is obliged, by error to use language which is not his own, which belongs only to legitimate children. Genet has neither mother nor heritage – how could he be innocent? By virtue of his mere existence he disturbs the natural order and the social order ... He is a fake child ...

Sartre continues as does Caroline with her choice of this long text, and I am left baffled. What is she trying to tell me? In what way does she feel identified with Sartre's long detailed description of a man born from violence whose life is that of "a fabricated creature, who will find his truth in solipsism"? She has also brought me a text describing Genet's biography including his perversions, violence and imprisonment. Is she telling me something of violence in her life? Yet, any questions on my part are met with the sound of silence. In the extract Caroline brought, Sartre continues:

> He is said to be "contrary to nature" ... We others who issue from the species have a mandate to continue the species. Genet, who was born without parents, is preparing to die without descendants. His sexuality will be sterility and abstract tension.

This is about the time Caroline is wanting to be sterilized (see Chapter 3). What am I to make of this? Is this how monstrously she sees herself?

Most of the texts were fascinating in themselves, yet I soon found myself at a loss as to what to do with them, other than read them aloud in her presence. There were moments where I wondered if the main point was that she mostly felt a "fake, fabricated child" and therefore unable to speak, because she had nothing real to say. If she had nothing to say because she felt empty inside, I wondered if the heaviness and boredom I was beginning to feel with these theoretical, philosophical texts was a way for her to distance me from her real experience. Perhaps she feared I would abandon her if I knew this.

As has often happened over the years, I was again overwhelmed with doubt about my continued persistence in giving her hope that this endeavour would lead somewhere. But when I tried to refer her to a centre for sexually abused patients where there was also group work and support, she felt I wanted to be rid of her. After all, she said angrily, if she was not able to talk to *me* how could I imagine her speaking up within a group!

A first narrative

However, as my doubts pass, as would often happen, I have fresh thoughts. I begin to see that there seems to be a connecting theme between the bits and pieces. They all seem to present suffering as a result of failure, neglect, abandonment or personality disorder in the mothers. One of the books Caroline had brought was called: *So the Witch Won't Eat Me: Fantasy and the Child's Fear of Infanticide* by Dora Bloch. In Bloch's book, the author–analyst describes several patients she had treated who had found out, while in therapy, that they were conceived as unwanted pregnancies, which their mothers had wished to abort but had never been open or honest about this. But since Caroline said absolutely nothing about the content of the book, I was left wondering if perhaps she had given it to me mainly because of the book's title – thus revealing her fantasies of having a devouring, frightening "witch" mother. In my mind I found myself developing a narrative of her life: Caroline had grown up as a lonely child, rejected by a narcissistic mother. She had found physical and emotional comfort in the arms of her silent father and this closeness had developed to an incestuous relationship, including a pregnancy and abortion about which Caroline felt very guilty.

This would be the first of several narratives I was to conceptualize over the coming years. Although it was mainly through the various written texts that she provided that this narrative was born I soon began to feel that bringing other people's quotes would lead us nowhere, since the narrative remained *my* creation alone. Caroline seemed to sense my growing discontent at this form of communication and, in the twelfth year of therapy, she suddenly surprised me by bringing a text of her own words. It was the first time she had done this.

I almost wrote "she would sound her own voice" – but no, no vocal sound accompanied these written texts. It was only my voice to be heard as, she, as usual, was completely silent, and I read aloud to her first, the texts of others and then her own words.

A borrowed voice

Yet, nothing is straightforward about Caroline and therefore as I write, I too must be accurate in my use of language. Although it is true to say "written by herself", this must be said with some reservation. What Caroline actually does is hide her words behind mine. How does she do this? She presents a page written in the first-person pronoun "I", but I soon discover that this "I" represents not herself, but *my* point of view, her therapist. She "impersonates" me and talks about herself in the third person! In one of the texts she even "explains" why she does this:

> ~... Caroline is likewise very careful with her use of words – not to use them loosely so that they be misunderstood but also with a specific meaning so that their reference is very precisely defined. In a related issue, Caroline also appears far more comfortable "borrowing my voice", as if to emphasize just how uncertain she still feels about asserting "realities" – particularly in reference to herself.~

So, in her writing, Caroline is giving me "a reason" for her "borrowing" my voice. I am not sure if I quite understand the reason, but I think she is wanting me to know that she is *not stealing* my voice.

I will now present a quite complex text Caroline brought at this time, in this disguised way. It exemplifies how her use of written language could be quite "maddening" at this time, yet one must admit, a far cry from the chaotic poetry which had been her earliest printed words. (see Chapter 2). First some background as to the content: Caroline had recently brought me two books by a woman who was diagnosed with Asperger's syndrome at the age of 25, who had written autobiographies describing her experiences in great detail. The first book is called *Nobody Nowhere* and the second *Somebody Somewhere*, both by Donna Williams.

The following is Caroline's text: an attempt to demonstrate how Caroline uses Williams' text and then her own words, disguised under her therapist's (my) identity, to communicate something to me – firstly about her compliant behaviour, and then reveals, as though inadvertently, a **secret:**

> ~A possible explanation for why Caroline "has no feelings" and thus cannot retain an emotional memory of events, which then disintegrates any sense of "realness": In reference to a passage in *Somebody Somewhere* which describes an experience with which Caroline is familiar from her own history:
>
> "...'the world' could force compliance even if it couldn't touch you. A mind that hadn't yet reached out for anything was being force-fed with what others called 'life'. The subconscious mind began to store

meaning that my conscious mind had not yet learned to reach for. I was still in a state of pure sense without thought or feeling. Feelings that had not yet met conscious awareness were being triggered. There were no words for them or even knowledge of where they come from. What poured in just sat there. The feelings were not ready (p. 6).[1]"

If the world impinges itself onto the small child before a sense of self has had time to develop, sensations exist but no clear feelings. This means that no clear *words* can form that represent the feelings. A situation is thus created which Caroline speaks of as always living in a vacuum:"It's like never being able to catch up. Something got created but it never had any feeling, nor any words for it. You're then expected to know what it is and to know how to use it – but no one ever gives you any time *to do* that."~

Then after describing how some of her siblings dealt with the parental "impingement" by active defiance she continues:

~.... Caroline, for reasons of her own, chose to "comply". Thus she outwardly accepted her mother's impingement but in order to "save herself" (save her "self") she had to close herself off from any real interaction with the outside world and not let anything inside.~

While it would be very pertinent to know how Caroline's siblings dealt with the family situation, for the sake of anonymity this cannot be explored here. Caroline continues to describe in her text how she would often hear her mother calling her names, such as "ridiculous" and would, to some extent identify with this because:

~Caroline could take that word "ridiculous" because it felt something (something – anything) was better than nothing. It was (and still is) better to have some certainty, something real to grasp, than to live in a vacuum, not having anything to produce from the inside to the outside (the "world"). Yet it probably didn't feel quite right – didn't match what Caroline sensed. The trouble was that since it couldn't be swallowed (completely taken in) nor vomited (completely gotten rid of) it simply "sat there" and Caroline was "stuck with it" – just as with all the other things that she assimilated for comparable reasons and also couldn't be jettisoned. (Although we didn't talk about it at the time, that feeling is very similar to that of being pregnant, ["feeling" here only being a metaphor; it has no meaning where being pregnant is concerned at all]. Here was someone sticking unwanted things into you and leaving them inside when you didn't want any of the "impingement" (penetration). While getting rid of that object inside was possible, even then there was a great deal of ambivalence, and the loss is "felt" far more acutely, perhaps because at one level it could be acknowledged as "real" (concrete) and not simply referred to as some sort of "make-believe" entity that "sort of existed".~

So what do I learn from this complex text presented to me in various forms of print, enclosed in brackets within brackets? I feel as though I am walking through a labyrinth looking for the path that will somehow lead me into an open space where thinking and breathing might become possible, then suddenly – in the innermost brackets – the centre of the maze, bracketed as though to hide the significance of the secret she is about to reveal – I am told of a pregnancy!

A precise choice of words

Caroline, in this complex almost debilitating way, has described how she had over the years in the home of her childhood, compliantly adopted a false self (Winnicott, 1960b) to the extent of "taking in" both what her mother attributed to her about her identity and passively received her father's impingements into her body.

Caroline is letting me know that today she will not repeat this passivity. And it seems to do things "her way" begins with the way she uses language with me. She struggles to be precise about her choice of words, for example to differentiate "feeling" from "a sense of things". This struggle is possibly one of the explanations for the split I experience in her different ways of communicating with me. When she writes she can take the time to choose the exactness she is searching for without it hindering the flow of the text and thus, with time, I will be presented with writing that becomes increasingly eloquent, verbally fluent and communicative.

But, meanwhile, in my clinic, the person I meet is mostly silent and denies any knowledge of having a memory of being sexually abused. Yet, she has written both of an impinging mother attacking her "self" and an impregnating father penetrating her body. So how can she be in total denial? Again, I find myself wondering if I really believe her. When I confront her with this, her response is a pleading stare – dying for me to understand her without her needing to say more. But I insist. I need to understand. She "explains" through use of yet another written text – again – *her* writings but still "hiding", writing as if she were me, using my "I":

~... The issue of remembering ... is in fact one with which, apart from the lack of memories connected with the abuse, Caroline does not have a problem. Yet here too the memories fall into the category of "store-up-repertoire": things which exist, as it were, on a ticker-tape and can be run backwards and forwards – not as an emotional experience or identity, but merely as a learnt set of data. If the characters (the various "faces" that behave in the outer world) are not real and do not express any emotions then what they say exists in a one-dimensional space; they represent the the stored mental repertoire of a "theory self", a kind of composite mental script whose only "reality" is as theoretical facts, information, knowledge – dissociated from any "real self". As such, while they can easily be manipulated, (remembered, referred to, quoted etc.) they do not "belong" to Caroline or help to constitute a "significant narrative". The latter apparently cannot be achieved until "the world" and Caroline's "my world" can somehow be integrated– and Caroline can stop living minute by minute with no links to join her self [sic] together and establish a true identity.~

Caroline here is describing how vulnerable and fragmented is the experience of non-integration, of not having a sense of identity. Not having a sense of self with a narrative that feels real and owned also affects the sense of time. If time is not experienced through continuity, but through only a *minute by minute existence*, how can anything feel stable or real or reliable?

No integration

Without conceptualizing it thus to myself, I was experiencing unreliability in her confronting me with "two Carolines" – the catatonic one when the two of us were present in the same physical space of the clinic; and the brilliant scholar who seemed to come alive only when she was far from me. No integration seemed possible. Retrospectively, I know now that the concept of extreme dissociation, the kind that causes a split into several personae, was not yet something I could emotionally know or believe. Only with future experience would I come to be convinced of the existence of such a phenomenon. But, meanwhile, I kept searching for possible explanations. A thought I had and expressed to her was that perhaps she experienced me as her father (in a psychotic transference) "the thing in itself" and was showing me the "freeze" response as a result of an eroticized transference. I received a confirmation of this when once, after she had refused to enter the clinic for a particularly long time, and I had been unsuccessful in deciphering anything that could cause this, I suddenly realized that this was the first time I had worn glasses (a sadly inevitable outcome of the ageing process over time). Thankfully I recalled, since I had met him that one time long ago, that her father wore glasses and I could say: "Even though I am now wearing glasses I am not your father." This interpretation "defrosted" her and she began to enter the room slowly. It took several sessions before she was convinced and entered on her own accord without my needing to repeat this interpretation.

The following is another example of just one of the many texts she gave me at this time. It is a written response, a day after I had, out of exasperation of anything ever becoming more certain, suggested that perhaps we could "let go" of searching for "objective" proof that Caroline had been abused. I said that I thought that since we were unlikely to know more than we did already, perhaps she could accept and be consoled by the fact *that I believed her* that this was most probably true but might be impossible to prove. Caroline wrote, again in the third person, as if from my point of view:

> ~The question "Why is it so important for Caroline to know for certain whether or not she was abused" is misleading in the sense that it refers to cognitive knowledge – although, that too, is important. What is more significant is Caroline's need for "emotional knowledge" – i.e., specific memory, in some concrete form, of the actual experience.~

I wondered if Caroline here felt she needed to remind me of Winnicott's lesson on how trauma is to be resolved.

How was emotional knowledge to come about? Throughout the therapy I welcomed any emotion that appeared spontaneously. I always made room and was empathic to any pain she revealed. Often, I found myself sharing my own feelings with her. Frequently, they represented her feelings, unable to be felt by her – as had occurred after she told me of the sterilization and I found myself with tears. Over the years Caroline gradually began to feel. I knew this because often, as I spoke, I would see tears rolling down her cheeks covering her whole face. Her crying was a great relief for me, indicating to me that I was able to reach her – meet her in the overlap between our worlds. This was a sign that she was human and I was not in the presence of a stone. Yet, even her heartfelt crying was in total silence.

Taking ownership over her voice

Then one day she brought me a page where she first used her own "voice" – where "I" now referred to Caroline herself. The following is the incident that precipitated this text. One day I had inadvertently left my car lights on. Caroline stood immobile at the entrance to the clinic. I saw she wanted to tell me something but couldn't. I encouraged her to enter and when she eventually did she stood in the middle of the room, immobile. After ten minutes she said: "Car ... lights ... on." I asked her if I could go out and turn them off and return, and she agreed. This took about three minutes. (In the idiosyncratic dictionary that she had given me, near the word: "Car" was written: "Body"; waiting ; driving – *killing*.)

I had several thoughts around the incident of the car lights. It showed perhaps for the first time that she could have some concern for me as a *separate* person. We were no longer only merged in a wished-for symbiotic union. Her words threw light on what our interaction meant to her and were most enlightening. The following is the text she brought on the day following the car lights incident:

> ~We had been talking about how to make things real – that there could be a reality that wasn't sexual, a way to get Tova to be real and not to be frightened of her all the time.
>
> Today we talked about how I couldn't be sure – especially talking about it on the inside – that Tova would understand that I was referring to her car in the present – and not Dad and the car in the past – which was eroticised. The fact that I couldn't differentiate – and that we were talking about it on the inside – meant that I was afraid that she would think that I was inviting her to do something sexual. Mixing the inside and the outside, instead of keeping them entirely separate to avoid any possibility of confusion, meant that I didn't have any way of knowing how she would take it. The fact that I was able to tell her was a symptom of my willingness to risk her misunderstanding – something which I think derived in large part from my wanting her to be real. But she actually knew off the bat – without even thinking twice about it – that I was relating to her car in the present. When I asked her how she knew she thought it was partly because that's her reality – that she doesn't think of everything in erotic/sexual terms – and partly because she sees me as part of present reality – and thus also as not as eroticised in the past.~

Another reality

Caroline writes further in this text:

> ~All this together made me realise that maybe another reality does exist – one that isn't defined in sexual/erotic terms. Not only that, but it's not a question of losing everything if that reality disappears, because it's replaced with another reality – which itself is real. And if I know that she can understand that with Dad I was never sure whether I was doing something "innocent" or was in fact doing something to lead him on, which meant that I could never know how to interpret actions – his or mine – then perhaps I can feel safer with her. If she knows how that happens she has to be in a different reality – because if she was in the same (sexual) reality she wouldn't be able to understand the confusion; she'd merely be as confused as I am. It means that she may really be real in that way – as she said at the door, "I am real in that way."~

***

Despite this insightful document our space stayed as it had always been: static. Caroline stayed "dead", made no sound, spoke little and never related to anything she had written. If I did – there was just an ignorant stare as though saying: What are you talking about? So, with time, I am almost embarrassed to say – I myself dissociated Caroline's written treasures from my active memory.

After death of mother, possibility of living with father

Caroline's writing continues to be a source of important insights that she shares with me in this way. In this written form, she shares with me her thoughts about her strange use of language; about the incest; and even about my contribution to her psychic development. If not for these written pages I might have given up on her.

Shortly after her mother had died (and 16 years into therapy) the issue of the possibility of her perhaps wishing to go to live with her father came up. I'm not sure what made me mention this. I think I had the thought that this might be a thought she was having but dared not say. As a result of my having raised this option to think about, she wrote an amazing description of her thoughts about this. The following is the total text unabridged:

~Tova had very pertinently asked me what I would do if Mom dies and Dad's alone – would I actually grasp the opportunity to say, "Now you can be mine and I shall make sure that you are." The answer was no, the first instinct being that I wouldn't go near him after what he did to the baby. But the fact that I wouldn't do that doesn't fit with the refusing to let go and the holding on. If I really wanted him as a "husband", why wouldn't I go and live with him?

That's already sick (pathological). I know that I wouldn't do that – knowing in the sense of understanding the implications and being sure that I don't want to do it. Tova very wisely thought we should try and understand how I have this knowledge – when I know so few other things. I tried to explain that some decisions you can make deliberately, knowing exactly what options are, the pros and cons, and the consequences. At other times, you simply follow one of the alternatives, not because you know that it's better than any of the others but merely because you have to do something. It might be the right thing, it might not; it's simply what you do.

That's what the holding onto him is like. I wasn't conscious of doing it at the time because I didn't really understand what was going on. It's like Winnicott's discussion of people who attempt to recreate the experience of death. They constantly look for similar circumstances in order to reconstruct the original experience, but because it wasn't actively registered (it couldn't be, being death) they can never find what they've been looking for. Trying to find the emotional dimension of the explanation embedded in the holding on is like that – it's not there, because it didn't get registered as a rational thought – it wasn't a conscious decision – at the time it occurred.

Tova understood from that that the holding on is so much a part of me that it's virtually impossible to isolate. It's become such an integral element of who I am, as a person, that it leaves no possibility of getting rid of it. To do that would be to remove part of myself. But going with the metaphor, Tova said that maybe we could get at the problem by looking at the holding on as if it actually were a bodily part – an arm. The trouble is that the arm is diseased – and if it's not amputated, gangrene will set in and infect the whole body. In other words, keeping the arm is life-threatening.

Then I have a choice: either I keep it, which I can, knowing what the risks are; or I come to terms with the amputation and the loss, knowing that I've saved the whole body which can continue to grow healthily. All this time in therapy, I've had a terrible conflict between a small healthy part which has been saying, "I know what happened was sick and I want to get out of that atmosphere (breaking the circle of incest by taking it out of the family)" – and the need to hold on (with all the fear of loneliness/rejection, humiliation, etc.). The holding on may originally even have been a healthy response: his love being the one positive thing out of the whole mess, and something good to retain. It was also probably the only way that I could get out. How otherwise would I have been able to leave the house – without anything?

In spite of all this, the leaving was good – an acknowledgement that the circumstances were really sick and looking to survive. Nor did I want any more part in the killings! The first had been more than enough; I wasn't about to let there be any more – which there may have been if I'd stayed. The first time I could have said, "I didn't understand, I had no idea what was happening." But that excuse wouldn't have worked a second time – I couldn't have said that I didn't know – and then I would have been a participant in the murdering. Evidently, I was sufficiently aware to know that I couldn't do that. I actually knew (in some form) that I had to get out – even if some of the sickness had to come too, in the form of holding on to his "love".

(Maybe that's part of the problem too, – that the knowledge of needing to leave is compromised by taking him with me. Since I couldn't make a clean break, the leaving becomes contaminated – not pure, in the sense that the good's mixed with the bad. It means that the "knowing" isn't clear because I'm not sure what the motives were – as though knowledge has to be black or white {good or bad?} The moment the action's tainted by a questionable motive, I lose the sense of what it is. Knowing is only available, as it were, when I know that what I did was either right or wrong. Put the two together, mix them up, and the confusion is too much to tolerate and the knowledge disappears.)

Putting the question of holding on in these terms at least makes it more of a choice – something which I can isolate (separate out) and of which I can say: "This is a decision I can make about myself – what I do about the holding on." Do I say, "It's too familiar, still too much a part of me to be able to agree to its amputation." Or can I get to a place where I can apprehend: "Yes, I understand why I did it – even that it was perhaps a good thing to do when I did it. But now is it still helpful? Is it not actually a health risk? Am I not in fact going to suffer more if I keep the arm than if I amputate it – with all the pain and loss involved in the amputation?"

That's at least a question about which I can make a decision/choice. As Tova said the time before: It's not a matter of choosing holding onto him altogether or rejecting him altogether. It's more a case of saying: There's no possibility of having him as a husband, of having him instead of M., of him choosing me over her. That shouldn't even be an option, belonging as it does to the incestuous circle. What I need to be able to try and understand is that while he's not available as a husband, he's still actually a father – and I don't have to give up on him in that relationship. If he's a father, then I don't have to be loyal to him as a "wife" – which makes room for letting other people in.~

Reading this text, I am moved and impressed by Caroline's development, by her clarity of thought. I feel privileged that she shares with me such *deep insights* about her way of thinking and feel this is so valuable for understanding the depth of guilt, confusion and overwhelming emotional complexity aroused by incest. I am optimistic from the proof she gives me in this written form of the development of an internal world within her where contemplation and introspection are evolving.

There is also the mention of "*a participant in the murdering*" and the "*killings*". At this time I thought that she is confirming what we already thought in the "hanging doll" incident over five years earlier – that she feels so guilty over the aborted or, "killed" foetus (caused by the abortion) and that had she stayed at home, more pregnancies may have occurred with similar outcomes. Little did I suspect at this time that a few years hence I would have much more gruesome thoughts.

Caroline came to the next session with yet another text. It seems our work had stimulated many thoughts in her, with a need to share them with me in the only way she could, by writing them, so she could still maintain silence in my presence

A new word for the dictionary: the development of language

~This is the first time I'd ever spoken in terms of Dad as a "father" not with a capital F or D (some godlike being, the be-all-and-end–all of everything). It was as though I'd been able to add a new word to my vocabulary – a word I'd never known before … that he could be/was a "father" had not been accessible; the concept had no existence. Not only had he not acted as a father, but I had refused to see him as anything other than a "lover" – especially after the leaving, since that was the only "love" available. If I was left without that, I had nothing; if he wasn't a husband he wasn't anything.

Being able to differentiate – to acknowledge that he could be not only a husband (or not even a husband, in letting him go) but also a father (what he should have been, and objectively actually was) – is a sign of being able to see the complexity of things. Both the ability to see the complexity and the capacity to separate the different aspects are important. As long as I only see him as a lover there's no room for him as a father. If I can see him as a father, then I can better understand that he shouldn't have been a lover in the first place – and that, all the more so, I shouldn't still want him to be one now.

Tova's understanding that I'd found a new word – and telling me about it – enabled me to see what had happened … not going back now (deciding not to go to live with him) is a recognition of the difference in generations: I won't go back as a wife because I know it would be inappropriate as a daughter.

Once I can see him as a father, I might be able to see myself as a daughter. That's another word that's been missing from the vocabulary – evidently because if there's no such thing as a father there can't be a "daughter" either.~

So, here was finally an answer to my long neglected question of why she would only use "Dad" and "Mom" (see Chapter 1) when referring to her parents. As she said: "father" had not been an option in her vocabulary, since she had no experiential knowledge of a father. And, as mentioned, Caroline was always very careful to only use meaningful words with me.

This reminds me of something I read in a book by Elie Wiesel, the Holocaust survivor and recipient of the 1986 Nobel Peace Prize. In the preface to his first book *Night*, he describes his need to "invent a new language". Words had betrayed him and lost their original meaning. "How was one to rehabilitate and transform words betrayed and perverted by the enemy?… All the dictionary had to offer seemed meagre, pale, lifeless."[2] And I recall how Caroline created a new dictionary for us to use.

***

The lost and found experience of the written words

In the 11-year period between the establishment of a sense of safety and the first appearance of the first persona – the Little Girl Caroline – Caroline continued to bring me her written words. She brought me about a hundred pages of typed text. Each one seemed to contain content of overwhelming value and insight about herself and the process she was undergoing with me. They were like precious pearls exposed in their shell but soon the shell would close and disappear from consciousness and lay motionless in the depths. This was because the texts were left for my use only. She will not relate to them in any way and it is a question I still find myself thinking about – where did I store these words? Most of the time they seemed to dissolve into nothingness in my mind after one or two sessions of trying to integrate them into the work with her, but since she seemed not to "own" them in any emotional way, they disappeared into the depths of my inner world.

The texts stopped arriving when the new persona appeared and Caroline would often acknowledge their existence only through relating to the pain over the loss of her writing self. It seems the personae enacted the past that previously the written texts had "reported".

Surprisingly, I found that what I had thought had disappeared from my mind – the contents of these written texts – was actually to become alive and available for use in my interaction with these personae. Since I found these texts extremely valuable, representing rare, inner, first-hand impressions from the experiences of this patient, I will try to weave them into this continuous narrative, that most of the time felt anything but clear and continuous.

A theoretical issue: object constancy

How could it have been that after knowing and seeing me for so many years Caroline could have responded with such fear when I started to wear glasses? How could I have become "the father" in her experience of me? Does this mean that Caroline never developed, in all her time with me, some inner sense of constancy or knowledge of who I am and that I do not change just because of outer changes? It raises the question as to whether internalization is developing. Object constancy is a developmental milestone in cognitive development, dependent on maturation and object relations. I cannot believe that Caroline does not perceive me as being of object constancy overall. Yet, it seems that an external change in my appearance can create doubt as to who I am. The stimuli that distort her perception are trauma related: as is seen in her response to my glasses – worn by father. When I wore different clothes, she did not respond in such a way. Yet, if ever there was a change of place – e.g. when I moved to a new clinic, she responded in a similar traumatised way. I take this to mean that her sense of safety was very precarious and dependent on external signs of sameness. A new place aroused all the fears of imminent danger. I was later to understand from her that she had no way of knowing that *I* would not change with the changing surroundings. After all, if *she* could change to different personae perhaps it was natural for her to assume I might too.

Part of the explanation for this was to be found in her written words of how she experiences life – almost as a two-dimensional film. This also goes with her initial description of "living as an observer of life" and not living/experiencing life (see Chapter 1). This sounds like a defence, both perceptual and by distancing herself, against perhaps being over stimulated by traumatizing visual scenes. This use of perceptual "blindness" as a defence will be met again after the father's death when she reports literally to be able "to see" some things for the first time.

In this chapter I have given a taste of Caroline's development in the use of written texts ranging over a period of about 12 years. It has been a brief mosaic limited only by lack of space. The texts written by her contain treasures worthy of deep analysis in treating the dissociated mind.

Notes

1 Donna Williams, *Somebody Somewhere* (1995) Random House, Inc.
2 Elie Wiesel. *NIGHT.* preface to the new translation, page xiii.

Chapter 6

How can I know that we are real?

> Feeling real is more than existing; it is finding a way to exist as oneself, and to relate to objects as oneself, and to have a self into which to retreat for relaxation.
> Winnicott, Mirror-role of Mother and Family in Child Development,
> *Playing and Reality* (1967)

Timeline: years 11–22 in therapy

I soon realized that I was serving the function of a witness in more ways than one. I was also accorded the function of representing Memory against the amazingly destructive force of Deletion that would emanate from the very depths of Caroline. Behind the mental action of deletion there were strong forces of repression and dissociation. The combined strength of these two forces seemed totally immune to any interpretation or intervention that I could think of.

What proved so frustrating was that the more we knew, the more deletion would occur and nothing I would say seemed to make the least difference.

"Working through" seemed a theoretical concept not applicable to Caroline's psychic makeup. It appeared that these oppositional counter forces could not be resolved – as expressed by Caroline herself in something she wrote a year before ending therapy: "…there are two forces in me – one that won't give up on knowing as much as possible and the one that insists on making everything disappear."

The stage upon which these counter forces was played out was in the therapeutic setting, the encounter that took place within the safety of the walls of the space she had created for herself.

How can one know what is real?

We were now contending with two vital issues:

a   How to know that anything is real, and
b   Once she knew something to be real, how to maintain a *memory* of it.

These were continuous themes throughout our work.

Over the course of time I realized that the therapy was serving as a way to help Caroline have a continuous history in which she hoped to establish a sense of feeling real in my presence. Since she could not feel certain that anything in her past felt real, she hoped that by feeling real in the present she might be able to learn about her past in a way that would feel tangible and convincing for her. According to her logic, it went something like this: if the present with me was real, and I could be a reliable witness who knew that this was so, then *by trusting me*, and my psychic processes, she might come to feel the same. It came down to finding a way to develop basic trust – something so lacking in her primary relationships. She hoped that I could be the object of this new experience. After all, she had put me through so many tests until now which I seemed to have passed and survived.

I had become the proof of her existence. It seemed crucial that she could hold onto the knowledge that *I* was real. Each separation from me "left her for dead". Not only did she fear I would lose memory of her, I think she feared more that she would lose the belief that I was real. Over time, this was to become a great concern for me, fearing she will always remain dependent on our meetings, dependent on my existence. After all the years of intensive therapy where Deletion – the force of Evil that seemed to conquer all – I could not imagine in my mind's eye that this analysis could ever come to an end. I recall at times pondering – what would happen if I was to decide one day to retire from work? Would I be motivated by guilt to see her until I died or became senile? I had chilling thoughts of her standing over my grave with her accusatory stare for having abandoned her to a state of eternal dependence and emptiness!

***

Now I will try and illustrate how dependence was manifested in our work together.

We are 12 years into therapy. She has brought me various articles expressing other people's thoughts (Chapter 5). Though the articles are pertinent to our work, we never break through the barrier where she can relinquish her silence and express herself in real time. We are getting nowhere. It's another dead end and we are both exasperated.

Unbearable guilt

C: I can't do any more. I can bring you the pieces but if you can't put them together then what's the point of bringing more pieces?!

As Caroline says this to me, my thought was that she has a point. Genet had a Sartre to tell his story so why can't I tell hers. But Sartre had the privilege of literary licence. He did not have to be faithful to the truth. Genet made no demands on Sartre to help him get to the truth and help him know that he was not making things up as my patient demanded of me. So am I truly guilty of something or is this guilt a reaction of the countertransference? After all, Caroline was always suffering from guilt about her very existence. And if she *was* guilty – would we be ever able to alleviate this guilt?

It seemed Caroline first needed to know about her past, to regain her memories so that we could know more specifically *what* she felt so guilty about. But – then, here we were back in the vicious cycle of her claiming to have no emotional memories. And to let me know of the extent of her unbearable guilt Caroline brings me a book that was to disturb me for a long time. It was called: *The Case of Thomas N.* by John David Morley. (The reader is never told what N stands for; I would assume perhaps Nowhere man or Nobody.) It is a strange story about an adolescent boy who is found sleeping near a murdered girl in an apartment. He is arrested, interrogated but suffers from total amnesia. He is hospitalized in a psychiatric ward for some time and much of the book is a description through the eyes of his psychiatrist. Here are some quotes from the book that Caroline picked out for me:

~At its most elementary level, Dr Ormond concluded, the boy's fear of exposure was a fear of anything that objectively demonstrated his existence ... In this undertaking the boy had been his own best ally. The solution had been absolute: he had lost his memory. All subjective evidence that he existed was obliterated. By his own peculiar logic, if nobody knew who Thomas N. was, it became rather doubtful **that** he was.~

And:

~The boy felt guilty about his own existence. He behaved as if it were a secret he was frightened would be found out. He had suppressed his memory, and in doing so had contrived a shift of emphasis from **what** he had forgotten to the fact **that** he had forgotten, this in turn eliciting feelings of guilt and unease, which took the form of remorseless inquiry into the antecedents of every here and now, day by day, minute by minute. It was **a closed circuit**, offering nothing but questions, endless questions.~

A closed circuit

I, too, feel I have more questions than answers. What is Caroline trying to reveal to me? For years now, we have also been preoccupied with searching for the reason that she has no memories. Her search always felt very sincere. Yet, together with this feeling of sincerity I would on occasion be confronted by a glimmer that gave rise to the feeling that Caroline was intentionally *hiding* something – from me, from herself and from some internalized voice threatening her. For example, around the time she introduced *The Case of Thomas N.* she said: "If a self needs a past then one way not to be a self is to erase the past and the future."

I found it very difficult to reconcile these seemingly opposite sides of her.

***

Can I tape our sessions so that I know they are real?

Through the enigmatic character of Thomas N., I felt Caroline needed me to know that she was dealing with guilt about unknown things, possibly connected to violence, and like him, she had no way of verifying if this was true. But that novel ended with neither Thomas N. nor the reader ever solving the mystery. Was this to be our destiny? I again found my detective side stimulated, my curiosity aroused.

It was not possible to know at these moments which one of us was more motivated to solve this mystery. She seemed to be leaving me cues in unexpected places for me to decipher with as little help as possible from her side. After all, the first definition in the dictionary that Caroline has written for me, was *Hiding*. I suddenly had an "answer" to one of the questions I was left curious about around the third year we were meeting. At that time Caroline had expressed a feeling that often the sessions themselves lost their sense of reality for her, as though she was not sure she had actually been in therapy after leaving me. One day she surprised me with the request to bring a tape recorder to one of the sessions and record a session so that she would have concrete proof of the meetings. I decided to agree. I think my rationale for this was the hope that it would help me understand her better and, after all, she rarely asked for anything.

I made my agreement conditional on receiving a typed transcript of the taped session. She agreed to this. However, when I received it from her I was shocked to discover that only *my voice* appeared in the transcript. How strange, I thought, until I realized that this was the outcome of her being mainly silent and relating to my comments and questions nonverbally! On occasion, when she said a word or two, she had requested to turn off the taperecorder and I agreed, without questioning her as to the reason. Actually, I had not been suspicious at the time, not knowing I was involved is some secret drama. She had done this so "expertly" that I did not notice it at the time! Her voice *did not exist* on this taped session of the two of us together. As with Thomas N. – there was no evidence *that* she existed.

The question – as always, was: why? The reason that this Thomas N. disturbed me so was that (a) he had been accused of murder that could not be proven nor disproven and (b) although the book ends with his acquittal concerning the alleged murder due to insufficient evidence, on leaving the court house, while distractedly crossing the road, he is run over and killed by a car! Punishment and death was the sordid end.

I was left with the foreboding that perhaps it was not by chance that in our work together we were not finding out the "truth" about the past. Perhaps it was best not to know more, and perhaps Caroline "knew" this in some dissociated part of herself.

***

Asperger's syndrome: that must be the answer!

Another unanswered question that at times plagued us was: to what extent could Caroline's difficulties be explained by some neurological condition? This had come up in the initial meetings with her (see Chapter 2, The Last Hippie). In the sixteenth year of therapy it surfaced again. This is how it happened: Quite coincidentally, we happen to be reading the same book at the same time. It was Mark Haddon's best-selling novel: *The Curious Incident of the Dog in the Night-time*. (2005) The book describes qualities of a boy with Asperger Syndrome that in many ways resembles Caroline. He is over sensitive, unemotional, has difficulty in reading social situations, is withdrawn from the world of people, and is very suspicious of everything and everyone. Now the need for a neurological testing seemed justified.

In my enthusiasm that we may have found the "correct" diagnosis for her I even go to a consultation with an expert in the treatment of Asperger. However, after this consultation I am convinced that Caroline does *not* suit this category of diagnosis. She is much too aware of inner life, both her own and mine, her abilities do not correspond even if her disabilities have much in common with Asperger and if I were to treat her in the behaviouristic orientation recommended for Asperger patients she would think *me* to be the one limited in the understanding of another's mind.

Despite my doubts that Caroline had Asperger, I did not think there was a reason to discourage her from taking the psycho-neurological tests. The diagnosis was inconclusive: she might have this syndrome but since Caroline could not give a history and had no memories of her past development, the same symptoms could also be caused by PTSD! So we were back to square one! Caroline participates in all the testing very willingly. When I relate to her enthusiasm she says: "If I have a diagnosis … that means … I have something … that other people have too … so it means I am … *human!*"

At the end of the psycho-diagnostic evaluation where no conclusive findings could be made with any certainty, I had expected her to be disappointed. But she surprised me by bringing me a gift! This was the *first time* she had ever done so! It took me time to understand the reason. Finally, I understand that it was because I had actually arranged a meeting of *three of us* together (the psycho-neurologist, myself and her) to discuss the test results. She had found this extremely moving and meaningful. It took several sessions to understand that for Caroline this act of mine carried the following meanings:

1. I was real (outside of her) and on her side – by having brought in a real third person
2. That I took her suffering seriously.

This meant that I *believed her* that she felt her suffering to be real – that her concern of having losses of memory and amnesia were *real experiences* for her.

This gift was her way of expressing her deep gratitude to me that I was taking her subjectivity seriously, and proved this by assenting to her being diagnosed!

Her gift to me was of great significance. It brought home to me the realization that *most* of the time when Caroline was *only with me* she remained in doubt about my good intentions towards her. The need to have proof of my trustworthiness in a concrete way is repeated over and over again. We had been together for 17 years and she still could not trust me. I could not really understand the depth of this suspiciousness and, especially, its resistance to change.

***

Silence is not to get lost in meaningless words

Most of the time we were not dealing with diagnosing her or other little dramas. Most of the time, I struggled just to "stay alive" in her death-like presence. But Caroline seemed to be helping me stay committed. There was also a communicative quality to her deadness and silences. Winnicott (1971) mentions that *commitment* is the most important quality in a good-enough mother. And commitment requires survival of the object over a period of time to allow for process to be experienced.

Since silence is what dominated most of the sessions, this would be what I often talked about, at times raising hypotheses, but often questioning her about her need to be so abstaining in her use of speech.

C: I need questions to get me to focus because I often come so empty ... If I feel I shouldn't exist in the first place ... then to speak about myself, to want to be the topic of interest ... if *you're* interested, *you* ask.

At times I felt Caroline wished to help me deal with my exasperation about her continuous silences.

C: Why do you assume I have something to say? ... most of the time... my mind is blank ... so I have nothing to say ... so ... I don't exist.
T: Why is that? Why is your mind blank?

Caroline says to me in a tone that is meant to appease me: "You get the better deal – there are places... I talk what is expected...of me ... to appear normal, but ...not real. Here ...you get the ...real me ...but ...no words."
And as I hear her words, I know this to be true.

***

Another month passes and we are at the same place. Again, I cannot bear the silences – not knowing what to do. Feeling my frustration she asks me:

C: Why are words ... so important?
T: What do you want to do in therapy – if not to use words?
C: It's the coming that is important ... a place to be ... to be seen ... Not to talk is not to get lost ... in ... meaningless words ... not grounded in anything.
T: So there is a need to find a way to feel grounded in order to find real words.
C: I don't know how to do that.
T: Maybe if you know what you feel it can lead to a thought and then to a word.

Here, I recall our beginning where she had used the words: "a stone feels no pain". But in our many years together she has felt much pain. I have been her witness to the most painful weeping. But still, she will not speak.

***

When a haircut makes you naked

One day (thirteenth year in therapy) I decide to change my hair style. I have my hair cut short after years of having long hair. For a whole session Caroline is speechless and a session later she shocks me with the following words:

You are exposed ... it's like having something stuck in my mouth ... can't swallow ... can't get it out ...

This is the first time she has *spoken* words implying involvement in oral sex. It`s as though the shock of seeing me thus, led to a spontaneous statement before her defensive control took over. I remember that in the intake she had told me that she could not eat anything in public nor ever use the public toilets, yet without being able to explain anything. It seems all the orifices of her body were experienced as eroticized zones that could be penetrated. I recall her distaste for using the phone to communicate to avoid her ear being penetrated...Perhaps even the physical act of speaking – which involved moving her mouth, making sounds, was a traumatizing experience arousing physical sensations reminiscent of oral penetration by a penis. I realize my haircut – exposing my neck – means nakedness to her. She always comes with her head almost shaven, as well as her sleeves rolled up to the elbows even during the cold days of winter. I noted to myself that she was exposing a body part inappropriately on "the outside" and this was obviously done with intention. Only years later would this body sign be deciphered.

If she is real then maybe what she says is also real

A text that continues describing the abuse soon follows:

> ~Tova for some reason hadn't opened the blinds so that when she opened the door the hallway was dark. I found it very difficult to go in and we talked about the problem during the session. When Tova asked about the "physical memories" of being in a dark place my ear blocked at some point and I started to feel sick. I presumed that the blocked ear – which happens fairly frequently – was a symptom of not wanting to hear or know. The feeling of needing to vomit went with that of having my mouth being completely filled and not being able to move because it didn't leave any space. Not only couldn't I breathe but I couldn't even say anything. My nose was also blocked and I couldn't move to do anything about that either.
>
> By the next session I was already questioning the reality of what I'd described –whether I hadn't made it up, whether it could actually be real. In exploring why it should be so difficult to keep hold of the reality – not only of the past but of the present (re)-experience – I said that maybe the very nature of talking about something whose reality is dubious makes the discussion illusory as well.
>
> Tova's response was that it seemed more likely to her that the distortion was a result of guilt feelings or some other reason to want the experience not to be real – especially since from her perspective I hadn't seemed to be making anything up or putting on an act in describing what I'd felt. On the contrary, it had seemed very real to her – not like other times when things were very disconnected and "distanced". (She also commented that the dissociation which occurs during abuse necessarily entails doubts later on about the reality of the original experience, the person not even being sufficiently there to register it as real – or for it to enter into one's "experience".)
>
> At some point during her remarks I was hit by a sense that what she was saying – what we were talking about – might actually be real – that I might actually be able to know something. It expressed itself in my question at the door as I was leaving – "Can you help?" – i.e. can you do something which will actually make things real?
>
> I opened the next session with the same question, to which Tova responded that it seemed as though it was the first time that I'd in fact

considered that something could. It's true – up until now the idea of "help" has been completely void of meaning (and thus the worth of "therapy" in general, I suppose)

I wasn't even sure what it was that made sense to me in the previous session. It had something to do with her being on the outside – involved and "in on things" without being within them – enmeshed in them. If she was on the outside – and she'd demonstrated that she was by being able to describe her experience of my experiencing myself – she could give me a way to know that was real because it wasn't compromised by her involvement. It could be real and I could **know** that it was real. All the time I was growing up I could not know because the only people I could ask were people who were themselves involved. How could I trust them to tell me the truth – what was real – especially when they had a vested interest in making sure it wasn't known? (that's why children are now encouraged to tell what's going on – to teachers, parents, anyone – so that it won't be a secret and thus an "illusion" – Tova remarked.)

I kept trying to identify precisely what made sense to me. It also had something to do with feeling that Tova herself is real. If she's real then what she says can also be real.

I think what probably had most to do with it (again) was being believed... Here, I'd described part of the actual abuse itself – having my mouth stuffed, not being able to breath – or even shout- or move and being/feeling utterly helpless. If I had felt that things were real in connection with those "physical memories" – because Tova had believed me and yet wasn't part of the problem – then the abuse itself was real. I could know it was because Tova could mirror back to me what I was experiencing without being a participant. Tova understood what I was trying to get at and added that she serves as a "witness" in this respect – something which she's been doing all along but which I never realized/ understood until now.

I still couldn't refrain from asking at the end whether I wasn't way off on all that I'd said. Tova's response was that despite the desire to experience reality, a part of me still wants to insist that the abuse never happened – partly in order not to recognize how it's affected all of my life and partly in order not to think that my parents weren't good.

In spite of my doubts, the session had made a lot of sense to me and I asked Tova if she would make notes for me.~

A lesson from the abused: on the importance of being believed

1 Being believed by a trusted other (outside oneself) is imperative to a sense of feeling real (Winnicott 1965b).
2 Bodily sensations help establish feeling real.

3 Physical symptoms (such as blocked ears) if taken seriously/believed to be a symptom – can open the way to memories (Freud's work on hysteria).
4 What contributed to Caroline's not knowing what was real was having her experiences made fun of, invalidated by those she was dependent on. Having the (trusted) therapist as an "outside" object while validating and empathising with her inner experience enabled Caroline to become acquainted with, to get to know her own experiences and trust them.
5 Applying recommendations for incest victims today: it is essential to find an appropriate way to protect the child from the abusive parents in order that ego strengths, such as reality testing, are given the chance to develop.

Chapter 7

The story of incest
Keeping it all in the family

Timeline: year 16 of therapy

The wise owl

For Caroline to bring me a present was a most meaningful move. Literally – she brought something from the outside world to the "inside". It was concrete proof that her fear of contamination, of the loss of boundaries, had subsided considerably. One could say it was a sign that she knew I was separate from her. I saw it as a gesture of deep appreciation and an act of trust in me, in our relationship. And it was an act of giving – to let me know I was of help to her. I was greatly moved. And the present itself was big too. She carried into the clinic a very large framed picture of an owl with big staring eyes sitting on a branch. It was hand-embroidered with the smallest of stitches executed with utmost precision. She managed to tell me, in bits and pieces, that she had begun making it shortly after beginning therapy because it reminded her of me. "An owl is wise and sees in the night," she said.

When she said this, I thought: She needs me to see the terrible things that happened in the night that she cannot tell me about but hopes I will be wise enough to see. Yet, she still needs this concrete proof of a third person from the outside (the psycho-neurologist in this case) to know I am on her side.

I couldn't hang Caroline's picture in the clinic because at the time I was sharing a room with another therapist. Caroline knew this. She also knew that I took it home and she asked that her creation not be exposed to others.

So it could not be in my home clinic. I hung it in the next room. She never mentioned it again. It's still hanging there – very austere and mysterious.

Thinking back on those staring eyes of the owl reminded me of Caroline's unnerving stares into me that I had often interpreted as her wish to penetrate me. Yet, if the owl represents me, her staring was also a reversal – her wanting to have me see better into her inside where she hid her secrets. After all, at that time, 16 years into the therapy, we thought her mother saw nothing of her suffering.

In this chapter I wish to look at quite a few samples of Caroline's writing in detail. In retrospect, I understand that in this way she could tell me some of those hidden secrets that even my "owl eyes" could not see without her help. They were brought to me shortly after the gift of the owl, over a period of about a year, often in a response to my expressing great frustration and despair about the way she talked and behaved with me.

Caroline's fear of contamination had subsided to a degree, but she continued to separate words and at times even syllables with long pauses in her use of spoken language with me. At times like this I found myself being separated from her by the very fact that language was used as though it was a weapon in a war where she would distance me by making herself impenetrable. I almost could not even understand the little that she did say! Paradoxically, this weapon was a double-edged sword: the softer she spoke, the less clear she became – and the closer I needed to get to her in order to literally hear her. Was I subtly being seduced to come closer so as to know her better? Eventually, I surmised that she had almost "succeeded" in making me want to give up on her. Only then, sensing my exasperation, did she explain herself in writing:

> ~The control which is exerted in keeping things apart may also function as a way of "protection" against invasion into one's body from the outside.~

From this I understood that, for her, closeness was associated with invasion and it seems that the impact of incestuous invasion into one's body can be so all-consuming that even letters and syllables need to be separated, not only people and things.

Incest leaves no space to be

Toni Morrison (1990), winner of the 1993 Nobel Prize for Literature, illustrates ingeniously through the use of visual impact of written language how incest can create madness. In her book *The Bluest Eye* (1990), we are told in the first chapter that Pecola is having her father's baby. But there is a preface preceding the story that comprises three identical paragraphs differing only in the spacing and punctuation of the words. The following is a sample of this text:

> (Version 1): Here is the house. It is green and white. It has a red door. It is very pretty. Here is the family. Mother, Father, Dick, and Jane live in the green-and-white house.

> (Version 2): Here is the house it is green and white it has a red door it is very pretty here is the family mother father dick and jane live in the green-and–white house

(Version3): Hereisthehouseitisgreenandwhiteithasareddooritisveryprettyhe isthefamilymotherfatherdickandjaneliveinthegreenandwhitehouse

Seeing this, Caroline's need to separate words as a defence against the all-pervasive experience of incest and enmeshment suddenly became so clear. When there is no space where space should be there is no meaning, and madness threatens. Language cannot be used to communicate. Instead, it is used to tantalize and create a sense of chaos and distrust.

Space is needed to allow for individuation, identity and integrity. Space is needed to have time to rest. Caroline, in her expression of both the need for the presence of a third person and for space is letting me know of the dangers of symbiosis and of incest that loom as threats for her when only the two of us are left together. Space allows for the entry of the third, who will ensure against the danger of incest. In Caroline's family, as in all incestuous families, there is no third present as a protector. The mother either does not know and thus does not protect her child from the incestuous father, or is in collusion with him and thus the father–mother are a single combined unit. The father, by entering the bed of his daughter, fails in the father's phallic function of separating the child from the danger of symbiosis with the mother (Bollas, 1989).

Space for the soul

In the Jewish religion, when a couple marry, the ceremony includes being blessed in uniting as a couple while making space between them for a third – the *shechina*: God's presence. It is this presence that ensures that the marriage will contain spirituality as well as a physical union. In incestuous families so much is missing that words seem insufficient as a means of communication. Perhaps Caroline's sense of self as being a worm rather than a Person, comes close to the devastating impact of incest on the little girl's soul. I recall Caroline having told me in one of our first meetings (see Chapter 1) that she came to Israel in the hope of finding God, after having lost the ability to believe in anything. She had no better words to describe her lack.

***

I wish to now quote pieces of texts from Caroline's own writings that describe in her words – written but never spoken – some of her experiences of incest. Her writing, most eloquent, I believe, can express for many speechless victims, the absolute devastation that incest causes.

The trigger for writing this text was that Caroline wanted to bring me an article she had written for her work that had been published and of which she was proud. She writes:

~… I'd realized that one of the big differences now was that I could give it to Tova without being afraid that she was handling me. As long as things were so concrete and sexualized – including Tova herself – I had no way of knowing that she could differentiate between physical objects and my body. The inside was so pervasive and all encompassing that it left no room for any outside. When I finally understood that she's separate, that she possesses a reality which is non-sexual … then I could also comprehend that if I gave her an article, that's what it would be for her – an article. It wouldn't be anything else/more – not my body, not any sexual contact, not erotic enjoyment, etc. Her reality would ensure that it remained a concrete physical object – mine, brought in from the outside, but not thereby made part of the inside and contaminated by it (in the sense of "contaminated evidence" – compromised by contact with the inside).~

On incest as being a sort of marriage

Caroline had tried to describe some difficulty she was experiencing with the fact that the girlfriend she now lived with was having her father live with them temporarily while his house underwent renovations. It was very hard for me to make sense of what she was saying. Only after having read her text I understood that having a "father" – any father, in the same house as she lived in, felt threatening. The anxiety aroused from the past trauma did not allow differentiation in her thinking capacity. Her experiences with an abusive father meant all fathers might be abusive if they shared the same roof. She wrote:

~Today I managed to explain that it felt like a marriage; a sense of belonging to someone else. Tova wasn't happy with the "metaphor" of marriage, marriage for her being by definition something mutual. She wasn't sure however, that I didn't have something more in mind, that she was missing an element.

I said she could think of it in terms of prostitution, if she preferred: someone who doesn't have the right to her own body and belongs to the pimp who owns her and can use her any way he sees fit (or un-fit), wasn't something mutual, not something which two people had agreed upon. It was belonging in the sense of being owned: of someone else having the rights over me, my body.

But the idea of marriage isn't simply the relationship between D/I (Dad /me)– it's the whole context of the abuse. He's married – so it's a question of him saying, my marriage isn't good; I need someone else. Not only is he married but he's staying in the marriage.~

Caroline continues to elaborate upon the confusion this situation causes her in her inability to know what is real in her relationship with Dad. It leaves her maintaining the hope that if she keeps faithful to him he might become hers. Reading this, I see how confused she must be – a woman in her forties writing like an oedipal child of six. She continues:

~But the whole situation is confusing with regard to belonging, because it's not clear what he's actually doing and how I should understand it. It also leaves me permanently an outsider because as long as he stays in the marriage I'm not going to belong – to him, to myself, or to Mum, because I'm betraying her. It's also an extremely humiliating situation – again. To be the "mistress", the "second wife", the concubine, or prostitute is an essentially degrading status. Maybe this is one of the reasons why the sense of being humiliated/laughed at is so pervasive – not that they behaved towards me like that but that that's what all the relationships themselves were based on.~

So incest creates the illusion of the child's being someone special, at least to her father, while actually leaving her desperately alone, belonging to no one. And from this deep loneliness Caroline continues to describe how her solution is to remain totally faithful to the father. This is taken to the extreme and includes not allowing herself to form an attachment to anyone, including her therapist. When I express my thoughts that she is resisting any influence of mine in order to remain faithful to Dad she presents me with an elaborate description that seems to confirm this:

~... being rejected so sharply and so abruptly – as I told her today, the abortion wasn't simply about the baby not living – as if that wasn't enough – but it was also a way of D's saying: "Nothing's going to come out of this relationship." Killing two "birds" with one stone.
The humiliation and rage generated by such a circumstance – being completely helpless to do anything to stop it, to stop D. from stopping it – must be huge. But instead of expressing it externally – which wasn't possible physically, emotionally or any other wise – one of the ways to hit back was to say: "OK, you think you can stop, just walk away. But you can't – I'm not going to let you. I'm going to hang onto you inside, and at least that will give me the sense of being able to control something." I reacted to the abruptness of the withdrawal – and the implication it carried of killing the relationship – by "simply" denying it: On one level by clinging to the thought that it wasn't over; on another, by creating the illusion that maybe he hadn't really abandoned me – he might still come back at some point.~

Caroline continues to describe how the ending of the incestuous relationship was, in fact, much more painful than the abuse itself. It seems that this led her to hang onto Dad desperately as is described in the next text:

> ~In the light of what I stand to gain or lose from the cessation, the relief somehow becomes negligible. Even though the abuse was awful, the living in constant fear/paranoia of being caught, the problem of not knowing what was real, how I had to relate to M., etc., etc., – the effects when it stopped were just as traumatic. Coping with the loss was in some ways far more difficult than dealing with the attention. If a large part of submitting to the abuse in the first place was to mitigate the loneliness, then the abandonment was not only going to reactivate the original loneliness – literally – amplified several times over because now I knew a way to offset it – but to do so mixed with: guilt for being so dirty (with all the reasons why I deserved it, the loneliness now being justified, if it hadn't been before); using the abuse for my own purposes (reinforcing the negative self-esteem); with the knowledge that I couldn't go to M. (plus, more than likely, in addition to all the rage at her failure to intervene, etc., feeling of wanting to kill her in order to remove the obstacle to him belonging to me); the humiliation/pain/rage at being "passed over". With all these bad feelings going around, it's hardly surprising that I should want to hang on to the one which makes me feel slightly good about myself.~

Caroline then brings another text that relates how she is unable to separate from her father. From her writing it is difficult to tell if she is in control of any of her actions or feels obsessed by something out of her control. I will give just a short example from the long, complex text she brought me:

> ~I don't have any existence independently of him. He goes wherever I go or I take him everywhere, including the therapy, where he gets associated with Tova and all the sexualisation etc. He's there in every relation because all relationships are potentially a betrayal of him, I even dress like him – as if I am him in a significant sense ... As long as he's part of my identity I'm part of his, there's no way to make him a subject of discussion as an independent entity ... The real trouble with incest is that it's all in the family: I probably wouldn't have survived if I'd stayed at home, but the only way I could leave was by taking him with me. Not only that, but by keeping him inside I kept everything inside – and inside the family. No one else can get in – including Tova – in any real sense.~

***

And as I read this over several times – I no longer know what I think. Has Caroline all this time been intentionally making things become unreal so as to "keep things in the family"? If so, has all her suffering about nothing feeling real been a sham – some lie to distract me? And if so – why? Why does she continue to come to therapy? After all, if she wants to keep her Dad inside as a way to deal with her unbearable loneliness – what does she want from me? And since I know none of this can be spoken about with her since the content of the written material is not related to as a separate entity to be discussed, not objectified – I will soon find myself dissociating from these incredibly perceptive texts. They will vanish into some inner place within me to be, stored in some subterranean strata of meaning to be made available for use at a later time.

Tohu vevohu: from formlessness and void to the word

One day, out of yet another moment of immense frustration that Caroline was not speaking to me in any "normal" way, out of pure despair I asked her to tell me in a couple of words why she thinks she does not use language with me. Her spontaneous answer was: ***Tohu vevohu!***

These words are from Genesis, the first book of the Bible:

> In the beginning God created the heaven and the earth. And the earth was without form and void; and darkness was on the face of the deep. And a wind from God moved over the surface of the waters. And God said, Let there be light: and there was light. And God saw the light, that it was good: and God divided the light from the darkness. And God called the light Day, and the darkness he called Night ...
>
> Genesis Chapter 1, verses i–vi

"*Tohu vevohu*" – are the Hebrew words translated into English as "without form and void". Not always do languages overlap. In this case the two Hebrew words needed four in translation. Caroline has an exquisitely precise knowledge of the subtleties of English vocabulary. Her vocabulary is as wide-ranging as it is deep. For her to choose a word in Hebrew as a response to my question was extremely unusual and I cannot put it down to chance. *Tohu vevohu* – although comprised of two words have that special meaning of utter chaos – unbearable confusion, disorder and non-differentiation, non-separateness. Only if these two words are spoken together do they describe this state. Each word is rarely used in Hebrew and has a different meaning from the joining of the two. Alone, each word signifies a desert, desolate emptiness, a void, unbearable nothingness.

Tohu vevohu. Why did Caroline choose this pair of words? The act of incest comprises a pair of bodies in sexual intermingling, which causes utter chaos for the child partner. The act prompts a sense of feeling alive – rather opposite from the desolate emptiness when she was alone, bereft of the source of being desired and desirable. So two desolate objects when joined together in *tohu vevohu* are at least not alone in their despair when they conjoin. It is also usually in the night that incest occurs. In the night one cannot see and being unable to see, does not allow one to differentiate forms and shapes.

Formlessness is often an outcome of a merger of one thing into another, where boundaries lose their clarity. Reality itself becomes questionable. In English, "to be kept in the dark" is an idiom that means: to intentionally be denied access to knowledge. It is a well-known phenomenon that children who have been victims of incest by their parents often are not sure that this really happened. The darkness of the night, the emotional turmoil, the fact that the act is hidden, denied, not spoken about – not named, all contribute to this state of not knowing.

In Genesis it is God's intervention that creates light. With the entry of light clarity begins. *Tohu vevohu* can be related to as the mystery of potential energy – the black hole of formlessness out of which creation is potentially possible. But for this to happen, there is need for light. "And God said: Let there be light …" God creates light, then differentiation and from this the Word can be born. "And God divided the light from the darkness. And God called the light Day."

Caroline's God was her dad. He did not introduce light into their darkness. He did not introduce words to clarify anything. On the contrary – he had motivation for maintaining the *tohu vevohu*. Out of this state Caroline decides it is better not to speak, especially when she knows she risks the danger of being humiliated by being told she is making things up. Silence is the only sane alternative. But she also wants me to know. This time she creates a code – she chooses *my* mother tongue[1] (Hebrew) rather than hers to reveal to me secrets about her family. And I feel I am living inside a spy story trying to decode the little messages she sends me.

***

The experience of writing this chapter was particularly difficult. At the end I was left insecure about its intelligibility. Mainly, I found myself not being able to decide if Caroline's texts were brilliant descriptions that sprang from inside the experience of a victim of incest, unique in their depth of understanding – and if so whether I would be competent to transmit her wisdom to an outsider reader. Or, if what she was writing was on the level of intellectual, logical analysis empty of any deep significance? Here I was again experiencing doubt, and not being sure if it was justified or again aroused from projective identification with her recurring doubt about everything. I suddenly felt the urge to communicate with an outside reader, and have a third person enter my inner space – between me, Caroline's words and my effort to communicate. I was experiencing the uncertainty of being inside the closed circle of incest where all outside objective perception is lost because there *is no one* on the outside. I, thankfully, had trusted others on the outside, who were available to help me and to whom I could turn. If only Caroline could have had someone to turn to …

Thinking more about the vicissitudes of my thoughts I realized they resonated with something with which I was familiar – sometimes feeling bright and original with a sense of competence, while other times I could lose my self-confidence and even wonder if I was suited to this demanding profession. The pleasure of feeling special at times, the excitement and sense of aliveness when I have insights and perceptions – took me by extension to thoughts of Caroline as a bright little girl: how special she must have felt at times when she was her Dad's chosen one. Even more special than her mom. And then the total dejection and humiliation that came with the rejection and the denial of any status or recognition; and how she would be again abandoned to the desert of loneliness. I do believe this aspect of "soul murder" was a heart wrenching repeated experience in her growing up.

Note

1   I am bilingual – I was born in Israel, my family emigrated to Australia when I was 7 and I was there till the age of 18, receiving English schooling. Since then, I have been at home in both languages.

Chapter 8

The danger of the good object

> If you don't do what he wants you lose his love and if you do ... then you are full of rage and lose your self.
>
> Caroline to her therapist

Timeline: years 16–17 of therapy

Dealing with madness means being able to simultaneously hold on to paradoxes. Bion (1991) wrote in one of his last works: "I cannot promise communication of pure non-sense without the contamination by sense." In this chapter, perhaps looking at the mirror image of this statement, I have struggled to communicate something coherently so that my moments of feeling that Caroline's madness made a lot of sense could be communicated to another person, and thus prove that she was not so mad after all.

So why make this effort? An apt question.

The answer I can best come up with is this: within the noise, confusion, and despair, certain moments of clarity cast pure beams of light into the darkness of the formless chaos, the *Tohu Vevohu*. The illumination of these moments, which I experienced, were I believe experienced by Caroline in a similar way at the same time. We were then – for a moment, in sync. The repetition of these occasional precious moments contributed to a felt sense *that for her, life could be worth living* ... Because, even for just one moment, one has been understood.

Reality perception becomes possible and then lost

Caroline had hesitantly asked about the possibility of there being a different reality. I asked her for clarification. She was able to "report" that there were times that she could see me as "real" – that I was neither the mother that she feared nor her father whose presence eroticized everything. "But I don't know how that happens and I can't manage to keep it", she told me. This chapter is an attempt to look at these two issues.

What Caroline had let me know in her concise but exact observation, was that she might be able to overcome her trauma! She was able to know that she was in the present and *even experience the present as present*. The pathological effect of unresolved trauma is that it has the power to take over the present and turn the present into the past. The debilitating effect on the traumatized person is that when this happens there is little control over it and anxiety takes over, and when this anxiety is experienced as intolerable, either psychosis or dissociative processes predominate. The traumatized psychotic patient cannot summon sufficient ego forces to know this is happening and lives in the present as though she is in the past. This *is* her reality. Diagnostically one of the symptoms of psychotics is a distortion of reality. Yet, here Caroline, for the first time, was able to tell me that there are times that she *knew* that this happens to her. *In vivo* I could witness her growing capacity to think and be able to know when she feels I am real and even know who I am. She is also *aware* that something happens to this experience that makes it very transient. Here is the nascence of an observing ego developing that is capable of observing what she is experiencing. I also understand that she wants to be my "research partner" to explore how this happens. I will soon relate some of our findings at this time but will say, that unlike many hours that started off with hope but ended in despair, at the end of this hour, standing at the door, Caroline said: "At least I know it's there to be found!"

On hearing this, I found myself feeling a slight, pleasant warmth inside. And this time it did not come from the hot coffee cup that I always cradled in my hands to prevent myself "freezing" while with her. I recognize it as warmth emerging from the impact of her words. From having made a safe place for her over these many years, where any uncontrolled gesture, misunderstanding or separation on my part have threatened the potential of total annihilation of all we had built up to that point. I realized something deep had shifted in her. Is this what object constancy is about? And from this place, inside Caroline, a place was being made, a place where thoughts would be able to be thought because she could feel and rest in a sense of safety in my presence. And as she said so simply, even if it's often lost "it's there to be found".

I realize she was experiencing a sense of conviction as expressed in her words "I *know*", a rare verb in her vocabulary. To experience this, even if temporarily, after having been continually in a state of pathological doubting, must have brought her some much-needed relief. I think of the delight the toddler experiences in playing hide and seek, which can only be fun, and a wonderful, exciting experience when she has the certainty of *being found* by the gathering arms of the playful parent. Winnicott (1963b) describes how

> In health the infant creates what is in fact lying around waiting to be found. But in health *the object is created, not found* ... A good object is no good to the infant unless created by the infant ... Yet the object must be found in order to be created. This has to be accepted as a paradox.

So, from whichever direction one is to look at it, this statement of Caroline's was a cause for some optimism. To know she can find something that was hers and then got lost, is indicative of the sense of conviction she is able to experience after endless years of pathological doubting the reality of everything.

Kindness arouses the vicious cycle of incest

I will describe what led to this achievement of seeing me as a real object separated out from her projections. In general, it was an accumulation of many tiny experiences over and over again in the therapy where she had survived the terror and found me there on the other end – not abusive, not retaliating nor seductive. But more specifically, in the last month we had "discovered" through my showing care for her and being able to talk to her about it, that she experienced *positive* feelings on the part of the significant "other" as a *threat*, a real danger. It happened like this:

One day I was sick. Unlike with other patients whom I can inform ahead of time that I will be absent that day, I cannot inform Caroline since she forbids any phone communication between us. (She experiences her ear as an erotic orifice for penetration, see Chapter 1.) Instead, I arrange that a note is left on the entrance door for her to see when she arrives. The next time we met I opened by expressing empathic sympathy for her having arrived to a closed door. I saw her immediate anger. Did I not know that I was not allowed to do that? To express *any caring for her made it unsafe to be here*. How is this to be understood?

Although I had noticed that she often blushed when with me, until that moment I had not "put those pieces together". To hear me express care about her arouses desire for more – more of that feeling that she felt when she felt my care. Perhaps she experienced this desire with a passionate intensity as a child deprived feels hungry for love. But the abused child of the past, allowing herself to respond to the "caring" parent, was met not with care but by an adult whose wish to fulfil his erotic desires took precedence over any real care for his child's needs. So my expressing care for her results in her becoming the guilty one: guilty for wanting to be loved. Within seconds I had been turned into a seducing adult arousing her desire and she became the bad one for wanting to be loved. The anger she must have felt at *not finding me* is also proof of her caring and her desire to be cared about. This is the rage I met when I mention caring. Caring threatens the protective defence against experiencing the pain and rage of disappointment. I recall how, in the first years I was not allowed to use words like "want" in speaking with her.

I conveyed to her that her desire to meet me, and thus her understandable pain at my unexpected absence, was not only *not bad*, but legitimate, in that it represented life, her desire to live. We had spoken about her sense of aliveness that she experienced often only in the therapy, in the here and now in relation to experiences with me. This was confounded with the excitement and sense of aliveness she felt in the presence of her father in the past. After all, he had desired her.

Would she be able to separate his desire for her from my caring for her and wanting her to feel alive in a non-sexualized way? We were facing a really complex challenge – how to break the vicious cycle created by incest. Incest had made her *desire to live,* to experience positive feelings, as invariably bound up with the *erotic,* and therefore *dangerous.*

I do wish to point out here, at the risk of being repetitive, that none of the above came about in any clear, orderly way. But after struggling with glimmers of understandings and transforming nonverbal behaviour into something with meaning – the clear beam of light came in the understanding *that if positive feelings pose a danger – then where or how can there be a safe place?*

It was after this process that she came in with the statement of knowing there could be a different reality.

How does therapy work? What makes transformation of the inner experience possible? Or, as Shengold puts it, "In psychotherapeutic treatment, we know what to do; the mystery lies in how to do it". Not only was Caroline in danger of feeling loving feelings in her abusive family, but anger at her parents was also dangerous. At any moment she could be abandoned by the mother she had deceived or replaced as her father's love object. There was no room to feel anything. *To feel was dangerous* and she had arrived in therapy as a stone, a stone that feels no pain. It is the therapist's ability to contain her projections which include being the seductive object for her, without overwhelming anger, retaliation or pleasure, that contributes to her developing sense of safety. So if there is room for hateful feelings, then loving feelings can have a chance to be experienced as not endangering the patient.

So when Caroline said, "it's there to be found" I was momentarily experienced as a good object: "a different reality" in her words (Brenman, 2006).

How a different reality is lost

Caroline wanted to know why she couldn't "manage to keep it". Here is how it "got lost" this time. I will go one step backwards to try and describe that moment.

In the previous session, as mentioned, Caroline had articulated her thought that she was able to see me in different realities. But I had not understood her and said something to that effect that since we had come to the end of the hour we could go back to this next time. In between these two sessions, apparently what happened inside her was that my not having understood her question made her regret she had asked me in the first place and then, once she was "there" (that is, feeling sorry about something she had done to me), she got lost (lost the positive experience of knowing who I was in the present). I interpret the guilt she immediately feels, taking all responsibility upon herself.

On *Oedipus Rex* and acting out

Caroline's response is: "It must be my fault." This thought is immediately associated with sexuality. In her mind, I became the mother she had wronged. *When guilt and fear take over, thinking stops.* She cannot hear my thought that the guilt she took on was so as not to feel anger *at me* for not understanding her. The taking on oneself the guilt of the abusive parent is characteristic of the abused child whose need is to maintain the illusion of a good parent. (Shengold, Davies and Fawley, Herman)

This mechanism is brilliantly illustrated in the Greek masterpiece, Sophocles' play *Oedipus Rex*: when Oedipus understands what he has done, his first spontaneous response is to act – to destroy his eyes. He destroys the origin of seeing – the organs of visual perception. Seeing was eroticized and the desired object, the mother, allowed the incest to take place. Not to see is not to feel the desire, therefore not to transgress. To act is the spontaneous gesture before thinking can come about. To act is a defence to avoid thinking unbearable thoughts. One might say: an act for an act, as "an eye for an eye".

Caroline willingly prefers to see herself as guilty so as to maintain the illusion of a good parent. Understanding this she pleads: "So how will we find a way not to have everything eroticized?"

My response: "Yes, that is our big task."

Incest and anorexia

Caroline asked me to write up this session. I agree but suggest she also writes up what she remembers of it. This was becoming a common interaction. These moments of "light" made Caroline experience that sometimes what she understood in therapy was important. But since she knew this could be easily lost in her mind, the request for me to write up this session was to have some record outside of herself. We were to call this "the written witness/evidence". Talking about this, she realized that since for her, everything was eroticized, she could not or would not keep anything (any thought born out of the two of us together) inside of her, because it would become bad through contamination by her dirty, sexualized inside. She would mentally evacuate it out in a bulimic way and thus *make it unimportant*, and therefore be unable to be kept as a memory. For Caroline, *verbal intercourse was equivalent to sexual intercourse* and any outcome (new idea) was an illegitimate foetus to be immediately aborted, vomited out and Caroline was in danger as all anorexia nervosa patients are. I recall that years earlier she had brought me an article that cited a statistical relationship between anorexia and incest. At the time I had not been able make much sense of it.

"Is it alright to feel something is important?" Caroline hesitantly asks after thinking this is important enough to want me to write it for us. And I reply: "It's what's called growth, creativity."

It is then that I realize that she has just given me the answers to another question I was left to ponder over at the time of the intake: that she had told me that she had the knack of turning everything into insignificant and meaningless stuff. And this contributed to her pervasive sense of guilt.

At the door, she thanks me. This she would do very rarely, letting me know that today I had given her something meaningful. I liked to think that this she could take inside her and keep there so as to be able to be found. Perhaps therapy could be a nourishing experience.

***

Despite all this, no linear progress seemed possible. If I was hopeful that I now had a "partner" on this therapeutic journey, I was to re-experience over and over, that only through *experiencing the past with me, as though it was real, could anything develop*. To talk *about* the incest never lasted long. But when on occasion she did – I related to her words as important. For example:

> … If you don't do what he wants … you lose his … love … and if you do … then you are full of rage…and loss of self.

Decoding some nonverbal signals

On another occasion I learnt the meaning of her nonverbal behaviour associated to specific places in the room – for example: often, on her way out, while standing on the threshold between inside and outside, she would turn to me in slow motion, and when facing me would say very slowly something like "thank you" or "so we will continue?" It was a very ritualistic behaviour, enacted always on the same spot. Not really understanding what had spurred her question at that time, I usually answered with a non-committal response. On one occasion she voluntarily told me:

C: You don't know what happens on the other side of the door. Mum could catch me if she opens the door and sees – but here … it's OK. I can see that you speak to me at the door – so you're not angry at me,"
T: So you can know I'm not mum and you haven't done anything wrong.

And I think to myself how the long experience with incest and fear of being found out, the threat of losing love – her mom's love, her dad's love, the impossible conflict – left her feeling such a bad person, that here with me she needs the concrete reassurance over and over again that I don't hate her, that I won't leave her.

While this is enacted in the transference, she brings me several texts she wrote at home about the incest. It seems these two processes need to go on simultaneously, yet stay separate while perhaps integration takes place at an unconscious level. As described by Winnicott in *Fear of Breakdown* – it seems there cannot be talk about the trauma. It needs to be lived – inside the transference.

Here is an example of how it was:

Inadvertently, I take off my cardigan because it is a little hot this autumn day. Caroline closes her eyes and keeps them shut for most of the session with no word or movement, as though fearing I will attack her and she is in freeze to protect herself from me. I am feeling exasperated, tired of this "childish" behaviour – feeling manipulated and from my anger I "demand" that she open her eyes "so that you can see the present – that I am not your dad who is undressing if I remove my cardigan, nor am I putting semen into your mouth if I am sipping my cup of coffee!"

I continue, not hiding the frustration I feel, "If you open your eyes it will help you be in the present in an active way, rather than let yourself be drawn into the past in this helpless way! You may then be able to see me here as someone who is trying to help you!" She remains silent and "disobedient" until the end.

The next day Caroline starts off with:

> It's not a matter of logic. Logic doesn't work! I understand the logic … to open my eyes is to see the present… You're way ahead of me… you're talking about the inside…talking about what goes on inside of me …on the inside…I'm not even in a state where I can think of you here…that you are here to help me…It's hard enough getting over the fear at the door.

And I wonder if she is also telling me that when I even *mention* her inside experience it feels sexualized so she must expel me and my words.

***

The death of the mother and the beginning of thinking

In this period, 16 years into therapy, Caroline's mother dies. With her death, Caroline notices a change in her inner emotional state. She tells me that she realizes that she has always been *afraid* of her mother. Although we had speculated about this in the past, the reality of her mother's death created such a shift in her feeling state that she said with great conviction, on more than one occasion: "I know that I always feared her because I don't feel that fear since her death."

Experiencing knowing with such certainty was a rare moment for Caroline in itself and here she was relating to it as a fact, not just a fleeting moment. This "knowing" with a sense of conviction will become the first of a growing list of "emotionally known facts" about her relationship with her mother that will lead eventually to her deciding to end therapy. With time it became clear, but discovered gradually, that this fear has contributed largely to her "frozen" state of mind.

A move to a new clinic makes the question of continuity pertinent

A few months after the death of her mother, I needed to move to a new clinic and knowing that for Caroline any change gives rise to anxiety, I let her know of this a long time in advance so that we will have plenty of time to prepare for the move. The issue of the move to the new clinic brings up questions around the continuity of the therapy. Any attempt of mine in the past to discuss this was always interpreted with the suspicion that I want to be rid of her, abort her. Although this comes up now as well, Caroline is able to allow herself to explore thoughts about what *she* wants regarding the continuation of therapy.

Danger in the desire to live

In the midst of our preparation for the move to a new place and the thoughts about it there is a one week Passover vacation and on return Caroline has again "lost" continuity and is silent. She writes:

> ~When Tova did seem pleased to see me after the break, there was something quite terrifying about its concrete expression. I got quite lost following that, no longer knowing what the issues involved with the move were – as though the fright had shut everything down so that thinking about it became impossible.~

I will now cite a relatively long text from Caroline's writing because it describes with lucid clarity how the desire to live as a felt experience, can become frightening and how, on this occasion, we found a way to deal with this anxiety. I could shorten the description if I were to put it in my words but I find that Caroline's writing is like a lesson that is most informative of her inner experience and could not be better described in other words.

> ~… it's certainly not possible to tackle the issue of "wanting to live" in two weeks before the move. What I needed was some way to reframe the terms of the move – so that it wasn't in reference to wanting, but to something more manageable.

> Tova saved things by reminding me that what we both know we've been doing in therapy all along is trying to strengthen my hold on sanity – to find a way to make me feel more normal and things to be real. If I could think of the move in those terms, maybe that would help.
> Really! As Tova said, this was another example of my need to have things stated clearly and explicitly. A large part of the problem was that when we started talking about wanting/being wanted, the anxiety became so great that it took over everything else. Tova took it for granted that the wanting involved in the move (to the new clinic) was simply that of going on trying to strengthen my sanity to make me feel normal. For her "wanting" was so obviously to do with that, that to say the rest of the sentence was redundant and superfluous. For me, on the other, not having it stated meant that it could be anything. It's as though the word "want" in and of itself, when left open-ended and unspecified, acts as a magnet which attracts everything to do with the past. It then gets totally confused with sexual wanting – with which I want to have nothing to do. Words are so ambiguous, so fraught with uncertainty for me that I need to have everything specified in detail, stated accurately and in full – so that there's no room for misunderstanding or confusion. I really don't want to lose this place where I can think, know things for certain, feel real and normal; I don't want to abort the therapy ....~

Hope

Reading this, I feel hope. If she can think so clearly and feel therapy as a place where she can think even though at times she is dragged into the past, then this path we are on is the right one. I feel like writing her last sentence in big letters and hanging it on my wall to show her next time she experiences me as the dangerous abuser.

> I really don't want to lose this place where I can think, know things for certain, feel real and normal.

This was the verbal equivalent to her putting the photo of the two of us smiling at the Hospital Donation Ceremony on her computer as her screen saver. She would look at it each time she left the house to come to therapy so as to remind herself that I was on her side.

Some thoughts on incest and psychosis

From Caroline's texts, it is painfully clear how the guilt created in the child by long-term, repetitive participation in incestuous sexual acts, and hiding this from the mother jointly with a need to be faithful to the abusive father, who is also the loved one – together create the potential for psychosis. The way

Caroline attacks her own mind and loses all capacity to think is reminiscent of Bion's description of psychotic thinking processes as being characterized by the hatred of reality, both internal and external, and all that makes for awareness of it (Bion, 1956).

The very act of incest creates a confusion in the sense of self by being treated as an object of love (lust) and also being abused by that same person. In this situation, to feel any desire is to confirm that one is bad and deserving of the hate. To feel loved without feeling bad is uncharted territory.

The closest Caroline can come to saying something positive is in her last sentence, "*I don't want to abort the therapy*" thus indicating that these 17 years together have built the foundations of a sense of safety. At least from her writing self I know this.

Chapter 9

On incest, blindness and paranoia

Timeline: 17–18 years into therapy

Winnicott: playing and reality

In her constant search to find herself Caroline was reading widely – any books that might be helpful for us to use in therapy. In that respect she was always "my partner" in the search for her identity. Her belief in the value of the written words as possible mediators to her experience was one of her strongest assets. Without this, I doubt I would have been able to help her. From our history together, she also knew that I knew and accepted the importance of her need to use books to help us on this psychoanalytic search for herself. Books were "the Third" for us (Ogden 2004a) providing us with the necessary space to think in and about her mental life.

As we were preparing to move to my new clinic, Caroline wrote the text that follows below. There had been months of preparation for the move to make it as non-traumatic as possible for her. She had discovered Winnicott's book *Playing and Reality* (1971) from which she was soon to quote, but first she asked me if I could bring the cushions from the old clinic to the new clinic. I couldn't do that, since they were part of the furniture and it was a shared clinic, but I suggested instead that I bring a cloth to cover the armchair for her to familiarize herself with and I would take that to the new clinic and put it on the new armchair.

> ~The last day before the move. Tova fortuitously suggested that instead of taking the cushions she could bring a piece of material with which to cover the chair – as a kind of transitional object. This made good sense, and led straight to the thought of playing which goes with transitional objects.
>
> Having got that far, playing became a possible way of using the move positively. Not only could it serve as an opportunity to leave the past in its concrete form behind – starting again in a new place without attaching to it all the fears and apprehensions which were associated with this

setting – but it could also be a new place in which to start playing. In this sense the old place had functioned as a preparation for the new, creating a safe environment in which playing can occur – a realization and freedom from the anxiety which has always been present; a sense of "normality" which will allow for moving; and a space for being in which it may be possible to find my "self".~

I was so moved by this most optimistic text, particularly as this tone was unprecedented in our actual meetings. The last quote of the several she brings from *Playing and Reality* is:

~"...In these highly specialized conditions (of therapy with a trusted therapist) the individual can come together and exist as a unity, not as a defence against anxiety but as an expression of I AM, I am alive, I am myself. From this position everything is creative."~

Different meanings of pleasure

Winnicott's writings confront Caroline with the importance of not only feelings, but the feeling of pleasure. Caroline has always associated pleasure with eroticization and her "badness" but Winnicott's writing opened a small window that allowed her to now "play with the idea" of there being the possibility of fun in living. Caroline approached the investigation in a very logical way – trying to look for memories that could explain how or why she connected pleasure with badness. Finding no experiential memories, she decided to go about it differently – searching for memories where she enjoyed something without the accompanying feeling of badness. She was able to define with a feeling of certainty unusual for her that *having her eyes tested* was a positive experience. This was a routine experience done periodically to adjust her prescription eye glasses.

The eye test: a sense of certainty

I found Caroline's scientific approach to trying to learn about her own mind most impressive. Let's look at how she approached this "inquiry". Although it seemed very logical, it had not occurred to me to ask such a question about the possibility that pleasure could be anything but a positive experience. For me, it was so obvious that I took it for granted. To take something for granted, means it is not thought about or questioned. Like gravity it is just there. Only if it were to be absent or abused would there be questions asked. Her need to be able to make room for this new idea in her rigid way of thinking led to a search for an experience she could own as hers where she had enjoyed something without feeling bad and guilty. The following is her analysis of this new finding.

~this was something which I finally comprehended as being an enjoyable experience because, on the one hand, I knew what I was talking about, and at the same time, what I said was taken seriously. The combination of these two factors is extremely rare – which is probably what makes the experience memorable ... Even if it's a case of saying "I don't know" whether the right or left eye is clearer, that's already an answer in itself – which the optician takes seriously.

Once we'd gotten that far, Tova suggested that therapy must be a "traumatic" framework for me. In contrast to the eye test, where the investigation is clearly designated and defined, the questions are unambiguous and have clear answers, and relate to a specific issue, therapy is by definition an invitation to think about all sorts of issues whose "answers" can come from different places, involve various levels, and aren't normally clear, specific or unambiguous. It's certainly no wonder that open- ended questions immediately produce a sense of confusion and fear in me – given that I don't know where they are coming from, where they're leading to, or what they involve ... Even talking to Tova about it (the eye test) was easier than talking with her generally is. The fact that I know what I'm talking about removes the fear of uncertainty. The latter involving all the issues of making things up, not being believed, making a fool of myself, etc. In that respect, talking has everything to do with my knowing and being sure of data which are clear and unambiguous.

Tova, however, raised the possibility of another factor. If I've now been able to identify what makes the eye test such a positive experience, it's quite likely that the reason is that I've allowed myself to stay with the feeling of pleasure, rather than cutting off from it immediately. Once I can be with the feeling, there is space to think about it – and thence to try to understand what it's composed of, what elements go into making it enjoyable, etc. ... the trouble is that in most other instances – perhaps particularly with Tova – the fear of enjoyment is so immediately associated with sexual feelings that it kicks in without giving me time to stay with whatever subject we've raised.

That made much more sense to me. In some ways, it may be connected with my determined efforts – which have been so frustrating to Tova – to slow things down to a manageable pace ... to try to avoid giving space to the fear to kick in .... Of course the fear of enjoyment or pleasure, which is the real issue which needs to be dealt with. But then I wasn't in any place to start talking about that. Now perhaps we are.~

One type of behaviour – such as extremely slow speech as demonstrated by the gaps in Caroline's speech – can slow things down to make sense. Yet, at another time that same behaviour can be there to hide, to conceal, what is actually going on. When language is fragmented to this degree, then words become "non-sense". What came into my awareness while writing this book was that, of course, this happens only when we are in live interaction and there is a fear she may lose total control over the situation. As seen in her writing, where she is alone, there is an amazing flow – in shocking contrast to her jerky, way of talking which involves being with another.

There was something remarkably liberating in being able to talk about Caroline's fear of experiencing pleasure. Insight was expanding into understanding her constricted existence. Where any form of pleasure in human interaction is immediately eroticized arousing guilt and badness, a defence against this is avoidance of human interaction. The vicious circle is created where isolation from others leads to an "emotional autism" where there is little contact with others, little communication and thus no input from the outside about one's perception of reality. Everything stays within the family or within one's mind.

In the next session we were rewarded by a rare experiencing of humour together – a non-erotic moment of pleasure. What was wonderful was that we both felt it at the same time and, thankfully, Caroline was able to put it into writing.

Here are some of her valuable insights:

~In discussing how difficult it is to stay with any feelings of enjoyment or pleasure, we began looking for ways to try and deal with the issue. I finally arrived at the point where I could admit that I need to confront the original experience which created the association between enjoyment and badness. As Tova suggested, therapy and the eye-test are analogous in purpose: both have the aim of seeing things more clearly. The problem is that in contrast to the eye test, which is quite straightforward and non-traumatic, looking in therapy involves opening up some really disgusting subjects. We joked about it a bit – I would have been quite happy if Tova had said that I wasn't making sense, but she was sure that the expiry date had come due on the diversionary and avoidance techniques I've been employing for so long.

Something about this session made a real impact. ... the fact of being prepared to acknowledge that the fear of enjoyment comes directly from sexual experiences with Dad had the effect, as it were, of legitimizing a part of myself which I'd never been willing to recognize. It was like discovering a reality which had, up until now, always been elusively out of reach – like finding one's feet on the ground rather than being "strung up in midair."

It seems as though owning up to the past – acknowledging, in however small a way, that it's a part of me, and admitting that it is something I know, had the effect of granting a sense of reality and legitimacy for the first time. (The word which comes to mind is "propriety" – which includes both "rightness" and "ownership".) The more I know –admit/ own to – the more I can be there, partly because more of me is there and partly because it's material that we can then deal with.~

I find myself feeling elated. Here is Caroline outlining the work needed to be done in therapy. And she is able to describe, from her own experiences, what is therapeutic in all therapies: the ability to know and own the painful truth about oneself on the way to feeling whole. She was able to recognize her mental functioning – *to take responsibility* – to own painful parts of herself. And here it is *she* who is defining this. I recall her first sessions where she came suffering because her friend had accused her of evading all responsibility. I was ready and willing to help her deal with this. I could see her becoming what I so hoped she would: a whole person with the ability to feel real feelings – of pain and pleasure, conflict and confusion the way of all humans. The renewal of hope was the source of my elation.

Then came the fall. Our understanding plummeting down. Such short-lived optimism. So sad and disappointing that the peak reached in the previous paragraph and the writing could not be sustained in our real-life interactions. We are immediately mired in doubt again. Caroline's writing describes this too:

> ~We came up yet again against a cloud of unknowing which frustrated the attempt.~

When you drink your coffee in front of me are you trying to seduce me?

In our sessions there is a regression to no memories, silences and staring, as though none of the above had been "accomplished". We experience again a block. This was Caroline's outward behaviour with me in the room. But her writings reveal that "behind the scenes" as it were, in the privacy of her room away from me, she is able to write to me about us. She writes about her motivation to now analyse the sources of her anxiety, which so quickly breaks down communication between us. The following is an example where she stopped talking because of a physical action on my part: I was drinking something hot and told her I needed to today because of a bad throat. Usually, I only hold the cup in my hands to warm them so as not to freeze in her deadening presence. At this session, she fell into paranoid silence. After the session Caroline writes to inform me why this happened – but in the session itself she was in "freeze mode".

Not to be is not to see is not to know

> ~Tova was drinking because of a bad throat so we started with that. It's almost as though it's not simply ideas which are uncertain, but also "things". In a somewhat paradoxical sense, the effort of not being there with Dad – of not seeing anything in order not to know anything – has created a preternatural awareness of all sorts of things. These have now become a series of occasions which generate fear....Part of the anxiety produced is not knowing whether innocent things are really harmless, or whether I should legitimately be afraid of them. So, for instance, with Tova's drinking, I can't sufficiently distinguish

between her need to drink in order to be able to talk – which in effect has nothing to do with me – and my sense that she's blurring the boundaries between inside and outside, so that "putting inside" represents a sexual act instead of a normal act of drinking.~

Incest creates an inability to have *neutral* experiences in the presence of the other. Thinking itself becomes a burden. Now Caroline had revealed why she always entered the clinic with her eyes closed. "Not seeing anything is not to know anything." And I am reminded of Caroline's familiarity with the Bible where the meaning of "knowing" includes sexual intimacy: "And the man knew Havva his wife; and she conceived, and bore Qayin ..." (Genesis 4, i).

The danger of anger

From recognizing the significance of the feeling of pleasure there was an expansion to other feelings. Now anger became a legitimate topic. Until now even the mentioning of it was forbidden in our space. I knew this from my countertransference – that mentioning even *annoyance* could make her feel accused and bad. An example: about two years earlier, Caroline had witnessed me having an argument outside the clinic (she stalked me so she was in a good position to see) with a man who had carelessly damaged my car with his. I was not "my usual soft-voiced self" with him but was very angry when he refused to give me his driving licence details. After seeing this she refused to enter the room and eventually when she did, she hesitantly told me that she now knew that I could be a very dangerous person because what if I were to turn my anger against her?

It was quite clear that, for her, anger meant danger and had to be avoided at all cost. Her compliance was evidence of this. On account of Caroline's alarm at anger, I often struggled with my anger at her in the sessions, especially around her staring and silences, looking for ways to modify my responses and express them in a way that she would not experience as an attack.

Feelings allow decision making

Legitimizing and recognizing the importance of having feelings, including anger influenced Caroline's functioning in the outside world. A rare incident occurred: she *shared with me* an outside event: her dissatisfaction with her place of work. To my surprise (surprise mainly because I knew nothing about her outside world), she decided to quit her job and described how she arrived at this decision.

> ~... Tova finally understood that work was an abusive situation – my description over how Mr. D [her boss] behaved made it clear to her that

he wanted to own/control/me. She said how impressed she was that I was standing up in public for my name and fighting for my rights. I told her that in large part it was because I recognized that it was an abusive situation and that if I couldn't confront Dad I could confront Mr. D. It was a way to bring things out into the open – not to keep them hidden and secret and something to be ashamed of. It also was a vicarious way of confronting Dad.~

Caroline was able to act in her environment in a self-enhancing way because she was now able to be in touch with her feelings, including her feelings of anger. She no longer needed to evacuate feelings the minute they came into existence. To allow herself to feel and stay with the feeling long enough to experience it and name it, enabled her to differentiate between past and present – between her father and her boss. This made thinking possible. Thinking rationally is a prerequisite for rational decision making. Caroline was no longer only a passive victim of outer abuse nor of her inner drives. She was becoming, as written in one of her texts: "a person with a personality". I told her that I was very proud of her that she had stood up for herself.

Although Caroline felt this development was a direct outcome of the therapeutic experience she also attributed it to the reduction of *fear* since the death of her mother.

This event coincided with her having witnessed my anger at the abusive driver in the car incident (mentioned above) where I did not allow myself to be abused. I wondered if this had contributed to her newfound ability, through identification with me, to stand up for herself.

***

Descartes' Error

I now wish to share here Caroline's deep observation of the effect of living without feelings. Accepting that to feel is a positive accomplishment and not something to be evacuated led Caroline to allow herself to think about having feelings. This was in response to a book she was reading by Antonio Damasio: *Descartes' Error* about the relationship between neurology and the psyche. In this sample of her text, I would like to show how Caroline used Damasio's book:

> ~(Damasio writes) "When emotion is left out of the reasoning picture, as happens in certain neurological conditions, reason turns out to be even more flawed than when emotion plays bad tricks on our decisions."~

She then continues, quoting a description about a man who as the result of a neurological illness which caused:

~"profound defect in decision making. The instruments usually considered necessary and sufficient for rational behaviour were intact in him. He had the requisite knowledge, attention, and memory; his language was flawless; he could perform calculations; he could tackle the logic of an abstract problem. There was only one significant accompaniment to his decision-making failure: a marked alteration of the ability to experience feelings."~

It is obvious that Caroline identifies with this description. She continues:

~This reminded me very strongly of Tova's recent comments regarding my ability to communicate with regard to the negotiations with Mr. D over the work agreement. She noted several times that in describing the events related to the negotiations I was far more coherent, composed sentences with a beginning, middle and end – one after another – and was generally more "alive". I put it down to the fact that I knew what the issues were with Mr. D; that I could think; and that underlining both reasons might have been the reduction in fear since Mum's death.

Tova, on the other hand associated the difference in my communication with my being in touch with my anger. It was as though the feeling of anger – its identification, recognition, and experience – allowed me to become alive.

When I could feel or be in touch with the anger, the decision-making process – knowing what I wanted out of the negotiations, what I was willing to do and what I wasn't, etc. – was made much easier because I had a focus and purpose. Without that focus/significance/meaning everything becomes apathetic, indifferent – the very thing I complain of with respect to having no interest in anything.

This description is just from reading the Introduction ... but even this much seemed to make a great deal of sense to me. It's a general feeling that's accompanied most of my life, so it's not just a recent phenomenon. I simply didn't have the tools to define or comprehend what was happening.~

Caroline, I think to myself, would make an excellent psychology lecturer.

On the sense of absence

Something in her writing implied that in her subjective experience, Caroline had some memory of once having felt differently.

Suddenly, I understand that Caroline knows in the depth of her being that she was once a person who experienced aliveness, and that the way she has been feeling most of her life, is in contrast to this. She carries the experience of having changed or lost something. Someone born with a neurological-based deficit of affect would not be constantly is search of what has happened to them. This realization validated what I seem to have intuitively felt when first meeting her. At that time I had the thought neurology wasn't the answer, that her condition was not primarily caused by a neurological factor (see Chapter 2). This was why, in the first year of therapy, I discouraged her from having neurological testing.

***

The advantages of a neurological diagnosis

But for Caroline, to give up the diagnosis of having a neurologically based amnesia was itself quite painful. A few months earlier, while undergoing the neurological tests to determine if she suffered from Asperger's syndrome, she had written:

> ~Having raised the possibility, I was then faced with confronting it. In many ways, such a diagnosis represents a relief. …~

But then her doubts creep in, and rightfully so. She continues:

> ~If much of my behaviour is to be explained neurologically, does that mean that all we've discussed about the abuse has been an invention, for lack of knowledge about a physiological base? While Tova's response was that she didn't really know what to say about that, she did seem to indicate quite clearly that she didn't see any contradiction between the two.~

When Caroline brought this text to me together with her announcement that she has decided not to renew her work contract with Mr D, there was a sense of freedom emanating from her that I had not seen previously.

***

Hiding from the neighbour: dissociation *in vivo*

One day I opened the door for our session but Caroline was not there. Instead, I saw a neighbour opening the door across the corridor. I searched and soon found Caroline hiding in a corner. It took a lot of persuading for her to come inside. At first she had no idea what had happened nor that she had gone into hiding. The last thing she remembered was that she had rung the bell and a woman had come into the hallway and from behind her had asked her to move so that she could pass with her baby pram. Everything that had happened after that was lost to consciousness. Fear had paralyzed her to such an extent that she psychically "disappeared", leaving a blank in her perception or memory of outer events.

Caroline was able to say that the combination of being between inside and outside (on the threshold of the door), having someone surprise her from behind and it being *a mother*, had been the worst kind of situation. We both thought that this probably aroused the childhood trauma of the abuse – fearing being caught by Mom after having done something forbidden secretly in the room with Dad.

If you don't know something it means you don't want to know so you are bad

To know that one does not know something is quite an achievement. Caroline had developed the capacity to realize she had dissociated. There was a continuity of being that included the dissociation. I had been a witness to something that we both felt was very significant and Caroline was motivated to have it recorded in writing for our use. This was on the day following the incident, since fortunately on this occasion Caroline did not delete the whole event from her mind. She began to slowly share with me her thoughts. I wrote them down, word for word while she "dictated" with long pauses between the words.

> There are literally ... missing bits ... first ... of all you don't understand what happens a lot of the time ... then ... you don't know if it's true ... or false which goes together with ... not knowing if you've made it up. ... you can't explain it and then ... it means you ... need to know as much as possible ... so there won't be missing bits ... it also goes with ... the automatic link of ... not knowing and ... having done something bad ...if you don't know things the first explanation is that you don't *want* to know ... or you did something stupid or wrong or bad ... because the not understanding does not make sense ... and then it gets connected to the secrecy ... things not being said ... or being deliberately mislead ... so it's almost as though the two themes are interchangeable ... being misled and my not understanding. So then, your not knowing always carried an element of having done something wrong or bad. Does this make sense?

What Caroline said made a lot of sense to me. I suddenly remember a very old film I once saw called *Gaslight* – a Hitchcock-like film where the evil husband wants to drive his wife insane so that she will commit suicide. The method he chooses is to turn the gaslight down every time he leaves the house, leaving her to experience semi-darkness, and then he would turn it up on his return, without her knowing this, of course. When she told him about it he denied the possibility of such an occurrence, making her doubt her sanity.

I think of Caroline as a young girl, being deceived by her abusers and then also blocking out her own mind so as not to know something. But then not knowing how to know anything. How easy is to become insane under such circumstances when there is nothing to hold onto and no one to bear witness to what is happening.

I share my understanding of this with her: "I think we can assume that the origin of your anxiety and the concomitant 'disappearing' in such an extreme way is probably because something bad was being done. And it was too terrible for you to *know* it."

Caroline then remembers that in the past this "missing bit" experience used to happen very often in our sessions, almost all the time, and now it rarely happens.

"But then I didn't even know it was happening" she adds. And I remember how she used to say nothing, nothing about it or anything else. And all I saw was silence and a blank stare. But now Caroline is able to experience a sense of self, recognize when she has "disappeared" and begin to introspect about this and in what is perhaps the greatest move: she *talks* to me about it. Eighteen years later.

Chapter 10

The hospital dream
A place to bring the madness

Timeline: year 19 of therapy

In Chapter 4 I related how Caroline, as a consequence of her mother's death, received a large inheritance and donated a significant portion of it to save the lives of neonatal babies in a hospital department.

This act in itself was of tremendous significance in her life and the process involved was itself most moving. I wish now to elaborate on some of the events occurring between the time of her *decision* to give the donation and its actual realization in an official ceremony that I attended. The whole process took about a year. This decision was a turning point for Caroline where she made the choice of opting for *life* (represented by the life-saving machines) over the pursuit of Death (represented by preoccupation with suicide or wanting a grave made for the doll).

On this day Caroline looked pleased when she entered and was holding a bag with some sweets in it and a typed page, which she took out. This is very unusual for her – to bring something into the clinic from the outside, and in such an open, unhidden way. In response to my curiosity she tells me that the sweets were a gift from the staff at her friend's office, to celebrate her new job offer. She then gave me the page to read and I notice that it is divided into three separate sections:

1   On one side, there is a copy of a contract for her new job offer, which is professionally more challenging than the previous one.

For her to describe to me this celebration in outer reality was quite new. It also revealed the sense of triumph she felt over her recent decision *not* to renew her contract with her old boss after recognizing his abusiveness.

So here was Caroline informing me about outside reality in real time, and telling me of a sense of accomplishment and joy, these being so important, considering the continual sense of humiliation she had experienced, in the proximity of her boss and her father.

***

2   On the other side of the page was typed the details of a dream she had had. It was the first time she had brought me a dream in written form:

> ~I woke up in the night in the middle of a very vivid and "real" dream. I've not experienced anything of this sort before: any dreams I've had have not had any feelings attached, but this was of me, when I was 5/6 and I knew it was real.~

In the dream she was being attacked by a mob and then found herself in a psychiatric hospital, being looked after by the staff who were kind and trustworthy, *but she could not talk to them.* She could only be silent and communicate non-verbally with a little boy who was also hospitalized. The dream became frightening when a man (the attacker) tried to force himself into the hospital.

Her first response to this dream was:

> The dream felt good because it felt *real*. It's better to be mad and feel it's real than to be mad because everything feels unreal.

The next day she said about the dream that perhaps the hospital represents therapy:

> Safe to be mad in, safe to bring the madness to, but becomes dangerous when *he* comes here too. Maybe it means Mom and Dad are here.

I recall at the time worrying that even in the dream she *does not speak* to the staff.

3   Under the typed dream, separated by a dotted line *** Caroline wrote the following:

> One of the BBC programmes by Robert Winston on the mind /brain, he indicated that one of the ways in which people get to know others is by seeing them move. Perhaps this has to do with my inability to move – not wanting to give any opportunity for being known.

***

Knowing Caroline, I understood that it was not by chance that she presented me with this visual format of three separate pieces placed together on two sides of one sheet of paper. I find myself wondering how to decipher the hidden meaning of the three new bits of the puzzle all joined together.

My thoughts at the time were:

On one side of the page a normal, adult Caroline has written about her progress in the real, outer world (the news of the new job interview). This is how Caroline is functioning outside the therapy and she is, for a rare moment, sharing her world outside the clinic with me.

On the other side of the same page there are two pieces. The first was the dream. It represented a new mental capability – a dream with feelings that feel real, and it is remembered and reported to me. She is becoming a *someone* rather than a *no one*. She is able to enjoy having an inner world and even tell me about it: the dream felt *good*. There is the experience of: *I exist*. And have feelings that last long enough for them to become material for dreams. Here is a basis for introspection – and in my presence. Surely these are the first buds of the possibility of Caroline being able to soon have the ability to have her own narrative of her life! To have a sense of who she is and maybe know something of where she has come from and even hold onto a memory of it. She is slowly developing increasing ability to contain her pain, not just evacuate it by deleting parts of her mind.

Yet, with the relief of being able to dream a real dream a fear enters the dream itself that is experienced as real to her; real in the sense of not being only in the dream, but a real event in outer reality: the entry of the threatening man. Anxiety makes the dream into a nightmare. The hospital (safe place) feels endangered by the man/her father, who at this time in reality is actually bed-ridden in a distant country.

***

Finally, the third part, as though unrelated, is the BBC quote that hints at a conscious need to hide her movement in order to hide others gaining knowledge about her, again indicating a sense of mystery and some uncanny secret, including the hint at sexuality. So, within the puzzle piece of the BBC quote is enfolded a riddle. This in itself creates in me the already well-known feeling I often have with her of my being subjected to a "cat and mouse" game, trying to decipher clever quizzes and yet never being reassured if I have found out the "correct" answer.

***

I think how these three pieces represent the different inner states of Caroline at this time.

Interpreting the hospital dream

At first, Caroline expresses her fear that the dream means she is going mad and will need to be hospitalized in a psychiatric ward. But she mentions an accompanying good feeling, since it has allowed her to get away from the abuser. The existence of *a place to go to* where she can feel protected is a source of comfort. But even here, the dream stresses, she remains silent I relate to the dream as symbolizing the fear that if she reveals to me her past acts with her father she may go mad. I add, the fact that "he" intrudes and destroys the safety of the place in spite of her silence, means that silence will not be enough to help her heal. It will keep her "institutionalized" (in a psychiatric hospital). So, within the dream there is the paradox of the safe place of therapy becoming unsafe in spite of/because of her silence. I find myself encouraging the necessity of "talking to the staff" (me) as being the road to healing and a sense of inner safety. It seems, unconsciously, I am experienced as being in competition with her father over her. He vulgarly attacks my space to take her away from me. Little did I know that this will be acted out towards the end of the therapy quite violently and that the violent dream was a precursor for real violence to come ...

Yet – in spite of all the above – the fact that this is dreamt and that she related to the dream as feeling good, I find encouraging. It means therapy is experienced as a transitional space where all this "impossibility" is brought to: a place to bring the madness to. "Do you understand that the dream means that the only way to be real is by being autistic!" she says, referring to the non-communicating element of both herself and "the silent boy".

Maybe I understand – but I cannot accept that it must be so. I am here in the function of the life force – believing in the benefit of therapy – of our togetherness and at this point in time I see her *silence* as the enemy. I say: "at this point in time", because over the course of what turned into our 26-year therapy, silence was a dominant feature and I came to learn that it served many functions: to hide secrets, to protect her from a murderous superego (Rosenfeld, 1987), to represent the unspeakable, Edvard Munch's silent scream, to prevent drowning in meaningless noise, to allow for time to think, among more meanings.

I decide to pursue the issue of silence some more, seeing it as a source for her stagnation and keeping her forever immobile and psychotic. I ask about the little boy in the dream – the silent one with whom she communicates, *in silence*. I wonder why with the staff – who represent me, she/he will not speak?

C: He's also been through something similar.
T: I remind her that at times she has asked me if I, too, have been abused by my father. (Not in the same way as you – not sexually, I had replied). Is this why I am "the staff", the outsider, because I have not suffered like her? Caroline reminds me that in the first book she gave me *The Promise*, by Chaim Potok, the therapist Danny, could only help the boy Michael, after he himself had suffered in a similar way: by being exposed to total silence, in a very sadistic way, by his patient. I then relate to the pain and rage she must often feel towards me, being the staff, who can go away and leave her with her imprisoning pain, and go off to my safe home and family while leaving her behind. So only with another "inmate",

abandoned like herself, will she communicate. At least with the little boy there is no humiliation involved. I relate to her fear of expressing any of this anger at me, out of trepidation that she might lose control and go mad and be put away, if she were to express any of this rage towards me.

T: If we were "in the same boat", like you and the boy in the dream, you wouldn't need to suffer this pain at the ending of each session. When I am the "staff" I leave you alone with your pain.

Caroline cries until the end of the hour. The crying represents not only pain but also the crying at the relief that there is someone to cry to. I think Caroline felt understood that I could empathize with her rage at me even if I could do nothing about it beyond understand her.

***

A comment

And, I remind myself, Caroline had come in happy to announce that the dream felt good because it *felt real.* To feel unreal seems to be the greatest threat of all.

Caroline is sharing the experience of hope in being able to face the fearful unknown future. To be able to dream about it, to know it is in fact a dream, remember the dream and have a person and place to bring the madness to – this transitional space created in the therapy is the source of her hope.

Chapter 11

The silence is not to be battled – but understood

Timeline: years 19–20 of therapy

Shortly after the hospital dream, and from the danger of drowning in the ocean of silence, I find myself making an unprecedented suggestion. It is a proposal for action. Knowing that Caroline's father is on his deathbed, I ask her if she does not want to consider visiting him and trying, before it's too late, to ask him about the past. I understand that she is telling me that as long as she is so terrorized by the man from her dream, her Dad, she cannot speak. Her silence will prevail. I wanted to believe that perhaps, at the end of his life, he would admit to the abuse he had inflicted upon her, and relieve her of the "not knowing", of the living in constant doubt. For me to actively initiate such an action is very untypical in my work with her.

Caroline is shocked at my suggestion and insists that I tell her exactly when this thought had occurred to me; she fears that perhaps I had had it before her dream and thus had influenced her dreaming.

T: Do you think my thoughts could create your dream?
C: Sometimes ... if together ... can influence.

I think – perhaps she's right. I have had dreams that I'm sure are affected by her presence. Is this so different? So it's frightening to be too close and frightening to be separate. I have often experienced her extreme sensitivity in being able to read my mind and we both knew how compliant she could be. Sexual abuse is being *one inside the other* with no separation, no sense of self/other differentiation. With such fears her silence becomes her only shield of protection but it does not allow me to help her!

But the silence cannot be beaten. It is to be understood.

***

To commit suicide rather than uncover the truth?

It is at about this time that Caroline becomes suicidal. My insisting that she try to give up the silence has given rise on her part to a mounting and intense anxiety. It has led her to considering suicide as an option. For the first time I feel she is in real danger of taking her life. This is after she had mentioned that she feared that if she were to "know" her morbid secrets, she might discover that she had been *inhuman*. She expressed being faced with a conflict between choosing to know her past and find out it's too unbearable to live with or choosing to die *before* she finds out!

I sense that she is serious and insist she sees a psychiatrist and together we meet with him. The psychiatrist puts her on a low dosage of anti-psychotic medication.

The threat of becoming inhuman

A vignette

Medication reduced Caroline's anxiety somewhat and again I resume encouraging her to speak with me. I fear that her dream represented her wishing to "institutionalize" herself by developing "hospitalism" and becoming like the chronic schizophrenic patients I knew from my residency in a psychiatric hospital. I share this concern with her.

C: You are asking me to do something impossible, something beyond the bounds of human behaviour.
T: (sighing heavily) I think you feel that you cannot tell me of the inhuman behaviour because you don't know if we will be able to contain it here.

At the door, she turns slowly towards me saying in a cold hard voice that sends a chill down my spine: "That much you *do* understand?"

T: (a bit timidly) I think so.

***

At the next session: for the first ten minutes she sits in silence, eyes closed, thumb in mouth, looking like a big foetus.

C: That's why I need to know that I can end it now. (We both know that she means ending her life.)
T: Because you don't know if we will be able to contain the secret here?
C: I don't want you to say that I didn't warn you

T: (I'm feeling somewhat scared because I know she means this.) I represent the voice that is encouraging you to tell me, and your telling me there might be irreversible devastating consequences if you listen to me. You don't know if you'll be able to go on living. That's very scary. (I am close to tears.)
C: What's scary?
T: Did you understand what I said previously?
C: Yes.

I try to repeat what I'd said and I'm not sure if I'm clear enough because I am feeling scared. I add:

T: Wouldn't you feel scared if something you did or said might cause the other not to be able to go on living?

Caroline looks at me very quietly as though from the other side of life and says very quietly: "It wasn't a threat."
    Hearing her say this, I feel an unspeakable terror. I do believe I am experiencing how she can become *inhuman* – cold, devoid of feelings. (I later think that the last statement I made was unconsciously touching in her some terrible crime she had witnessed or even participated in and her inhuman-like coldness was the expression of the emotional dissociation from this, both then in the past and now in the present. I was the one feeling her unfelt terror.)

T: (needing a few moments to recover) I know it wasn't meant as a threat. I heard it as you telling me that that's how it is – as a fact about how you feel. That's why it's so scary. You really don't know – if you decide to tell me … how it will be for you afterwards – for us here together.

She looks at me for a long moment.

C: It's not about then … It's deciding to end it … now.

I am petrified. What can I do, or say? She is deadly serious and I can even understand it and there's nothing I can promise her. Then I start to think: but what is better? Is it better to continue being a living-dead thing? I realize now I need to reduce my anxiety about the potential consequences of my encouraging her to continue by reminding myself and her why we are doing this.

T: Tell me, how do you think it may become different here if you do tell me? What will it change here between us in your mind? The thing itself you already know so the fear is that *here* it will be intolerable?
C: I don't know what it is.

I'm again stunned. Is she again going to make us mad, go into the area of not knowing what is real? I find it exasperating that she wants to take us back again into that "no man's land" as though she really knew nothing. At this time I have no way to conceptualize what I think: perhaps a confusion of belief and disbelief in what she is telling me.

What suddenly arises for me is an association of scenes from spy movies I have seen where the victim is being interrogated and tortured in the hope that he will reveal his secret. I am the interrogator, and she is the captive, who has no answer.

T: Caroline – I think you are feeling anxious and again being vague ... because you're scared to reveal ... I thought it was clear that you know something and can't tell it, because to bring it from the inside to the outside and share it here with me feels too scary.
C: (emphatically) I don't know what it is.
T: You did say that it was something much worse than what we had thought until now.
C: But I don't know *what* ... I think there is something ... much worse coming ... and what if I will know about it?
T: What will happen?
C: Then I'll cross over from here to the ... *inhuman*. That's why I don't know if it isn't better to put an end to it now.
T: You are afraid if you find out and tell me, we won't be able to meet as two human beings. Here there have been precious moments, crying your pain and there we met, as two human beings. And now you are afraid that if you tell me about inhuman things – that I won't be able to bear being with you, that I won't be able to understand
C: And then I'll be left there ... on the other side ... *inhuman*.
T: I understand – it's scary. I can only say Caroline, that if you decide to tell – whatever happens, I'll do my best to try and be there for you, to try and understand how this happened. I won't abandon you.

(She starts to cry inconsolably. It is the end of the hour. I too am choking back my tears. But I feel a relief that she has human tears. It was the cold sphinx-like state of moments earlier that was most frightening. I apologize for needing to send her away in this state.)

A nameless dread and a nightmare

What is this "inhuman" happening in her life that Caroline is so afraid of uncovering? Is it real or imagined? I don't even at this time have an image or thought to express what it could be. But as I feel this sense of a "nameless dread" I recall a frightening incident that occurred between us a few weeks earlier

I had become used to Caroline stalking me. It was as though seeing her quickly hide behind some wall or shrubbery from the corner of my eye as I entered the clinic was so familiar that it had become part of the therapeutic setting. It did not occur to me to talk to her about it since I had learnt not to "touch" her with my words that related in any way to her body, posture or physical presence. So, while I was preparing myself a hot mug of coffee in the kitchen of the clinic, I was totally unprepared for what was to happen next. I approached the window and suddenly saw her face glued to the window pane, staring into my kitchen. I received such a fright that I dropped the coffee cup. She vanished with the speed of lightning.

This incident enabled me to speak to her about the stalking, explaining that it disturbed me. When asking her why she did it, her answer was: "So as to know that you are the same person on the inside as you are on the outside."

I was not sure what she meant by this and she could not say more. I requested that the stalking stop. The stalking ceased and at a later time I would understand better why she did it. But on the night after that scary incident I had a nightmare. I dreamt I was in my living room, looking out the window into the garden, when I suddenly saw that the branches of a nearby tree were slowly growing in the direction of the house. The tree had a life of its own and it did not stop at the boundary of the living room window but penetrated through the glass into my house. This was happening with the slow robotic force of something totally not within my control. I was terrorized by this invasive "alive" tree that threatened to consume me in the imagined safety of my home. My screams awoke me. I had felt the fear of being faced by something inhuman – something of nature yet unnatural, something I could not reason with, having no language for communication, yet a force much stronger than myself.

Body language

The next time Caroline comes she slowly passes her chair, picks up her cushion from it and sits on the floor, her back leaning against a wall, her body crouched over while holding onto her cushion for protection. Caroline on entry would chose a certain physical place and posture and then stay in freeze for the whole session. Only her crying created some bodily movement, "giving away" that she was alive. Over the years I had accepted that this body language was a way of expressing the extent of her anxiety, pain and other unspoken things. Whenever she made a move to sit on the floor I already knew to anticipate something particularly difficult.

Freud's "Uncanny"

Caroline opens the next session surprising me by asking if I had read Freud's paper on "The Uncanny" (Freud, 1919). I was familiar with it, so she continues as though teaching me how to use Freud's article to understand her:

C: He describes there that you know something ... through *not* seeing... only by looking sideways ... Genet couldn't know of his past... because it was behind him ... he needed someone else to know... and write about it... that's why we won't get anywhere by asking me about my past... only indirectly ... by reading the dream.

I say that the dream describes the psychiatric hospital and silence as a refuge from abuse.

C: Going mad is the safest.
T: Yes – but not really. Usually, if you are mad you can say anything and no one will believe a mad person. But here in therapy with me this is a safe haven. You know that I *do* believe what you tell me. But if you tell me, you feel you are in danger because of an inner voice forbidding you to tell. So, paradoxically. you can only feel safe if you *don't* speak. But, at the same time, if I were *not* to believe you – you wouldn't trust me, and then again it would feel unsafe here.

Moments of madness

I think to myself that there is no way that I can be for her that can feel safe for her. She then tells me that in "The Uncanny" Freud tells us that the boy in Hoffman's story saw the dreaded Sandman who came to visit his father. Then shortly afterwards his father was killed.

I wonder if Caroline is giving me a clue about some murder she knows about but can't tell me directly without endangering herself. Or is she afraid we will "murder" her companion–father who she fears giving up? I also find myself wondering if Freud was doing the same – giving the reader some hint about something uncanny of which *he* knew about but could not tell. And to think such thoughts about Freud created an uneasy feeling in me wondering if I could be sure I wasn't going mad.

***

Some further thoughts

1 While writing this book, I had another association to my "invading tree" nightmare. Perhaps this was an indirect way (as implied in "The Uncanny") of my experiencing in my sleep Caroline's terror: the growing non-human tree representing the erect penis invading my/her private, inner space with no way to stop it's overwhelming forcefulness. And all this happens at home which should represent a safe place.
2 I had promised Caroline that I would stand by her no matter what we found out. When I said it I meant it sincerely. On the other hand, I had

never been confronted with the "inhuman". It seemed that Caroline had. How was I to evaluate if Caroline was strong enough psychologically to be able to contain such a truth if it were to be known. What I relied on was her wishing to continue in her search for her lost past. In later years I came across words that described my overall inner belief in a book, written by Michael Eigen: "Work with madness and trauma requires faith. A faith allied with skill and caring. Faith in what? It's hard to say. There are many breeds of faith. Perhaps there is something we might call psychoanalytic or psychotherapeutic faith. Faith in being together, that in being together something good will happen" (Eigen, 2010).

Chapter 12

The death of Dad
Loneliness

> All the lonely people – Where do they all come from?
> All the lonely people – Where do they all belong?
> From *Eleanor Rigby*, The Beatles

Timeline: 21 years into therapy

Caroline's father dies. She decided not to go to see him before his death. She feared that if she were to ask him to admit to having abused her he would deny it, and that would leave her forever with the feeling of not knowing, thinking that she might have made it up. If he denied it, there would be the added humiliation for having asked. But she does decide to fly home to attend the funeral. She needs to know for certain, in the most concrete way, that he is dead. She has a need to see his grave. There had been no doubt about her mother's death some five years previously because she was there; she was present when she died. We discuss Caroline's need for concrete

C: What does it mean about me that I need to see it concretely otherwise I don't know? That I'm mad?

I say that when she feels uncertain she feels mad and having a sense of certainty helps her feel more in contact with reality. This seems to calm her somewhat before her trip. She misses two sessions because of the funeral.

On her return, I am shocked to see Caroline's eyes are *wide open*. This never happens. She always enters with her eyes closed. I say something about this.

Then, with her eyes wide open she asks if I have changed anything in the room. I have not. She then realizes that for the first time *she can see the door*! In what seems like genuine amazement she says: "When he was here I couldn't see a way out. Now I see the door!" Then she adds, "Maybe now there is a possibility of a way out."

Caroline describes a sense of relief, and says that this is different from what she felt when her mother died. That death was experienced as an end of the fear associated with her mother.

***

There is so much more than what "meets the eye". Years had passed since she had asked to leave the door to my room ajar so as to be able to feel safe with me at moments when she could not separate me from her dad. Now she tells me: "You can't be him. You're here and he's gone."

At the next meeting Caroline brings me a text she has written about the impact of her father's death on her. In her text she interprets her dramatic reaction to now seeing the open door:

> ~... until then although I knew that the door was open because we had agreed that it would be left ajar ... this time I could see, I could really see, that in fact it was ajar ... I said that it was as though finally there was a way out. With him no longer alive, I could know that Tova wasn't him – and hope that maybe I wasn't trapped or caught in the cage forever. ... I raised the possibility that the "way out" might be out of the not-knowing: of actually being able to "see" things and thus "know" what had happened ...~

Her father's death has a dramatic effect on Caroline. To my surprise, she writes of a *fear of loneliness* now that her father is dead. Her association is a fear of being left totally abandoned on the inside because of the father's death in outside reality. It's as though, in spite of everything, she had nurtured a hope that one day they would be reunited. She writes:

> ~... if I was actually to recognize the possibility of finding my own voice, it could only be at the expense of giving up listening to his. All this time I've had him there. Now, if I say I'm going to have my own memories, find my own version of the truth/ past, find my own voice/ self, I'll have to give him up to do so. That's a very scary thought.~

When I think of the reason for my surprise, I understand that it is still difficult for me to let go of the concept that incest must be only abusive. To think of it as something comforting for the lonely child is hard to fathom perhaps because of my own upbringing where the incest taboo is such a strong moral command not to be trespassed. There was another important change after her father's death: Caroline asked to add another session a week. We were meeting three times a week and she now wanted to come four times. She now had the economic means, having been left an inheritance. Her wish for another session was so as to feel less lonely and to have a place where she would not be alone with her potential memories. She told me that she was afraid she would go mad if she was alone with them.

I found myself hesitating before agreeing. The reasons I gave myself were mainly practical: it would be too complicated to change my schedule and would inconvenience me considerably. I was less conscious of the deep underlying *anxiety* that the practical issues represented. I was at the time seeing her in my town clinic where I worked three times a week and where I worked with colleagues in adjoining rooms. On the other days of the week I saw patients at my home clinic. I knew I would not come a fourth time to town and to suggest that she come to my home clinic filled me with the fear that she might stalk me there, invade my privacy. Even though the stalking in my downtown clinic had stopped since we had talked about it, the aftermath of the scare I had received when I saw her face in the window as I was making a cup of coffee in the kitchenette was still fresh for me. So my first response was to come up with a most unconvincing reason for my hesitation, saying something to the effect that it might not be for her good to come more often to therapy because it might make her more dependent. She became enraged. How dare I reject and humiliate her to this extent after having led her to feel that I had made a place for her! Her rage was expressed mainly in an accusatory and hateful silence.

It took a few sessions before I became more conscious of my mixed motivations and realized how much rejection she must be experiencing from my response to her request. I felt I had touched on deep, very primal knowledge she had that from her very conception she was unwanted by her mother. Once I saw my part in her pain I was able to apologize and tell her some of the truth for my hesitation in agreeing to add an hour. I told her about my being concerned with the inconvenience of coming to the clinic a fourth time since I only worked three days a week there.

The enactment of rejection in the transference

My reluctance to see her more often opened a path to emotional memories of humiliation from Caroline's past. The following is a vignette of this event, which was to become one of the turning points at this time. I wish to present it from the perspective of two voices: first mine and then hers as described in writing:

Therapist's description

I am confronted by an enraged Caroline. My hesitation at her request arouses in her a sadistic attack of silence and ruthless staring at me, the like of which I had not experienced so far. She then tells me I have humiliated her. I feel her enormous rage and contempt of me She becomes an angry, cruel, unforgiving abuser. The extent of her fury is total and I am not sure I will not be completely "burnt" for her as someone who can help her. I am accused of being an idiot who is despised for making mistakes; how is it that I do not recall every word I had said in the previous session! She says that either I am a liar or an imbecile or just evil. I experience how murderous her rage can be. I am not sure we will be able to survive this and express concern about her being able to use my help anymore, fearing that the 20 years of slowly and painstakingly building up trust will be ruined in a day.

"You can't help me if I'm angry at you" she dares to tell me. The next session she throws at me: "It's like being aborted!"

I tell her that if she chooses silence when she is angry this may happen again since I cannot read her mind and there are bound to be more misunderstandings between us.

C: It's not always like that. But this time because it was to do with *wanting to live*.
T: (now understanding something) In your mind you held the link. You knew why four times was important. Your father died, you now saw the door. It was a way out. You could think: "I want to live", and now you had the financial means to add a session. So to ask to add a session was a way of saying: "Now he is dead I am free to choose life!" and I did not understand that. But in my separate mind I was preoccupied with thinking how to technically make room for another session. So our minds, being separate, were thinking differently at this time. And this caused you great pain.

Caroline's description

~I was on the point of despairing when suddenly – overnight between Wednesday and Thursday – Tova told me that she'd realized that she'd not been understanding me …

Her apology meant a great deal. It meant, first of all, that I wasn't the person who'd made the mistake. It meant that I wasn't wrong in thinking that perhaps there might be a way out, that there might be a way to see/know, and that there might be a way to live. It also meant that she wasn't still Dad, something had happened to her – and to the therapy – with his death … It meant that she didn't actually not want me to live – that I hadn't been mistaken all along thinking that that's what she wanted when in fact it wasn't.

The whole process got so bad that in the end I'd stopped being honest with her, because she wasn't understanding and I didn't want to be misunderstood. I wasn't about to tell her the truth if I couldn't trust her not to misinterpret what I meant. Not having anywhere where I could be honest, and being dishonest with her, was an extremely painful place to be. It meant that there was nowhere for me to be truthful, to find out where the truth lies, what the truth is, who I am.~

So here was Caroline's explanation for the long abusive silence that I experienced in the session with her. But when explanation is split off from the session, transmitted in a different media of communication, it makes it so hard to hold onto all the pieces together and feel the whole person.

What struck me was that Caroline stresses how essential it is for her to be honest with me. This is something I always felt when with her. That is why I was thrown into confusion when she often denied so much I was sure she was sure of and could remember. It was incompatible in my mind that she was both honest and dishonest at the same time! I did not know then that I lacked the missing bit in the puzzle – the bit that would have given sense: the belief in the existence of DID as a real phenomenon. This confronts me with the limitations of one's own mind. I now understood that by my *not even knowing I lacked this knowledge* all I could experience was confusion.

Caroline continues in her writing to describe the humiliation she felt by actually needing to tell me how painful it was for her to feel what she did about my response. It revealed her neediness of me. She then has a vivid emotional memory of this feeling of humiliation in relation to her mom's having "made fun" of her by refusing to relate to her seriously when she asked for help. She now *knew experientially*, for the first time through the here-and-now repetition in the present that the humiliation was a *real memory from her past* anchored in a specific memory involving her mother. Caroline's rage at me for having not taken her request for help (an extra session) seriously had its origin in her neediness of her mother's help, followed by rejection and deep humiliation.

To feel anger is to know I'm real

Reflecting on this, I think that the ability to express this anger at me in the transference and it being legitimate to do so, together with the sense of trust already established between us over such a long period of time, enabled Caroline to *feel real*. To feel itself had a liberating effect. To feel anger, specifically, is to feel something strongly and this contributes to feeling real.

Being in touch with her angry feelings aroused a real experiential memory of the past humiliation to submerge from the deep. The memory from the past made separating past from present possible. Truly a significant achievement of ego strength.

My having acted as a *real person* – initially rejecting her request because of my own inconvenience, allowing myself to recognize my empathic failure at understanding her asking for an extra session, being able to apologize for my blunder, all this triggered the process that led to this development of a sense of Caroline's own realness.

Her father's death allowed her to make room for a new kind of relationship with me, her therapist. Her requesting to have an additional weekly session was her way of making more space in time in the holding environment she sensed she would need for what was to come. I am impressed by her deep knowledge of how therapy is to be used for her growth.

The splitting of the father: an external abuser and an internal lover

One of the dilemmas I found myself confronting was the seeming split in Caroline's view of her father. I tend to think the split was concretized in Caroline's way of communication with me. In the live interaction, she lets me know, and this will happen more and more from now on, how abusive and frightening her father was. It cannot be talked about but only enacted. Soon horrific scenes from her past will be acted out in front of my eyes.

On the other hand, in her written texts, "the writing Caroline" describes a fathomless loneliness following her father's death. In reality, I know she has avoided her father for years. When she had visited her home town to be with her siblings when I was away, she had made this conditional on *not seeing him* or being in his vicinity. As was mentioned previously, she had decided not to go to see him before his death but only to his funeral. Yet, the writing Caroline admits holding onto her father on the inside all this time. His voice controlled her. Furthermore, it seems to have been out of choice. Her silences with me were an expression of "obeying" his inner voice to remain faithful to him and not tell. She writes how her having *"no knowledge"* of her past was her extreme way of remaining "faithful", so as not to betray him or lose him by revealing the truth.

In this excerpt from one of her texts written shortly after his death she writes:

> ~... without his voice, and still without having found mine, I'm cast into the yawning gulf of loneliness.~

The loneliness of the orphan – widow

Caroline then describes in her writing how the therapeutic setting has contributed to her feelings of unbearable loneliness. Another paradox for me to contend with.

For many years the days on which we met were Sundays, Wednesdays and Thursdays. She had once asked if I could change Wednesdays to a Tuesdays but I was not able to. She had never mentioned it again – since for her to ask for anything was associated with desire. To be denied a request had always been experienced as unbearable humiliation as well as the sexual innuendos implied of wanting anything in the first place. Now – in her asking for the fourth session she is able to share with me how she needs me. She does this in the following way:

In the session, she asks me if I know what the computer "Word" programme designed to keep the flow of a text together and to prevent a single line of a paragraph being isolated on the top of the next page is called. I have no idea, of course. She is an expert at computers.

"It's *An Orphan and a Widow*" she tells me. "That's what Sunday feels like. It's been orphaned from Wednesday–Thursday and they are widowed from the Sunday."

She now dares ask that we set up the four days into pairs: two days in town and two in my home clinic, so that she might feel less lonely. I am very moved. I think how lonely she must feel that any "thing" that is alone – a Sunday, seems to touch off her "yawning gulf" of inner aloneness; that she needs to merge with another so as not to fall into the empty abyss. I recall her fear of contamination – and see it in a different light. Now I see how much energy she needs to defend against her desire for merger. I understand how powerful the force of the seductive father who invited her to merge with him must have been. Furthermore, I realize how much guilt she carries for this fulfilled desire. The extent of the guilt I always felt when leaving her now became more understandable in light of her overwhelming loneliness. Yet merger, any merger even of empathy, evoked for Caroline the merger of incest, and therefore also aroused guilt. So guilt predominated as an existential accompaniment to being.

***

I recall how some years earlier the word "loneliness" had first entered therapy. It was during year 14 of our work together. It was after I had been on a week's vacation and she had again fallen into deadening silence, which felt agonizing for both of us. I had wondered aloud if perhaps she might not be better off without me, the separations being so painful. Her response touched me. "Do you know how lonely that would be?" she had whispered.

***

A vignette

I have read aloud a text she brought describing the fear of letting go of her father's voice, before she has found her own voice. I am moved and say, "To give up his voice is to be the lonely line on the empty page". She cries and cries.

T: To hold onto "no – memories" (his internalized "command") – was to be the faithful wife, and in your mind you maintained the hope he'll come to you, be yours, because he was also the only source of affection. And you now fear that to give up his voice is to lose all of that.

Caroline nods in agreement and cries relentlessly until the end of the hour. And just before it's time to end I say softly, "Caroline, I've stayed with you all these years to help you gain your sanity – not go with the madness. Now that he's gone, I know you fear the loneliness. I won't leave you and we'll find a way for the fourth session."

It was then I decided I *must* reschedule to make the fourth session available for her – and in two sets of pairs if possible.

At the next session she opens with, "If he is dead I don't have to be faithful to *not knowing* anymore?"

But by the end of the session some deep need or habit to remain faithful to the internal Dad takes over and Caroline expresses her feeling that she is a coward in remembering this now, when her father is dead and cannot defend himself. She said that maybe she is therefore making things up now that he can't deny anything. I find myself thinking that perhaps it is *because* he is dead that memories are awakening in her.

***

A piercing insight from the writing Caroline

~...Tova said that it was the first time that I'd been able to distinguish between the past and the present in therapy: having the actual memory of something as it had happened in the past meant that there was a past to compare with the present. This allowed me to differentiate the present from the past. Without memories like that, without the feeling of being in the past, all the "memories" I have actually feel as though they are in the present. They aren't in the past at all because they never occurred there experientially. Without the connection to the past, without having a past event to which they were anchored, there was no space for them except in the present. They could only have an existence in the present because in my experience they had never actually happened in the past.~

Chapter 13

On pimps and prostitution

Timeline: 21–22 years into therapy – the year before Little Girl Caroline will first appear as a persona

With her father's death it seems that Caroline is well aware that a new phase in therapy is now possible. It seems she feels compelled to launch this new phase as quickly as possible. She adjusts the setting. Time and space are expanded. We now begin meeting four times a week and "closer to home" (twice a week in my home clinic). Along with this change, violence slinks into the analysis. Not all at once with some momentous occurrence, but rather subtly and incrementally until soon it will become outright violence. It seems her father first had to die, actually die in the most concrete way before Caroline could dare bring the violence connected with him into our sessions – therefore making room, literally, for her past memories. One may ask – why does Caroline need to know he is dead and buried to allow the memories in. Why could they not have been given admission earlier? We have now been working together for almost 22 years.

Some of the answers to this came from Caroline's writings. As long as her father was alive it seems she continued to nurture the hope and wish for a reunion with him. She was afraid that to reveal his violent side would jeopardize that. And now that he was dead, she no longer had anything to lose. I will now describe how she went about "preparing" the new place so that there would be a concrete space to contain what needed to be brought to it.

In the preparation for the move to the "new territory", to the clinic at my house, Caroline appears both agitated and excited, expecting something different now to happen. She asks endless questions about what the new setting will be like. There is a particular concern about how will I know who I am if I am also in my own home. Will I not get confused about my own identity? Although I try to reassure her, describing the setting – how there are clear boundaries between my work space and my private home space, she is still anxious. Everything is susceptible to the possibility of being eroticized. For example, the inconvenience that she will need to wait for a bus rather than ride her bike means she does "want" to come; waiting implies wanting and wanting means she has desire and having desire makes her guilty because it means she is responsible.

Caroline keeps asking, "But how do you know that you will be *you* if it is also your home?"

I find myself needing to give answers to questions I had never before been asked. How *do* I know? And more difficult still – how can I describe to her what I "know" by intuition? I feel that she is trying to know something from *my* inner experience – as though, there is something she doesn't get: how one knows who one is, and is trying to learn it from me! I find myself feeling sorry and limited that I don't really know how to "give" her that wisdom which to me, to most of us I believe, comes naturally without even noticing it. It's as though not having an inner sense of a self, a person can change because of a change in location. I recall her answer of a few months earlier when I had asked her why she stalked me and she had said that she did so because she needed to know if I was the same person on the inside (the clinic) as the outside. At this time I still had no thought of her as being with DID which retrospectively explains the reason for these questions. If she is more than one person, from her point of view, perhaps I, too, suffer constant change and lose my identity.

With all the apprehension that Caroline harbours, she also hopes that because of this move to my home clinic – we will find her memories. At the first session in my home clinic, after having stood outside the front door motionless for all of 40 minutes of the 50-minute session, on entering she finally says: "Coming here feels too close to home – but it makes feelings and memories more accessible."

With the preparation for the move she has brought me a book containing violent descriptions about slaughters in World War I. The author is Sebastian Barry (see Chapter 4). She comments that he uses animals to make it possible to describe something indescribable. After being reminded of his sordid descriptions of animal slaughters I accidently spill the coffee from the cup on my table and spontaneously comment, "It must have upset me more than I realized."

Caroline responds sharply. "How will you be able to help if just reading about it upsets you?"

Caroline obviously knows that violence is about to enter the therapy and she doubts my ability to be able to contain it. I suspect that she might be right. If to just read about the violence makes me spill my coffee will I be able to handle more? When I try to cover up my clumsiness by saying: "We need to understand how the scenes in this book are related to things you experienced in the past." Caroline responds, "It's not a matter of understanding. It's a matter of finding *where* it is!"

It seems the experience feels literally one of finding, within some inner "space", something that has been long lost. And I find myself feeling hopeful. After all, she now uses the word "finding" where in the past she spoke of "hiding". This expansion of inner space will allow for the mentalization of what will be found. The father's death will not leave an empty vacuum; the newly freed up space will become a spaciousness that will allow for memories. But what kind of violence will we "find"? What will we encounter, and how exactly is this to occur? I am feeling quite apprehensive and realize that Caroline's interpretation of my spilling the coffee as a sign of fear was quite accurate. Her extreme sensitivity and attunement to my unconscious has picked up my fear before my awareness of it.

A dream of pimps and prostitution

The violence comes. It does not even wait for the move to an additional day in my home clinic. It announces itself in a dream she has with the entry to this new "home" territory. This is what Caroline dreams just before the move:

> There were two brothers. The older one was a pimp for the younger one. He asked me and I agreed. But I didn't feel anything. As though nothing had happened. Then he asked me if I wanted to go to him again and then I realized, or knew, that I didn't want to. Then I was in the car with Dad. I wanted to go back to the house, downstairs because the lights were on and I wanted to turn them off. He didn't let me. He insisted driving around the whole way to the front entrance. It wasn't a nice dream.

Caroline's association to this dream was that she was a prostitute. I recall being quite shocked that she should use this description about herself. This was a new word in the therapy, as was the word "pimp".[1] What was marked now was the new expansion of Caroline's use of vocabulary in my presence. I notice that she in contrast to myself, seems to be unaffected by the word, as if something has inured or habituated her to it. Until now she has been so constricted in her use of language with me. What surprised *her* in the dream was that she was able to *know* that she did not want to do this. This felt new to her because up to very recently, she had had *no* feelings. I wonder if she is worried that coming to my home clinic, which does actually involve going down the stairs, would get confused in her mind with her home environment. From her dream it seems, at the manifest level of meaning , that the downstairs of her childhood home was where bad things happened. Would coming to therapy become equivalent to prostituting herself, and I would be experienced as the pimp–father. She is so frightened of coming to my home, terrified that she may not be able to separate me and my place from her father and the home that she grew up in. The fact that she gets so easily over-stimulated both sexually and by anxiety leaves her vulnerable to experience the chaos that was mentioned in Chapter7, the *tohu vevohu* of primeval experience.

I am concerned that perhaps this need to know more by "bringing things closer to home" also carries the risk of her becoming psychotic. I tell her that the stairs going down to my clinic are at the front entrance of my house, and they are not at some hidden back entrance as in her dream. She is suspicious but there seems to be no going back now. One thing she seems pretty sure of – that she wants us to continue the search and that, in spite of the accompanying fears, she really wants it to be in the vicinity of "home".

As has been mentioned, her dream about the prostitute and the pimp is dreamt the day before the move to the home clinic. The incident that follows will exemplify the intensity of *my* emotional state with the change of the setting to include two sessions a week in my home territory.

Prelude to violence: the cat's poo

It is two weeks after the move. Caroline is late. This *never* happens. I open the door to see if she is not hiding outside, as can happen. I am surprised to find that the pot plant I have at the entrance to my clinic has been knocked over and some of the earth is spilling out and the plant is slightly damaged. Instantly, I suspect Caroline, thinking that she must have come early, did this and is now hiding. After all, she had been "complaining" that she could not find the violence here in spite of the move. So I surmise that it is now being enacted, and directed at me. These are my spontaneous thoughts.

Caroline arrives ten minutes late. She says nothing. I ask her about the pot plant. Her response: "I don't think I did it. Were you hurt? Did you hear anything?" Most of the session is about her not knowing if she might have done this or not. There is a lot of speculation based on my assumption that she had done this to communicate some message about herself to me. What is very clear is there is no feeling of her sense of being unjustly accused. It's as though if I suspect her of having done it, then it means she must be guilty even though she has no recollection of having committed the crime. Her instant subjugation is obvious and painful to see.

After Caroline leaves I examine the area again and find some *cat's excrement*! I realize that our cat must have wrecked this havoc, and am shocked at realizing how easily I jumped to the conclusion that Caroline was at fault. Not only that, but I am also shaken by how easily she was able to "own" guilt over something she did *not* do and that for her *not to know* if she did something or not seems to be a normal state of mind, which she takes in her stride. It is, however, a state of mind that leaves Caroline open to accepting guilt irrespective of what she has done. I recall the book *The Case of Thomas N.*, which she gave me years ago and think how much like Thomas she feels. He, after all, even accepted that it could be that he was guilty of murdering a young girl of whom he had absolutely no memory. The "circumstantial evidence" was all that there was to convince him of his own guilt. I also realize that I have been influenced by Caroline's expectation and her own preparation for the onset of violence. I, too, am expecting something to happen here. So, when a pot is overturned and broken and when this coincides when Caroline happens to come late – this coincidence is interpreted as Caroline's culpability.

I feel shaken when I think how easily I suspected Caroline of being violent. In the not too distant future, when a forest fire breaks out near my house – she will do the same – suspect herself to be the arsonist to have possibly caused it. I wonder how malignant and contagious this paranoid tendency could become. I am not often in the habit of suspecting my patients but in this case I must have been unconsciously affected by the anticipation of violence she had warned me about.

Here is another example of incipient violence from this period: it is at this time that Caroline had her first clear blackout (as described in Chapter 4) for about 30 minutes in my presence as a response to the noise made by a neighbour. It took place in my downtown clinic. Caroline had associated the neighbour's shouts with her mother and this was the cause of her "blackout". But in contrast to the past, she is now aware of her own disappearance–blackout. She realizes she has lost track of time since the session ended without experiencing her own presence. We began to use the word "dissociation" to describe those moments when she "disappears".

Shortly after this incident another event of noise in outer reality provides an opportunity that Caroline has been furtively "waiting for" – a way to experience her terror in my presence. It so happened that I had ordered some furniture to be delivered to my house, although I had specified the hours when this should be so that the delivery would not coincide with Caroline's session. Of course, Murphy's law came into play here ... Just when we were in the middle of her session, the men arrived and made a considerable noise outside. Before my eyes I witnessed how the noise of the men outside paralyzed her. She cringed into a constricted ball as though hoping in this way to totally disappear. My attempt to reassure her by spelling out the reality – that they were simply delivering some furniture – in no way diminished her anxiety. So I decided, (with her consent) to go out and tell the men not to approach the clinic door. This has no effect on her. I urge her to say what she feared might happen to her, even though I was protecting her. Her surprising response was: "I never knew what Mom knew – if she knew or was part of it."

T: So I am Mom, and you don't know if you can believe what I say. You don't know if I haven't arranged something with these men, as in the prostitute dream.
C: Yes.

It was near the end of the session and we could hear my dog scratching at the clinic door, asking to be let in. I realize that the delivery men must have left the garden gate open and the dog must have got out and come to my door, seeking refuge. He was also frightened by the delivery men. With her permission I let my dog into the clinic, quietly soothing him.

It is very soon after this incident that Caroline brings me the book *Me & Emma* (see Chapter 4), which establishes dissociation as an existing fact. Caroline tells me she now believes she uses it as a defence. It can be named at last. At this time she asks me to prepare a place for her to sit on the floor in both clinics. She explains, "It's so I won't fall off," she says. She is very apprehensive because she is convinced that she will soon experience intense regression, and is trying to ready herself for it. The last time she sat on the floor was when she was under the table in a foetal position 12 years earlier. Then she came "out" to hang the doll and stayed out until this time.

***

In the next session Caroline probes the extent to which I was in control of my surroundings. Was I really going to prevent the workers from interacting with her?

T: You aren't sure if maybe I'm involved too – just as you said about Mom: you never knew what she knew.
C: I need a safe place for the madness.

It took another four sessions to work through what to Caroline was the "terrifying" incident of the delivery men coming to deliver furniture to my house. Caroline insists on knowing every detail, especially my thoughts, in order to be able to make sense of it in her mind and thus try and re-establish some sense of safety. It is a painstaking dealing with details. I answer all her questions, hoping this will help her know I'm on her side. The feeling is that she needs to have total control over every tiny change in the environment or of me. For her, having control means having a logical explanation for everything. Also, logical means understanding the connection between cause and effect. There is no room for chance or accidents or the unforeseen. When something does "happen", then someone must be to blame for it. Someone must be guilty. Caroline tries to discover if I am responsible for the men coming or if I could have prevented it. She seems to be looking for a way to *know* if I can be trusted.

When we are discussing the incident I remind her about my dog, how he came to me for comfort, for he too had been frightened. I hope this will help her restore her trust in me. She seems very moved by the dog:

C: The dog was frightened too? Were you frightened too?

It seems that I and what is mine have become one. I tell her that I was not afraid because I knew who the men were, and why they had come. But I say that I was annoyed at them for coming at the wrong time and disturbing us although I had specifically requested they come at a different time.

C: But how can it be safe here if you are angry?

The issue of the fear of my being angry has come up before and here I ask her if *she* has ever expressed anger. She tells me of the one incident in her whole life that she can remember. It had occurred a few years back, at a time when the danger of terrorist attacks on civilians in Israel was particularly acute.

There was an atmosphere of terror and danger because suicide bombers had killed civilians in public places such as buses and malls. Certain safety regulations were imposed, such as keeping gates and doors in public places closed so intruders could not enter unchecked.

Caroline had entered her work place and had left the door open. The cleaning lady, concerned for her safety and the safety of all, reminded her of the regulation. Caroline described how she was so angry that she banged her fist down on the table. "No one is allowed to do that! Worry about me, want to protect me."

At first, I do not understand. It was the cleaner's act of concern that had aroused Caroline's fury. What sense is to be made of that? It seemed completely unreasonable. And then I thought: Could this be the obverse of everything she herself had experienced, knowing no protection from danger for her well being? And perhaps there were more reasons I did not yet know about to explain her one incident of outward expression of rage.

An unnoticed visit by The Little Girl Caroline

Another meaningful incident from this period: She had knocked on my door too faintly and I suggested she pull the bell next time so that I could hear her. It was a little goat's bell at my front door. Surprisingly, she said that she cannot do that because *the bell was just like the penis that was stuck into her*. I was absolutely taken aback. She *spoke* these words to me. This time it was actual words, in real time and not written words written when alone. She had just told me in the clinic, face to face, that a penis had been stuck into her!

However, Caroline has left so I cannot ask her more. The next day I mention this incident and she has *no recall* of it. But I insist, saying,

> It's as if another Caroline is here now, and this Caroline knows nothing of what the little girl Caroline told me yesterday. The little girl got frightened and hasn't appeared today. Instead, she sent *you* – the One who Knows Nothing.

Caroline agrees with me. Then I realize there must be some awareness within her of the existence of herself in an altered state. Caroline says to me then: "How can you know which one you are speaking to?"

Her question bewilders me; it is so unexpected. So strange because it never occurs to me to question who I'm speaking to. After some thinking I respond:

T: I think I know that when things are said that have nothing to do with the present reality, then the little girl from the past is here. And yes, it's frightening, because maybe the adults told you: "Don't tell anyone anything." Maybe she is afraid of me because I'm an adult too, and I could become like them – I could be bad.
C: (agreeing) How can she know it's safe? She didn't feel safe yesterday.
T: Why?
C: Maybe because you saw her.
T: Yes I did – and that frightened her. I hope if she comes here more often, and can experience that nothing bad happens to her, she'll learn to feel safe.

Caroline nods in agreement. That evening I received an email from her. *"She says thank you for acknowledging her existence – even if she's too afraid to come back right now."* And I answered her.

Soon, she brings me a typed text that summarizes the momentous events unfolding before our eyes:

> ~On the Thursday, we somehow understood that the day before I hadn't been the person talking to Tova about the prostitution. I hadn't been there at that point – it had been someone else. Tova finally started to realize that there's another real person involved: the "little girl Caroline" who knows about the abuse. I can't tell her anything about it because I wasn't there – it wasn't me. When I asked her how she knows who she's talking to – which one of us –she said that when "I" start talking about things which don't match reality (my reaction to the neighbour's argument, for example), she knows that she's not talking to me but to her. Tova wanted her to know that it was safe in the therapy – she was the only adult there and she wasn't going to do anything to her. She was safe with Tova.
>
> **Having the little girl's existence acknowledged and accepted as real was the most significant event which has occurred in therapy.** It means that Tova knows that she exists – that she knows she's a real person; that she's the one who knows. Tova can't talk to me about the abuse because it happened to her not to me. I can't tell her anything about it – they're not my memories. When I got back I sent Tova an email saying that she thanked her for acknowledging her existence – even if she is too frightened to go back right now. Tova wrote back saying, "Please tell her that I was glad to finally meet her. I do hope she will come more often and experience that she is safe with me. Hopefully with time she will be less afraid." I'd half expected simply that she would write back (if she did at

all) saying "You're welcome". To get such a response – to have her taken so seriously – was huge.~

I am most moved by this email. Caroline's appreciation and gratitude is not only for this small act of writing. I feel here she is letting me know that the agony of our "sterile" interaction over years of barren silence has been transformed into fertile soil from which new life is growing. I experience her words as a gift, like a rare gem.

In the next session Caroline asks me why it has taken so long to recognize and find the little girl Caroline. It soon became clear that until both parents were dead and buried there was no way, she could come out of hiding – no way she would have dared to reveal the violent secrets of her past. Caroline's fear of her parents amounted to sheer terror.

"They were much stronger than you" she tells me. It seems she feared for my safety as well. Perhaps they would harm me if I were to know her past. I could only conjecture what kind of experiences she must have had that only with the father's death could she feel it safe enough to start telling me of prostitutes and pimps!

T: Even though you spent years making sure this was a safe place you could not feel safe until now. We were so careful – not to make things up, not to jump to any conclusions, to differentiate the real from the imagined, yet she, little girl Caroline didn't feel safe enough to come forward until now.

***

In the next session Caroline surprises me by *coughing!* This is so striking that I am rendered speechless. It's like a burst of thunder in the midst of a cloudless day. I have become so accustomed to the tense silence that it takes me a moment to realize that it's "only" a cough. I mention my surprise. She tells me that prostitutes never cough nor vomit. If they gag, they learn to suppress their responses. I am even more shocked. So the prostitute dream was not just a dream! She is telling me she is an expert on prostitution!

As though reading my mind she says: "I don't think you know what you are getting into."

There is silence in the room. Then she adds, "Everything will come out of nowhere."

I remember how I had spilled my coffee in fright. I become anxious that I won't be able to deal with her if she "makes a mess" by spilling out her guts "over me" recalling the time she brought a bag containing real faeces together with the doll that was hanged. With a sinking heart, I visualize her defecating in my room and wonder how I would cope with that.

Then Caroline speaks, as if honing in on my visceral fears, "In the dream I was in a hospital."

"Yes," I reply:

> Maybe that's what we need to think of. I find it hard to deal with such things without becoming nauseated, like when you cry and let your nose run and you don't wipe it. You remember how when you refuse to use a tissue, I need to turn around for fear of vomiting.

At this point Caroline started to cry disconsolately and asked if hospitalization would be instead of therapy. I could not answer. I could not think. I needed time and space for myself. And when I have it a new clarity comes to me. *This is what I have to go through: it's either me or her.*

Now I was facing a most difficult professional dilemma: if I didn't allow her to regress fully, then I would be betraying her, leaving her stuck in limbo; she would be both unable to "know" the trauma, and unable to become fully alive. Yet, if I allowed her to regress the way she wanted to or needed to, not limiting her in any way, I wouldn't be able to function, I would lose my sense of control, my professional identity. And I'd also feel that I was made to give in – against my better judgment – if such a thing exists.

Guilt paralyses me but then I recover somewhat by reminding myself that the reason I didn't become a nurse or doctor was precisely this. I was not suited for that kind of work. After all, I had chosen *psycho*therapy and not a physical therapy. I tell her that my limitations mean that I cannot cope with her bodily fluids and if she really *does need* to spill it out in order to heal, then we have no choice but hospitalization for her. This kind of confrontation with my own limits, and needing and being able to talk to her about it openly and honestly – was turning into a characteristic feature of my work with her. She had confronted me with many challenges but I knew that this challenge: dealing with her concrete physical secretions was an extension of myself I was incapable of.

After she realized that I was serious about the option of hospitalization, she cried again and she said:

C: I wouldn't want to put you through this but I'm not sure I'll be able to control myself (my body).
T: I know that.

Then I add that I thought: that she was also nervous about what might come out from her. Inside her is the actual knowledge that will be transformed into words, and perhaps she even "prefers" that physical shit will come out. I said that we did not "really" know what happened in her past. The one thing that we knew was that whatever it was, it was so awful that it made her panic and lose control of all her bodily orifices. And now with me, rather than "spill the beans" as it were, she would spill out her guts and the liquids inside her.

We have reached the end of the session. Caroline stares at me very quietly. She is very serious and then reminds me that we had talked about arranging a meeting with the psychiatrist, something we had discussed as a contingency measure if things got worse with the addition of sessions and coming "closer to home". Hopefully, that meeting would put measure in place that would act as a safety net for whatever would emerge from her.

***

In the next session Caroline asks me why it has taken so long to recognize and find the Little Girl Caroline. It soon became clear that until both parents were dead and buried there was no way, she could come out of hiding – no way she would have dared to reveal the violent secrets of her past., as expressed in her statement comparing me to her terrifying, absent, but dead parents, "They were stronger than you". Caroline's fear of her parents amounted to sheer terror.

Note

1 However, these words had appeared in her pornographic poems.

Chapter 14

When trauma has no witness

What's past lies still ahead and the future is finished.
Rainer Marie Rilke, *The Book of Hours* II, 3 (1905)

Timeline: a few months before Little Girl Caroline appears – 22 years into therapy

The previous chapter covered the period between Caroline's father's death and how this enabled her to "prepare" the therapeutic space for the return of memories. But Caroline must have known that she also needed to prepare *me for* the persona who was soon to make an appearance. She did this ingeniously by her written texts.

While nothing changed outwardly in the autistic way Caroline was with me in the clinic, behind the scenes she continued to provide exceptionally fluent texts, which I read aloud to us. The texts presented in the two months preceding the entry of Little Girl Caroline seem to have been written precisely in order to help me understand this strange phenomenon of DID: these texts are an invaluable description, coming from her inner experience of a dissociated person describing how it was for her. I think Caroline's writings are worthy of being text book material for understanding the phenomenology of DID.

I will therefore now present quite a detailed account of her texts.

Where there is no one to witness

The text below was written at the time when Caroline was bringing to me chapters from a recently published book in Hebrew (Seligman and Solomon, 2004) describing the treatment of patients who had been sexually abused. These sessions were conducted in the following way: I would read aloud the text she had marked in the book while she would listen attentively and on occasion would motion for me to stop so that she could ask me questions and hear my answers. It is as though we are studying a text together to help her create a narrative of her life. This interaction was a far cry from her catatonic mode – from the way we had "read" the books she brought years earlier. Then it was only me reading aloud, with Caroline listening but neither reacting nor commenting. Now we were like a couple of researchers at work on a common project: searching for the buried memories of her childhood. We had just read together the chapter describing the need for the therapist to be a witness to the patient who had no inner witness to her experiences (pp. 240–254).There had also been a description of DID diagnosis and Caroline had asked me if I thought this applied to her. I affirmed that I thought this might be the case.

As I read what I have just written I notice something I never noticed in real time. It's true there is a feeling of "we" – being a team working together to unravel a complex issue; however behaviourally, *only I speak*. Caroline is very much part of what we are doing but in fact the only words she uttered were those when she asked me if I thought she had DID. This absence of her verbal participation was done so subtly that only as I write this book do I notice this.

The next day she came in with the following text:

~Tova understood the idea of not being able to be a witness to my own experience — and my own self: If there wasn't an "I" there to experience it, there wasn't anyone to be there and therefore to be a witness. The event may have occurred, but I wasn't there when it did. It's like putting your whole existence in doubt, because it's saying that you weren't there when something happened in reality. It's not just that outside reality itself is destabilizing but that my reality – my existence as a person – is called into question. How can something have happened – "objectively", in reality – when I was assumed to have been there, but I don't know anything about it? Perhaps I made myself up.

When we got to the part about the "two histories" [Seligman and Solomon, 2004] Tova said that most of the time during the therapy she'd been treating the "Caroline without a history". That was the "person" who was present most of the time – someone defined by not having a past, by not knowing, by "omission". Sometimes – although we'd not known it at the time –the little girl Caroline had come, but I hadn't known who she was, or even that she existed. When Tova related to the things she'd said – or her responses to what LGC had told her, I'd thought she was crazy. She was referring to things as though I'd said them – and I had no idea what she was talking about. There was no communication or contact between the two parts and Tova's relating to her frequently made the therapy very difficult, because either I had to be mad or Tova was.

At that point, Tova added that it was more complicated even than that, because there was also another "Caroline" – the one who wrote down what Little Girl Caroline had said in the session and was able to remember and relate to it. In other words, there's another "Caroline" who is somehow in connection with the other two (or just LGC?) – at least outside the therapy room. In writing, that Caroline can "move" and communicate freely – something which I can't do in Tova's presence.

This confused me, because I was just getting used to the idea of their being two – let alone three parts. I needed to be able to assimilate the first aspect without having to contend with another part. Tova understood and said that we could leave trying to understand that part until another time.

I told Tova in relation to the latter part of the passage that it's like the event can't be known in any way whatsoever, there are simply no conditions that let it "be" – "be real" – because I wasn't there to witness it. I don't have any memories. I don't know if I dreamt it, because I don't know if I was awake or dreaming. No one else is going to admit it – it's like someone says in another chapter – it's the perfect crime because no one wants to acknowledge that it ever happened. No one wants to be a witness and the conditions make it completely unknowable /uncertain/ nonexistent. I also said that if there's no communication between the two parts because there was no one to talk to them, if I can talk to Tova that might be a way to get in touch with Little Girl Caroline. She agreed and said that since my sense of self has grown stronger, I've been able to allow myself to acknowledge that she exists. Now that I can allow that – allow her to be – we can try and put the pieces together and put the parts in touch with one another. That way, I might be able to find my self and my history – be a witness to my self/my existence, an existence which has a history and a reality.~

At the end of the session something very strange had happened to me. I suddenly lost my certainty about the correct time – thinking there was something wrong with the clock and I checked it with my cell phone clock so as to ascertain the correct time. I'm sure it was some countertransference reaction to the uneasy atmosphere in the room. Here is what Caroline wrote about this:

~At the end of the session Tova looked at the clock to see what time it was. For some reason she wasn't sure whether the clock was right ... she had to check against the clock on her phone to know which to go by. I told her at the door that she had to take us back to not knowing – not being sure what was right or true. It's as though she enacted precisely the phenomena the chapter's describing: my not knowing what's real – my experience or what everyone else says/what they want me/everyone to believe. I'd got her to experience that feeling of not knowing – and of not being sure what/who to believe. If she can know that experience – and not just tell me about it but also help explain how it happens and what causes it – perhaps she can be a witness to my history/past. If I can't experience things like that for myself, because I couldn't comprehend them when they happened, perhaps she can and try and explain them to me so that I can grasp them now.~

Caroline ends this text with a comment that will be reiterated again until the very end of the analysis three years hence. She gives a possible explanation about this sense of uncertainty and doubt that I had just experienced in her presence:

~... Perhaps it's also connected to the fear of losing Tova the closer we get to disclosing the trauma. I had to make her doubt what was real so that the reality we'd established during the session – the reality of my reality – was kept in doubt.~

About the importance of the writing and the meaning of being dead in my presence

We are still reading obsessively the chapter from this book (Seligman et al.) continuing to the section about the outcome when there is no witness to the trauma and how the body carries the memory of a trauma when there is no mentalization. It's obvious that Caroline has an excellent grasp of everything we are reading and I have the feeling that she really could have written this herself. She contributes deep understanding of how she dealt with trauma by elaborating her thoughts in the following text:

~...Tova understood that the need is to constantly live as the dead self from (buried in) the past – but that doing so makes living in the present impossible. It's a case of living the dead past so that it won't be forgotten or be pushed aside by new experiences before it's had a chance of life itself. The past becomes the present and the present becomes the past – because that's the only way that the trauma can be registered and have any hope of being told – given its own existence.

Unless and until the trauma is transformed into a narrative – the story of a lived experience – that's the only way it can exist: not having a living voice in the past, it invades the present and takes over the whole self – in much the same way as the original traumatic experience was so overwhelming that it flooded everything and made the self fragment. Without a voice or words, the only way to preserve the trauma is to re-enact it – constantly, continually, repeatedly. That's why the issue of writing is so important – of being able to construct a written narrative of my self.

In the past, Tova has frequently expressed a lack of understanding and /or frustration over the fact that nothing seems to change, even when we seem to gain some insight into my behaviour – especially, perhaps, the not moving. But as long as we've never been able to translate this comprehension into a coherent narrative – as long as I've never been able to feel the knowledge and know what the words actually mean/referred to – nothing much has helped. That's what we're really looking for: to be able to create an integrated narrative in which the past finds a voice and feelings. If we can find that, maybe we can loosen the grip of the traumatic past on the self and the present – put it into its proper place as something which happened in the past and can become part of the experience of the present, stop it erasing the present in order to preserve the past; bring an end to the internalization of the parental threat against speaking out …

… Paradoxically, as long as I've felt (and still feel) that I haven't found a way to "tell the story" there's been no way to "dissociate" the past from the present. Even if the present has been a dead life, it's one saving grace has been that it has preserved the death ("burial") of parts of the self which occurred in the past – not letting the abuse go unacknowledged in some form, at least.~

So here is the Writing Caroline giving me supervision as to how I am to treat her. It seems she knows better than anyone, and like a diligent, and responsible practitioner, she has done all the reading and not only knows the diagnosis but the treatment of choice.

As Caroline has written – the body remembers trauma even if the mind does not. That is why she needs "enactments" to occur and *for me to experience through these enactments her traumas* so that I can then empathize and return them to her in such a way that her narrative can be formed.

Part II

Living the past in the present: dying, to get somewhere

Chapter 15

Enactment instead of memory

Timeline: the last three years of therapy

A note to the reader: chronologically this chapter continues where Chapter 4 ended.

Enter: the little girl from the past

After almost 22 years Caroline was still bringing me countless books to read together. She would bring in a text lightly underlined in the hope that we would find her experiences in other people's words. But by now, after so many years of therapy I knew that we had exhausted this avenue. I knew that we had to return to the lived experience in the present to find her past and to uncover her traumas in order to heal them.

So when she brought me another chapter from the Seligman and Solomon (2004) book I told her "No more!" My words must have struck her like lightning. Caroline did something she had never done before – she suddenly picked up her papers and walked out on me! Her first spontaneous movement in the 22 years I had known her! When I reached my car, I found a note from her on the windscreen saying that she would not be coming to the following session on Sunday.[1]

In the intervening time, I wrote her an email saying that while I realized that she was very angry with me, it was important that she come because therapy was a place to bring her anger as well.

It was on that Sunday, while waiting for Caroline, that I heard the bell ring loudly. My blood froze in fright. Who could that be? It couldn't be Caroline who always hesitantly tapped almost inaudibly on the glass door so as not to disturb the universe. And besides, she had recently told me that she could not use the bell because it reminded her of her father's penis that he stuck into her. So who could be ringing my doorbell?

When I opened the door, Caroline stood there but immediately I knew it was "the other one". Her dress was the same, except for different spectacles – white framed. What was most strikingly different was her facial appearance.

Her eyes were wide open – in an "unbelieving stare" and her attitude and verbal communication indicated that this was the first time she had ever been here and the first time we had met.

The following is a partial verbatim description of the session with Little Girl Caroline, who I will refer to as LGC (Little Girl Caroline). T represents Therapist /Tova.

LGC: (in a cheery, mocking voice I had not heard before) Is this the right place?
T: Yes. Do you know where you have come to?
LGC: Why would someone come to see someone they don't know?
T: Why would they?
LGC: Right time, right place, right person? (in apparent avoidance of answering, looking around suspiciously)
T: Where did you think you were coming this morning?
LGC: Sounds crazy?
T: Would you like me to tell you who I am? (I say I am adult Caroline's therapist) I'm sure you know her because she sent you here.
LGC: What's *her* problem?
T: She suffers a lot. She has no memories and she feels like a dead person. She thought you may be able to help. She wants to help you too.
LGC: (in annoyance) She doesn't care about anyone.
T: What makes you say that?
LGC: She won't talk to me.
T: (...?)
LGC: Why do you believe *her*?
T: She seems sincere. I've known her for a long time. She's very upset that she's not in contact with you.
LGC: We live separate lives.
T: Did anything traumatic happen that might have caused that?
LGC: How can *you* help?
T: I'm looking for a way. I will try and get the two of you together again.
LGC: Why now?
T: I think because, as you know, both your parents have passed away now. It's something to do with that. Before, I think she was afraid to be in contact with you.
LGC: So she's not angry at *me* – she was angry at *them*?
T: I think so. No – she's not angry with you. You know, she's been feeling very guilty about everything, and especially about having abandoned you and she very much wants to make contact with you now after so many years of not talking to you. She needs help and that's why she asked you to come. Can we meet again tomorrow?

At this, Little Girl Caroline seems to nod in agreement and leaves.

***

The next day: again the bell rings. (Both yesterday and today she went and sat in the chair, and not on the floor where Caroline has been sitting for years – another way for me to know who is here today.) I immediately recognize her as Little Girl Caroline, wearing her white rimmed glasses. Her facial expression is still the disembodied stare, as though she's seen a ghost. Perhaps it's the way I feel, that maybe *I am the one seeing a ghost.*

LGC: We said we'd meet again today, yeh?
T: I wonder – how did you feel after yesterday's meeting?
LGC: (with humour) Is that the kind of question that gets asked here?
T: (I smile.)
LGC: (in an annoyed voice) Why did *she* get all the attention?
T: You're asking – why not *me*, why only *her*?
LGC: Yes, why didn't you give *me* attention – why all to *her*? You said you've been seeing her a long time.
T: ... Maybe she didn't remember you before ... or was afraid to talk about you before.
LGC: So that's my fault too! And why did *you* neglect me?
T: Well, I didn't know about you until now.
LGC: So that I suppose is my fault too. Why didn't you think of looking for me?
T: You seem to be wondering why everyone abandoned you, why Caroline left you *dead and buried* for so long, as though you never existed.
LGC: Yes. That's the *perfect crime* isn't it! (contemptuously) And she says she has "no memory". And you believe her!
T: Well ... yes. I did see how she suffered. She's been trying for years to get her memory back. Struggling. I know she feels very bad about abandoning or neglecting you. That's why she wanted me to meet you.
LGC: A bit late isn't it! So it's my fault is it?
T: It sounds like you feel – you've suffered enough. It's unfair to expect you to forgive her.
LGC: Why should I after what she's done?
T: From your point of view I can see it's unreasonable to expect you to do that. But you know, she's suffered for many years; punished herself; actually become like you – "living a dead life". Maybe that's punishment enough.

It's the end of the hour and when I suggest we continue in the next session she says: "You won't be seeing *her* again?"

And I'm suddenly not sure – who is my patient. I say: Oh, I think I will ... if *she* turns up on Wednesday ... I'd like to let her know about our meetings.

She assents and leaves.

During the last part of the session I have had an uncanny feeling that this Little Girl Caroline is not only the abused child but the *ghost* of a child who was killed, who has been dead and buried – in *the perfect crime*.

Caroline came to the next session in the guise of "her old self" and took up the thread of Thursday's session as though the two previous sessions had not taken place. I struggled with how to let her know what had occurred in "her absence".

I tell her somehow. Her response is to stare at me in disbelief.

C: How do you know *you're* not going mad?
T: ... You're not sure you if you can trust my judgement.
C: If someone thought they were going to be *killed* and they wanted to survive ... that would lead them to make their presence felt?
T: I think so. You felt last Thursday (when I suggested that we dispense with all the reading matter) that I'd said: "Let's forget the past"... so that would mean to stop searching for her, so she had to come forward and say: "I'm here. You can't just get rid of me." Otherwise there'd be no evidence, and no one would ever know she had existed. She's a part of you; she's a memory that your mind can't contain because it's too awful. You want her to know, because you didn't want it to happen, but you couldn't prevent it.

Here Caroline cries and cries. After some time she speaks:

C: Is she going to get hurt?
T: You're afraid they will want to shut her up for telling ... and kill her again. No she won't be hurt because they are dead and they can't hurt her, now that she's speaking up ...

***

After this session the adult Caroline became suspicious of what I knew and whenever I referred to the existence of Little Girl Caroline in my memory, she would cringe in physical pain. This would abruptly make me stop talking – I did not want to be experienced as a sadist and cause her pain.

Again, I felt that we had come to an impasse, a dead end. If I spoke it was as if I was physically harming her, almost assaulting her, if I kept silent she experienced me as persecuting her. She interpreted my silence as the desire to "shut up" and forget everything. There was no space to even interpret this experience.

During one of the sessions, after there had been a very long silence on my part, because I had been paralysed between these impossible choices, she said:

C: One of the worst things in the book (Davies and Fawley, 1994) is that the adult part doesn't want to believe the little girl.

T: Yes, That's what's happening now, here. You're identifying with the parents who want to shut her up and that's why you don't want me to tell you about Little Girl Caroline. That part of you is protecting them but they don't deserve that and she does need you. (Caroline cries and cries.)

***

What was astonishing was that all this happened after 22 years of therapy! The impact of having "met" Little Girl Caroline in this way is virtually indescribable. Again I felt, as I had felt on seeing the "Hanged Doll" ten years previously that *"Seeing is believing!"*

If I had to encapsulate in one sentence my feelings, it would be to say that I was filled with conviction that Caroline, my "walking dead" patient had once been a very lively, even cute little girl with a sense of humour and lots of spunk who "went missing". This was no Asperger's child. She was bright and lively. So what could have made her disappear, go into hiding – lost to herself, lose her memory, yet remain so determined to "be found"? For over 20 years she had left me little clues so that I would not give up the search. And now, when she had thought I was about to – she came out of hiding! At long last!

Only the most terrible trauma – some deep and unspeakable – terror could have caused this little girl to have gone missing in this way.

In this interaction with Little Girl Caroline I had become a witness to my own self experience. It was through my felt sense – a knowing based on input from my senses of seeing, hearing, and gut body feelings that I now knew how Caroline had been as a little girl.

Dissociation in dreams

One of Little Girl Caroline's questions was: what had prevented me from knowing about this little girl earlier? After all, before her appearance the Writer Caroline had written to me explicitly about this dissociated little girl. Two months before her dramatic appearance she had written:

> ~I asked Tova if it had perhaps been her (Little Girl Caroline) who had been under the table. Tova thought quite possibly it had been. She'd known lots of things about the abuse, and tried to tell her/us through the doll/paint/hanging, etc. Tova had understood then that she was a different part of me, one which I wasn't in touch with, but said she hadn't quite put it in terms of a separate person.~

It's true. Today I understand that my mind could not really grasp or believe or understand or accept that such extreme dissociation of a whole separated system (Sinason, 2002; Van der Hart et al., 2006) could be taking place.

Through her writing, Caroline continues to teach me a lesson in depth psychology: she analyses her dreams in terms of the dissociative defence: for example, she reveals that in the "Hospital Dream" (see Chapter 10) where she and the little boy understood each other without talking:

> ~The hospital dream was an expression of Little Girl Caroline expressing her voice and existence. The fact, too, that there was another patient there (albeit a boy) who knew exactly what I was feeling is perhaps an indication of the existence of both personalities – who could only communicate with one another within the silence of the hospital.~

So in her writing Caroline is letting me know that dissociation can be dreamt about. It seems she is raising the idea that the host or Adult Caroline tried to *inform me* about the existence of a Dissociative Identity Disorder (DID) by *dreaming about dissociation*. This introduces another way of relating to the analysis of dreams. Dreams can be related to and interpreted in innumerable ways, which will not be dealt with here. But, at least for me, this was the first time I was being invited to think about a dream as containing the message that the dreamer unconsciously is aware of suffering from DID and is dreaming this in an attempt to communicate it. She also calls the "personae" – personalities. This must be how she experiences "their" presence.

***

Between Chapters 5 to 14 I described aspects of the process that developed over a 12-year period, between the scene of "Hanged Doll" and the entry of Little Girl Caroline. However, in spite of the accumulation of much material about Caroline, mainly through her writing and enactments, no working through of the incest and abortion seemed to be taking place. This was a cause for concern. It was as though the knowledge was kept separate and not available for integration. At times it felt as though *I* was left in charge of the knowledge and memory in the hope that one day she could own it.

Over the course of these 12 years and in the chapters that cover this period of time, I have tried to describe the process that led to the dramatic appearance of the Little Girl Caroline persona. During the last three years of the analysis the appearance of Little Girl Caroline would turn out to be quite unpredictable. Sometimes, she arrived as Little Girl Caroline at the beginning of a session, in her white rimmed glasses. But this happened only a few times. Soon "my" Adult Caroline would arrive and somewhere in the midst of a session she would be "transformed" to the little girl often with no prior warning. I found myself needing to learn to recognize who was with me. At times this took me a while until I "found" who I was talking to. I will attempt to demonstrate some of this often confusing interaction.

If I could have introduced a movie camera the process could have been caught live. To describe it verbally, rather than visually is next to impossible. It was predominantly a visual and visceral experience. Often, I ended such sessions where she was in an altered state of consciousness by relating to her as I would with a hypnotized patient by "grounding" her – by asking, for example, that the little girl call Adult Caroline to come back into our present space and time, since it was the end of the session. And to my relief, Caroline always "returned" and then left the clinic at the end of the hour, with Little Girl Caroline safely tucked inside her in some way.

We were soon to notice that with the arrival of Little Girl Caroline, the Adult Caroline *stopped writing*. The texts, which had been such a valuable source of information for many years, were no longer brought to me by Caroline at the beginning of a session. Caroline expressed great sadness at the loss. She said that it was as though she had lost an important part of her self. I, too, was curious as to the reason for "her" (the writer's) disappearance.

***

A vignette from one of the first meetings with Caroline after having met LGC "in person". (She is wearing her regular glasses.)

C: Is it like … in … the books?
T: Becoming more than one person? Yes.
C: What did you do?
T: I invited her in and listened to her.
C: What's … her … name?
T: Actually, I didn't ask. I assumed it was Little Girl Caroline,
C: (nods in agreement.) She … told you … she didn't want to be … *killed*?
T: Yes
C: How … did you know she was … someone … else?
T: Oh, there were several signs. She used the bell. You look shocked. Yes, I was also taken by surprise when she did it.
C: The bell … on the … door?
T: Yes, the one we spoke about that time when I had suggested you use it when I hadn't heard your knock and you had explained why you couldn't use it. So I knew then that something had happened. She also wore different glasses. Maybe you have some clue about that. Have you seen different glasses in the house?
C: I … had new glasses made. These … ones I'm … wearing.
T: No. They were different – white frames.

Here Caroline goes into a terrible state. She first stares in disbelief and eventually bends over into her cushion crying in anguish, holding her arms tightly and not being able to come out of this state. It takes a long time and a lot of encouraging to get her to be able to end the session, which has run over time. Something of my describing her white framed glasses has shocked her.

***

At our next session Caroline stands with her back to me in the centre of the room. It takes me a few minutes to see that she is holding a small photo in her hand, pointed in my direction. I slowly take the photo from her. It is an old black and white photograph of two small children. One of them, a cute little freckled-face girl who is around five or six years old is wearing *white framed glasses!* They resemble the ones she had worn in her appearances as LGC! In a whisper she asks if the little girl looked like her.

Could it be that this sweet, slightly neglected little girl in the picture is the child version of my head-shaven ghost-like Caroline!

From this moment on violence will enter the room. Session after session something happens that I am not prepared for. I will soon feel that I am on a rollercoaster where at any moment an unexpected jolt might throw me off balance.

Enactments of violence

The first enactment: from masturbation to self injury

These violent enactments can be triggered by the slightest event. For example, when my shawl slipped off my shoulders. Caroline became suspicious: did this mean that I was "undressing"? She suddenly started rocking intensely in a very repetitive, ritualistic way, the movement becoming more and more rapid with her feet banging on the floor. There is no talking, and I begin to think that she might be masturbating and having an orgasm. There is fusion between aggression and erotic stimulation and at the same time she seems to be in physical pain. I am feeling overwhelmed and I want to stop her doing this; I somehow succeed in getting her to desist. The next day, however, she accuses me of not letting her find out what happened in the past. She says that by not allowing her to continue this enactment in the present I blocked her path to the past. She pleads with me to let her continue and I become like a prohibitive parent, forbidding this addictive behaviour. She also insistently wants to know what *I* experienced – was I turned on sexually? I am reluctant to tell her, not being sure of anything. Also, I realize how confusing and overwhelming sexual stimulation in inappropriate conditions can be. The next day Little Girl Caroline rings the front door bell. She is wearing her white framed glasses.

LGC: Am I still welcome here?
T: Yes, you're very welcome.
LGC: Has it helped her?
T: She wanted to hear what you told me.
LGC: But she didn't talk to me.
T: Well, I know she'd like to be able to. She asked about everything that happened between us. She even brought a photo to show me. I think it was of you when you were a bit younger.
LGC: Why did she do that?
T: She asked if you looked like her. **She needs your memories.** She has only the bodily memories and **you** know what happened. Last time you were here you had started telling me about nasty things jumping up in a nasty house ...?
LGC: His thing jumped out ... Confusion about Mom ... He liked it and she didn't ... He kept doing it all the time. I don't know if I had anything to do with it jumping out ... I don't want to talk about it any more.
T: It is difficult for you, confusing and making you feel bad. But it's very important that you are telling.
LGC: I couldn't stay there when it hurt too much.
T: It hurt too much when he put it into you.
LGC: Not just him.
T: Not just Dad? (It is the end of the hour and I am reluctant to end our session. I end by reinforcing her on her courage at being able to come forward and tell such painful memories.)

After she left I noticed that today, except for the first few sentences spoken, in facial expression, posture and voice Little Girl Caroline had actually become very much like Adult Caroline. In fact, only the glasses she wore and the content of their words distinguished between them.

The next day, at the start of our session, I found Caroline outside the clinic door. She was sitting on the floor, curled up into a human ball. It took a lot of empathy and encouragement to help her continue. She had only a partial memory of the "masturbating" enactment of two days earlier and seemed to have no memory of the previous day's session with Little Girl Caroline. She insisted I tell her everything. So I tried – describing her physical actions, suggesting that in this way she was letting me know about sexual acts experienced in the past. Then, to my dismay and considerable surprise she verbally attacked me for having told her.

The danger of knowing: head banging incident

With Caroline's attack on me for having told her the truth of my encounter with Little Girl Caroline, I find myself wondering whether this path towards exposure of past pain is truly wise. While I was turning this over in my mind,

Caroline suddenly initiated another enactment – this time of dangerous self-injury. When she had come in she had refused to sit and instead stood leaning against a wall. Now she suddenly started banging her head against the wall with the slow repetitive movements of a "masturbatory" act. I felt a rising panic inside me. I insisted she stop. She didn't listen or didn't hear me. I shouted at her and threatened to end the session. Eventually, she stopped but repeated this behaviour a week later. This time it took me much longer and a much more frantic effort to stop her.

These incidents left me exhausted. I had been made to feel fear helplessness, rage and total loss of control. Since when do I ever yell at my patients? Knowing that she wanted me to feel what she had experienced in the past was becoming overwhelming for me.

Our next session opens with Caroline accusing me of having threatened her. I concur but add a proviso: "Yes, I did threaten that our sessions would have to stop if you behave in this way. But I will not allow you to injure yourself like that."

C: You can't stop me.
T: Now who's threatening?

The rest of the session is a very difficult one where I realize that I cannot stop her and at the same time I know that I will not be able to let her continue in this way.

We have reached an impasse. I feel utterly helpless and give voice to my feeling:

T: This is not therapy. I have my limits as to what I am willing to go through. I know that *you need me to feel the feelings you went through* and I have: fear, loss of control ... but I can only do therapy if I have certain conditions. If I don't have conditions where I can think, I can't be of help to you. So we have to find a way to solve this.
C: So we can't go on?
T: Maybe, But not like this. We'll have to find other ways.

***

Before our next meeting I find myself quite frightened about seeing her again and even wishing that Little Girl Caroline would "arrive" and not the Adult Caroline. At least I can handle the little girl! But Adult Caroline has surely turned into her abuser. Desperate and in search of more information, I read the chapter on self-injury in Davies and Fawley's book *Treating the Adult Survivors of Childhood Sexual Abuse*. The chapter called "Exposure to Danger, Eroticization of Fear, and Compulsive Self-abuse" proves on the mark.

The opening paragraph explains what is going on with Caroline:

> The relentlessness and drama of survivor's self-destructive enactments can overwhelm the therapist as well, endangering the therapeutic alliance and, ultimately, jeopardizing the treatment. It is thus crucial that the therapist ... be familiar with the purposes and meanings of violent enactments ...
>
> (1994, p. 129)

So, at least I was not alone in grappling with the terrifying sight of Caroline's self-abuse and self-injury. I thus tried to be "prepared" for whatever or whoever might turn up at the next session. And it was fortunate that I did so, since to my surprise, and relief Caroline comes armed with the book to attack me:

A vignette

She enters and in a somewhat threatening way gives me to understand that if I don't let her continue then it would be the end. It is a veiled threat of suicide and actually not even so veiled.

T: You mean if I don't let you go on injuring yourself you feel we can't continue. I don't think it has to be the end. I think we have to look for other ways.

C: (Speaking *contemptuously* to me) Haven't you read ... the chapter in the book ... where it says that the therapist ... has to be ... prepared for ... self- injury by ... the patient.

T: (Feeling so relieved that I had) I have. And I have also read there that the therapist has to put a stop to the behaviour, even if it is self-soothing, like masturbation. It is the therapist's job to help the patient find alternative ways to relieve stress, and help her get out of an addiction, which fuses aggression and eroticization.

C: (taken aback that I know the book well enough to refute her claim.): But ... only if the behaviour ... is ... life threatening.

T: Yes. And in the book it doesn't specify what is life-threatening because only in real time can one know what feels life-threatening. I felt your behaviour was – if you would have kept banging your head, you could have caused yourself brain injury. Your back bashing could have broken your ribs and then you'd be hospitalized and then what would we do?

C: (pleading) If it happens today it means ... it happened in the past and ... that way I'll be able to know ... what happened then. Please ... let me go on. Don't stop me now.

T: I know already. I can tell you there was fear, helplessness, anger, a loss of control. I know that these are the feelings you were subjected to over and over again. It was terrible what they did to you.

C: (with a tear rolling down her face.) Please ... don't make me stop doing it now ... I must go on.
T: You want me to go through this over and over again, just like you were abused over and over again, and somehow survived it. You feel I have to go through it, that I have to be subjected to it as you were, and see what happens to me, how I survive it.
C: It's the only way.
T: (after some time) You know what I think Caroline? I don't think we will know more this way. On the contrary. Maybe we'll know the feelings, through my feelings, but we know that already. But we won't know the facts of what happened. It will help bypass that knowing. This masochism started just after you were on the verge of finding out something. You had asked about your mom – what did I know from Little Girl Caroline about your mother and the thoughts that there were more men involved. But since this self-abuse started, it's taken over, and you've stopped inquiring about what your mother knew, stopped "sending" Little Girl Caroline here who had just started telling me what she knows.
C: No, no ... you're confused.
T: Maybe I am. When one feels all this fear and panic it can cause confusion in one's thought processes. So go on – you tell me. Where am I confused?
C: (after a pause) *I'm* confused.
T: Yes.
C: (crying) I don't know ... who to ... believe.
T: Caroline, I think they must have said to you something like: "Listen to us, do as we tell you; you're being such a good girl, it helps us feel better, it's enjoyable too, you are also enjoying it. What a good girl you are."

She nods her head in consent.

At the end of the session, when she is at the door, she suddenly turns back to me and whispers, "Please ... don't say anything ... to anyone".

I am left with thinking of the fortunate coincidence that I had thought of reading that chapter before our meeting, thus managing to be "one step ahead" on this occasion.

***

The following sessions Caroline drifts in and out from past to present, from being Little Girl Caroline to Adult Caroline and back. She's constantly shifting. I try to follow, adapt, changing my way of being with her accordingly. She asks me if I remember what I did to the doll, and I do – describing how she wanted me to write "Fuck" all over her (Chapter 3) and how I refused to stick things into the doll's vagina.

"Is that what they did to you?" I ask, adding "They shouldn't have done it to you. It was wrong. It was not your fault."

And Caroline becomes a little girl once again, and in her childish voice she says: "They did love me ... they had to do it."

T: Why?
LGC: I don't know. Sometimes parents have to do it.
T: As though punishing you for something you did. That's what they said. And you had to believe them.
And I tell her that there was no one else around to say that it wasn't true. And I think how this little girl had to believe that her parents did love her, to believe that there was goodness in them to protect her from knowing of their cruelty.

***

The next day Caroline turns the tables on me by asking me why I believe everything she says. In this way she is undermining and attempting to undercut any certainty the previous session had established. Yet, she no longer only annihilates. She is also curious and wants to understand. I can see that her repertoire has expanded. With anguish she conveys to me that she had no idea what we talked about on the previous day ... all meaning lost, wiped out.

T: That must be so confusing – not being able to make sense of what you said yesterday ... Do you want to hear what *I* think happened here?

Eventually, she nods her head in agreement. There begins a sort of dialogue between us about this strange experience. She questions me about how I can recognize who is here in the room with me. I try and tell her what helps me "know" e.g. tone of voice, talking from the past, saying things only children think. She tries to convey to me how unreal everything feels when all experiential memory of the previous day is erased.

It is at this stage that the importance of my writing down the sessions verbatim in real time is established and talked about. At moments like this I do feel so much progress has been made: here we are – two people, talking *about* her mental functioning and about trying to make sense of it. There is a sense of "objectiveness": two real people discussing the existence of a real internal world.

But this sense of development is never long lasting. Towards the end of the hour Caroline starts the rocking again. And I find myself relieved that at least the self-injury has not returned.

Rocking to disassociate from herself

In this dissociated way some form begins to develop. We begin to recognize that the rocking behaviour is part of the dissociative process that leads her to "disappear from herself". "But then I'm ... not here and I ... don't know what's happening... and I... don't know where it's coming from." We understand that the voice that speaks feels estranged and adds to her feeling of being unreal. She asks if I think it's something "*she*" (Little Girl Caroline) is doing to her and I say that, on the contrary, I think it is the Adult Caroline who is identified with the parental punitive voice that is responsible. And she asks me to write this down as well. She then has an insight: "It's not making things up. It's allowing things to be said."

I agree and she asks: "I can't write... because that would... be... knowing?"

T: That makes sense. When you write you have to know something – to know even what you want to write, to make it communicative – transmit it to me too.
C: You know ... because you write?
T: I think I can write because I can know – because I have the advantage of not being part of the trauma. That makes me think of what we spoke of a few months ago, when you left me that article about the need for a *witness* ... where it said that often one can know the trauma when one can tell it to someone who wasn't involved. That's the importance of the witness. Writing is an auxiliary to knowing.

***

So this is why Caroline can no longer write! Since Little Girl Caroline has appeared she has been revealing the truths of the past in a very "alive" experiential way. This has replaced the Writing Caroline. If she was *to write* what the little girl actually revealed to me it seems she would experience knowing it to be real. She is letting me know that she is not ready to take ownership over these as yet, unknown happenings of her past; she can only "show" them to me.

***

But slowly some memories return. One day she reports a "real" memory that she just had from when she was about six years old. She recalls having been cruel to a much smaller child, perhaps a neighbour. She could say no more. She then suddenly seems afraid and asks if her mother was here and starts rocking again.

The next day:

C: I don't know anything ... so I can't tell you anything. It's not a matter ... of not being able ... to bare the knowing ... it's the going back itself ... that's *not being*. You go there ... and that's beyond the bounds of the human ... and it doesn't leave any option ... for living ... there's no chance for surviving ... the violence ... you don't survive ... It's a *killing field*.

***

A nightmare

The next day Caroline tells a dream:

> An animal is being ... attacked ... a small animal ... I don't know what it was ... it's being mauled ... by two big ... animals ... one was like a cat ... the other was ... bigger. It started tearing its ... limbs off ... the cat took ... some of the parts off ... and the other animal started ... all the entrails ... spilled out ... but I don't think... it was dead.

I interpret the dream as representing what she feels I am doing to her by insisting she tries to remember. I suspect our work is stirring up the unbearable conflict – for to know is to die and not to know is to die in another way. She cannot make a move and cannot stay where she is.

Her response is, "Don't you understand ... if that's true ... then the violence ... was there and if ... you're not the source of it ... then ... she (Mom) must have been ... and if ... do you know what you are asking me to do?"

The following day she remains silent for the duration of our session, saying only: "I've said ... too much already." It seems the realization that her mother was involved in the violence is unbearable.

Since she is silent I give voice to what I believe is her concern that she does not trust me enough to feel safe with me. To this she does respond with: "You don't know that this is ... nothing compared to what's coming ... if we go on!" And I understand that she is in great trepidation of some potential danger the content of which I am unable to even imagine.

The second enactment: undressing while I renovate my house

One day, as if out of the blue, Caroline suddenly starts to "undress" very quickly. It is so rapid that I barely notice it at first. She takes off her shoes and then her socks and is about to continue when I stop her. I again turn into a disapproving prohibiting parent. I "win" the struggle again, with firm words and threats. I try to give explanations, although I understand nothing. My not understanding seems to be "the right response" since she says this: "You don't understand ... so that means ... you're not involved ... so you're not doing it deliberately."

I'm relieved. She's seeing that I'm on her side. Perhaps she is experiencing my intention to protect her that lies behind my aggressive behaviour. The next day she brings our "reference" book (Davies and Fawley, 1994), and she has marked the word "anticipation". I read and understand that the anticipation before the sexual abuse she was to experience was so unbearable that she would "take control" over her anxiety by undressing and offering her body so as to get it over with already. She agrees but repeats the above scene saying, "What if it doesn't ... stop at the shoes!"

I am at a loss for words. After some time I tell Caroline that though she wants me to suffer the unbearable experience of being forced to do something I don't want to – being exposed to her undressing, so that I can experience how she felt – I cannot allow this here because I think it's bad for her and for me and for our relationship.

The next session she comes in attacking me:

C: What are you trying to do? ... How can you say you help if ... you won't let me ... stop the pain ... the only way that helps?

I tell her that the only way she knew to reduce her anxiety was by this addictive sexual activity and I am now experienced by her as the abuser who is causing her more pain by not allowing her to masturbate. However, we must help her find another way; that I know that this way does not really bring her relief, but leaves her feeling bad and guilty.

Meanwhile, simultaneously, there has also been an external event that may be associated with this "undressing" enactment. I was having my home kitchen renovated. Although I continued work in my home clinic Caroline refused to come there until there was absolutely no sign or reminder of a house being "damaged" in her words. The renovation would take several months. She was extreme and obsessive about not coming to my home clinic at this time. She "used" this event to act out with me the experience of "covering up" the violence done to her body in her childhood.

First, she accused me of "pretending" everything was fine when, in fact, in my house terrible things were happening and I came to work and did not even talk about it. (I meet her during these months only in my town-clinic and three times a week instead of four.) So she had good cause to be suspicious, she says. But since she also was able to keep in contact with reality at some level, knowing that this place was her safe therapy room, we were able to decipher that the undressing together with my home renovation represented her coming to school and wearing her school uniform in a way that nothing of the injuries on her body could be seen by the teachers. No one suspected the nasty things being done to her body in her home (represented by my "damaged" home). While I say something about this she, unexpectedly starts *banging her head* on the glass door on which she often leans while sitting on the floor. I start shouting at her to stop and I feel there is confusion between abuser and abused and manage to say:

T: You are now acting like the adult abuser to Little Girl Caroline and I will not allow it.

She admits that she couldn't tell anyone out of fear of not being believed since her parents were known in the school as upright citizens.

C: If the house is damaged ... and you're not talking about it ... then I don't know ... if I've made it all up.
T: In the past no one saw. Mom was respected in the community and you were alone; you had no one to talk to. So it was easy to think maybe you had made it up. It was confusing but also very adaptive on your part, because if you've made it up then it's all right to return home.
C: (agreeing) So "not being real". was ... real?
T: You had to make the memory of the nasty things in the nasty house be unreal, because you had no other place to go back to.
C: So ... I didn't make up ... the idea of ... making things up?
T: No. You had to think "I made this up" in order to survive. But that's a very complex mental state – you have to believe you can't trust your own mind – and then how *can* you trust your own mind!
C: To be crazy ... was something ... that might be real?
T: Maybe that felt preferable to thinking that what you experienced in that "damaged" house was real.
C: But ... it also meant that ... it went on!

***

The next week I tell her that there are still some signs on the house from the renovation so if she wants a "perfect appearance" it is not yet time to return and resume our four-weekly meetings. On hearing what I have just said, she begins to undress quickly. Again, I say things that are intended to stop this immediately and sound prohibitive and strict. She stops undressing and I interpret her behaviour as a trying to offer me the parent something "worthwhile" – sex, as though the fault is with her. And I add:

> Children desperately need to believe that their parents are *good*. And my not allowing you to return to the house to resume our four-weekly meetings feels that you are the bad one. But we can return there and resume our meetings.

Caroline nods in agreement while tears silently course down her cheeks.

***

The multifaceted task of the therapist inside enactment

I found my task as a therapist most complex. Although, as a child therapist, playing different parts in a play directed by one's child patients was something

I had extensive experience with, Caroline challenged me in ways I could never have anticipated and had never experienced.

Some of my tasks involved:

1 An actor whose role has been prewritten by the patient and transmitted to the therapist's preconscious;
2 The role as the outside audience (therapist) participant observer.
3 A witness to what is being "performed" while trying not to lose my grip on what is real and what is "the play", what is real and what might be fantasy.
4 While doing all the above, trying to understand and make sense of the experience so as to find a way to share the understanding with my patient.
5 At the same time, striving to protect Caroline from being hurt by her self-abusive behaviour.

Note

1 This paragraph is intentionally a repetition of the end of Chapter 4, to indicate the chronological connection in time.

Chapter 16

From "hanging the doll" to "death by hanging"

> At the moment of trauma, the victim is rendered helpless by overwhelming force. When the force is that of nature, we speak of disasters. When the force is that of other human beings, we speak of atrocities.
> Judith Herman, *Trauma and Recovery* (1992)

Timeline: 24 years into therapy

Death of the dog

The renovations have been completed but before resuming therapy at my home clinic, Caroline wants to see that it is safe with her very own eyes. She asks permission to come and see the house before resuming therapy there. I agree. Words of reassurance are not helpful. She remains anxious; she requires more proof. She wants to know if I would be willing to do something that might help her feel safe again here. Hesitantly, she asks if I would be willing to call my dog so that she would be able to see, by his friendliness towards me, that I was good, and that would mean I had not become one of the abusers. It seems Caroline has some inner experience of herself changing into different people so how can she be sure that it does not happen to me. How unnerving to live like that! Interpreting it doesn't calm her. She needs proof.

I am devastated. I know she needs concrete proof and I would call my dog if I could. But alas, over this month of renovations, my dog passed away. I knew she would never believe me that he died of a natural cause. But what could I tell her except the truth? And so I did.

After a long silence she quietly says, "The boy ... was afraid of his father ... because he killed the dog" and I immediately recall Mark Haddon's book, *The Curious Incident of the Dog in the Night-Time*. We had both read this book two years earlier. It is about an Asperger's boy who runs away from home because he loses all trust in his father, who killed their dog. She asks me if I have *buried him in the garden* and I suddenly remember the Hanged Doll incident from over ten years earlier where she had wanted us to bury the doll in the garden, and I had almost agreed. I tell her the outer reality – how my dog was very old, became ill, was taken to a veterinary hospital where they couldn't save him, and where he died.

Caroline glances at me with suspicion, and I add,

> You're telling me of violence. Ten years ago you wanted me to bury the doll in the garden. Then we thought that represented an aborted foetus – now the only way you can tell me what you were involved in is in this way ... killing, burial in the garden.

Just as I have finished speaking, Caroline does something completely unexpected, something she has never done before. After violently pulling at her shoelaces she lies down on the floor, creeps under the couch and for the first time weeps *aloud*, in a heart breaking way. The silence is shattered by the sound of her pain.

The only consolation I have to offer her is that we have now set up five sessions a week – a return to the four as before and added make-up sessions at her request for the time missed during the months of renovations. I find myself hoping that this will be a sufficient adjustment of the therapeutic setting to contain what is to come.

***

After this session Caroline writes me an email asking me if it is safe to come. I reply to her, assuring that it is. She arrives at the next session not as the Adult Caroline but as Little Girl Caroline. She wants me to leave the door ajar, acting as though she is in captivity and suddenly asks, "Where's the rope?"

When Caroline says this, the visual image of the Hanged Doll returns to me. It had been so strong that I had at the time photographed it. The image was of her swinging from the string tied around her little neck. I pluck up my courage and ask her if she ever saw someone hanged – executed – and if this makes her afraid this will be done to her. Caroline replies not in words but with her body. She slowly walks to the slightly open door and lifts up her arms and by holding the top of the door sort of "hangs herself" while making jerky kicking movements with one leg. As she turns to go, she tells me I must produce some rope the next day. I refuse. She asks me to bring the photographs I took of the hanging doll. That is something that I am willing to do, and I let her know this. I find myself needing to judge all the time what is safe and what might turn into a dangerous situation where she may actually hurt herself while in the regression. This is becoming more and more difficult.

An enacted hanging

Vignette 1: a rope

(Before she entered I had put the photographs of the "Hanged Doll" on the table.) Caroline insists on standing near the door the whole hour.

C: Are you sure no one is buried in the garden?
T: I'm sure. Not my dog nor anyone else. The dog was very old and he died a natural death. There was no violence.
C: But what if they're not old?
T: Maybe you can tell me about that.
C: (after a long silence) But why would I know about that?
T: Maybe you were exposed to something like that when you were small. It left you very frightened and left you living in fear most of your life.
C: (after a long while) Can you tell me more ... about the pictures. (She is referring to the photographs of the hanging doll I had set out on the table)
T: I took them after you finished dealing with the doll in the way you needed to.

(While I am describing this she, still standing, begins stretching her neck back in agony as though it's being pulled by an invisible force.)

T: Caroline, would you like to sit down in a chair. This is most difficult for you.
(She goes slowly towards the door and leans on it, with her back to me.)
C: I need the rope.
T: You can't have the rope. In the past you wanted a rope because it seemed the only way out. You were all alone with no one there for you. Now you have me to help you deal with this.

While I am speaking Caroline "hangs herself". She does this in a similar way as she had the day before. The sight creates a cold chill down my spine. She looks to me as though she is trying to mimic the posture of someone who has been hanged.

T: This is what you saw when you saw the child hanged, the way that leg jerked?

While she stays in this agonizing position as if strung up in the frame of the door, I go on talking. I talk softly, slowly, trying to be calm, calming myself, calming her ...

T: In the early years, when we met, you used to hold a red paper clip in your hand (see Chapter 2). And then one day you changed it to a different colour, remember? You told me that you had left it in Auschwitz. Did you know then about your past? (She shakes her head.)

But deep down in your unconscious you knew something. Deep down you *knew* that you had gone through something so terrible that it made you identify with those victims of the Holocaust. As some of them survived to tell, so you have survived to tell. First, it had to be acknowledged. *I am your witness.* I have the photos and with time we'll find a way to help you deal with it. This week we have five sessions. That's good. Tomorrow is Holocaust Memorial Day. Remember, there will be a siren in our session.

I need to ask her to move from the door so that I can open it for her to leave. As she leaves I have a horrible foreboding that she may try to hang herself.

Suicidal danger and medication

The next day I decide Caroline must see the psychiatrist since suicide cannot be ruled out. Anne, her partner, comes with us and tells the psychiatrist that Caroline has been talking about endangering herself while riding her bicycle. This is the first time that a concrete thought of how to commit suicide has come up. Caroline agrees to an increase in the dosage of medication.

In the sessions that follow the visit to the psychiatrist we continue to search for Caroline's past. We realize with more "evidence" that her mother was involved in the violence.

Vignette 2: mother's involvement

C: You said yesterday … "Go put it in the bath."

(I had not, but it was a reference to our very first sessions when she had told how her mother would cynically answer her if she asked a question when she was little. We are in a time regression at age six.)

C: Did she … make you … do that? Does she make … you do things … like that too?
T: No. But you are telling me she made *you* do things. You had no power to disobey.

As I am speaking, to my horror I see Caroline starting to hit her head violently with her fists. This seems to have become a substitute for the dangerous head banging on the wall. I continue to speak, sympathetically describing her loneliness; I say how devastating it must have been for her to have had no one on her side … no will of her own because they had crushed any she may have had.

Caroline stops hitting herself and makes the gesture of "hanging herself" with an outstretched arm. (From now she does this from under the sofa, no longer needing to "concretely" hang herself on the door. One arm, protruding out – stretched high above her neck, symbolically represents the hanging rope. This is clearly a "body-sign" introduced into our nonverbal dictionary.)

T: Caroline, if you are remembering anything now through body memory, try and put it into words. Tell me, I'm listening, writing it all down.
CAROLINE BECOMES LGC: Did you hide the rope as well?
T: I think you're asking your mother: "Did you hide the rope as well as bury that little girl that was hung?" What a frightening situation you were in; not knowing what to do ... with the rope; perhaps asking her: where shall I put it? ... and getting a cynical reply. "Go put it in the bath!" ... It's most painful to think that a *mother* can do that to her own child.

Caroline collapses under the sofa, hiding herself from herself, from me, from the world. I hear her weeping.

Vignette 3: unbearable guilt

The next session she stays outside, needing to be urged to enter. She enters but stays erect near the door.

C: What did ... she think of me ... to do ... something like that?
T: If she got you to do that? Like put the rope on the little girl?
C: Yes. (Caroline "hangs" herself in the frame of the door).
T: When you do that – "hang" yourself, it's because you are feeling very guilty and want to die. But it means, I think – that she thought she could ask you because you would do it.

Caroline remains immobile in this hanging position. (I think: she is both Little Girl Caroline showing me a visual memory from the past, and /or Caroline feeling guilty in the present. These kinds of metamorphoses of age and shifts in time keep occurring and I adapt as best I can.)

T: It means you had no separate will of your own, because it was crushed, annihilated. You were an extension of her that she used ... How that came about we need to understand. I know you are different from her; I know that you wanted to remain humane. That is why you are suffering so much.
C: Can you read me what you just wrote?

She then expresses the thought that since Mom had told her to do things with Dad in the past and she had (implying her agreeing to participate in the incest) her mother knew she could ask her to do this. I am enraged at this mother; what kind of "mother" is this? I tell Caroline that I am devastated by her mother's actions.
    The following day Caroline again throws into doubt everything that was said the previous day, this time blaming the medication, as though her

psychiatric medication is having the effect of a hallucinatory drug. I realize she wants to "undo" yesterday's most painful revelation of her mother's involvement in the atrocities. But I feel she might be ready to know the reality of her past. I tell her that on the contrary: because the medication is reducing her anxiety level, memories are returning

Caroline again starts hitting herself with her fists and I intervene by an interpretation. I say that it is her identification with the abusers that is making her attack Little Girl Caroline and that she is hurting her more and this does not make sense. My words reach her. She stops beating herself.

C: But how ... can you ... see her? She's ... so small ... and ... she's covered with disgusting things ... and you can't see inside.

Vignette 4: going too fast

The next day, everything seems too much. Caroline feels we have been going too fast.

C: It's been different ... because things have happened ... which didn't happen before ... and all in a rush ... lots of things together ... we've said things ... and not been able to talk about them, because something else happened ... not been able to ... put the pieces together ... but not even time ... to know ... what the pieces themselves are ... do you understand?
T: I think there is also an issue of trust here. Because when I say, like yesterday, "I believe you", that's not good enough, because I'm on the *outside*. I can't know objectively about the past, because I wasn't there ... as no one can ... that is, it's not *proof* of anything if I believe you.

Caroline assents – we understand one other! I, too, need to get off this rollercoaster at least for a while. From what I have just said, it seems I also need to leave her the opening that the element of doubt is an option.

***

Further thoughts

What has been too much for Caroline? In Vignette 1 Caroline is in the past, showing me a hanging and the next day, in Vignette 2 she is seen actually having retained the memory of the previous day and the gruesome enactment of hanging, while relating to it both from the past and in the present. It has not been deleted from her mind. A sense of continuation has been maintained allowing for memory, at least for now. But something about this seems too much, too fast; too frightening. I cooperate with her need to slow things down. I fear she may lose her mind if she admits too many of these horrific deeds that are being enacted in front of my eyes into her full consciousness. It was too much to know that her mother was implicated and then made use of her in committing the crimes. And the words "Go put it in the bath" had been first spoken when I had just met Caroline, now 24 years earlier. Little did I realize then that this was "the smoking gun" presented in the first scene of this increasingly violent drama.

***

What's in a name: Violet

There is now a lull in the enactments, during which Caroline brings a written text after not having written anything for a year. This occurred after she had asked me if I thought we could *talk about the violence*. In the written text she lets me know that the medication is helpful. It enables her to separate the past from the present. She introduces the idea of wanting to meet Little Girl Caroline. She decides to give her a name: Violet. By naming her it means *she*, the adult or host Caroline has been able acknowledge the existence of Little Girl Caroline. She was no longer an anonymous "she". The name Violet was chosen as an appropriate name because of its association with Violence and Violation By naming her she could be externalized. I added that her name was also that of a flower.

"Playing among the ruined languages" – a transitional space

Over the years Caroline repeatedly brought the same poem to therapy, with different lines marked for me to read. It was by W. H. Auden. "Hymn to St Cecilia". On this day the following lines were marked:

> Oh dear white children casual as birds,
> Playing among the ruined languages,
> So small beside their large confusing words,
> So gay against the greater silences.

***

To this she added something of her own writing:

> ~We'd been talking about language in general this week, in relation to Auden's poem: I'd said that the violence had become the language – the language used was the violence; as well as "murdering" language, because it isn't possible to talk about violence, and the perpetrators of the violence won't allow it to be talked about. I might have words throughout

the therapy, but I'd never had language. That's the large part of the reason for the silence – Auden's "dreadful silence".[1] All that's left then is the "beast" of "Dread born whole and normal" which has no language.

It's as though the ability to separate past and present has not only enabled a conceptual distance to emerge between the two but also a linguistic one. When past and present are the same, everything's concrete because nothing is symbolic: the past isn't something different and therefore can't be symbolized; it's right there – direct, immediate and unmediated. When there's a distance between past and present space is made for language. When the two are so closely intertwined, there's no room for distinction between them and thus one can't represent the other (or anything else). Tova called being able to name "Violet" as a way to distance her from me so that things wouldn't be too close/much, finding a "transitional space". That's precisely what the symbolization enables: a place in-between which intervenes between the past and the present and gives them each their own space ... When I thanked Tova and said that that had helped, she responded by saying that she was able to do so because I'd been able to share my ideas with her. As long as I can't tell her what I'm thinking she can't help me understand things. But this is really the first time I've been able to do that.

The thought of being able to talk about the violence is heady – both alluring and frightening.~

***

But although Caroline wants to *talk* about violence – it is again through enactment that violence appears. "To talk about" the violence seems an impossibility. As she wrote, "*... the perpetrators of the violence won't allow it to be talked about*". It is becoming clearer that the writing is the only way Caroline can "talk" to me.

A vignette: Enactment of the unsafe place.

Caroline stays outside on the stairway most of the session, eventually coming in on condition that I leave the door open.

VIOLET: You can't go there. It's not safe.

(It take me a while to "recognize" who is talking to me, in terms of time, space, age. I blunder about, searching. She tries to direct me:)

VIOLET: (reprimanding me): Don't you understand, it's not safe. If I tell you it's not safe why won't you listen!

T: Maybe I was led to believe it was safe, and that is the reason I came back. (I finally realize I need to enact the part of a little girl.)
VIOLET: But it's not!
T: You're saying: I really should listen to you; you're the one who knows. You really know it's not safe. You must have been there and experienced the danger, and now you want to protect me, the little girl, from being hurt.
VIOLET: Now you understand!
T: I understand you know about the danger and want to prevent other little girls from being hurt. That's very considerate of you. But, maybe you can't have control over that.
VIOLET: What are you saying?
T: You're not them – the other little girls – you are doing your best to protect them. But maybe you don't feel that that's enough. Do you think you could tell us what kind of danger is awaiting us, maybe then we'll believe you. Come in to the therapy room and we can talk about the unsafe place.

(At this point, I have returned to speak as her psychologist talking from the present into the past, both in terms of time and physical space while at the same time I am also "we": some little girl victims from the past.)

VIOLET: Will you leave the door open?
T: Yes, if it makes you feel safer.
VIOLET: (entering the clinic) You know what you are doing?
T: I do. I'm trying to work with you on knowing what's safe and what isn't.
VIOLET: So you don't know?
T: I know some of it – and with your help we'll know more. You also know a lot.
VIOLET: There's a bed!
T: It's an analytic coach. Not a bedroom, it's a therapy room where we do therapy.
VIOLET: You know that?
T: Definitely.
VIOLET: There's no one else here?
T: No one. I'll leave the door open.

(She walks in slowly, opening her eyes, suspiciously looking around corners and behind the door. She has never done this before.)

VIOLET: You won't do anything on your own?
T: I won't move from my chair
VIOLET: How can you stay safe?
T: I'm not from the past. I'm in the present and there's no danger in the present. But you experience the past as if it's *now*. You've experienced danger

in the past but it's *inside* you and attacking you, because you haven't been able to speak about it. You have a conflict about that. So you want me to know about the danger without you having *to tell* me, so you won't feel bad feelings for having told me.

Caroline assents.

We are three minutes before the end of the session and she is about to make the "hanging herself" movement on the façade of the door,

T: It is a very painful place to be … needing me to know, knowing I can't without you telling me, and fearing to tell. You've let me know today about the danger and the terror you suffered, even though you can't tell me the details … maybe with time.

***

Inside language, outside language

It seems that when I enter the trauma and speak from within – entering into the past and speaking in the present tense – I speak in definitive terms, thus giving a sense of certainty that this really happened, since it's happening now. Caroline seems to need this. When I speak from outside the enactment, then I use more careful, hesitant language like "perhaps …", "it could be that". This adds to the uncertainty Caroline feels about everything. I try to be as experience-near as I can. Also, this hesitant language of mine is expressing some deeper need to want to believe that none of these atrocities really happened.

***

Shortly after the above enactment Caroline has her first bike accident. She falls off her bike and is injured and taken to an emergency ward. Her injury requires stitches and she has a fractured bone. It is the first physical injury she has suffered in the 24 years I have known her.

Note

1 It is worth noting that she replaces Auden's "greater silences" with "dreadful silence".

Chapter 17

The cult dream

> For murder, though it have no tongue,
>   Will speak with most miraculous organ. I'll have these players
>   Play something ...
>   The play's the thing ...
>
>   Shakespeare, *Hamlet*, Act II, scene ii

Time line: the last two years of therapy

Before Caroline actually fell off her bike a lot happened both internally and externally. The rope incident continued to be re-enacted over a period of ten sessions. I found myself representing a little girl, or several little girls, while Caroline became a child who was trying to warn "us" that this is an unsafe place that we shouldn't enter. Nothing was talked about but rather happened as a present experience. Through enactments I "knew" that rape and killings were a possibility and I experienced the atmosphere of danger and fear verging on terror. Then there was an accusation that if I (her/they) entered this place, in spite of her warnings, I might be "getting a kick out of it", otherwise why didn't we heed her warnings (thus implying that the victims of the abuse were perhaps enjoying the sexual excitement.) It was unclear to me if this was perhaps her experience at the time of the abuse that she felt terribly guilty about, or that these were things said mockingly by the abusers that she was repeating. I spoke here from the "outside" (by sounding my normal voice of the therapist) saying how guilty that makes the child feel, because together with the danger she also feels excitement and erotic stimulation. Then there are sessions of her denying that she had said anything and it is obvious that she is torn between the wish to tell and the fear of revealing gruesome secrets. I recall her last nightmare of two animals tearing a little one to pieces.

I am left with the certainty that she had been in terrible danger and had witnessed endangered others while trying to warn them. Yet, never does she actually verbalize what is done.

After each *revelation* (revealing through the enactment of an atrocity of the past) and each *realization* (that this is what she experienced) there is the already familiar pendulum swing to *derealization*. If Caroline does remember what had occurred in our session, then she has no idea where the words came from, who uttered them, and there is no "ownership" of them. At other times she has no memory of what occurred, what she had said, and if I repeat her words, she expresses doubt in my judgement. Why in the world should I believe her! This tantalizing way of being with me is very stressful for both of us. I find myself in conflict about encouraging her to "own" her enactments or to let her detach herself by disassociating from such horrific events. How can I really know what is safe for her and what might be too much? What might be too overwhelming in its horror for her mind to take in and retain its "sanity"?

Fortunately, I am not the one who needs to take the responsibility over this most difficult, decision. It is Caroline herself who resolves my conflict by introducing new material. Here is an example: while I'm still perplexed as to how to relate to the derealization she has just done to the "rope" incident, I need to unexpectedly cancel a session in order to attend a funeral. Her response to my cancellation is to produce an enactment – becoming Violet who tells me that she won't tell me where things are buried and that she won't have anything to do with funerals and then accuses me (as "Mom", her mother) of burying the evidence about a little girl who could have been kept alive.

This is followed by a most "normal" conversation where Caroline tries to understand what is happening to her and to us in a brave attempt at introspection.

A vignette:

C: What do you do when something like that (yesterday's enactment) occurs and I don't know where it comes from?
T: That's a good question. I think because I've know you for a long time I relate to these events as post traumatic – as a re-enactment of the trauma from the past.
C: So if I don't know where it comes from you still have a way to relate to them?
T: Yes – I relate from my understanding from our work together of what the trauma was about.
C: You weren't part of it.
T: No, I wasn't part of it – I was someone on the "outside". I saw how you re-enacted the trauma of the past. But it's more complicated: I also had to take on the role in the drama (of the past) that you needed me to play out. You were the writer/director, and you needed to enact this play.

I was also the audience, the witness of that drama – making me both inside and outside at the same time. It was something I could do because it wasn't me who was traumatized. Does this make sense to you?

Caroline confirms that she understands.

c: Did you know you were on the inside? You weren't hurt if you were on the inside?
t: I knew I was in "the play" of the past events – transitional space. But you don't know and think you're in the past when it happens.
c: You could tell me what the play's about if I asked you?
t: Yes
c: Do you think I should know?
t: Yes – but not before you feel ready.

Some origins of constricted language and silence

In between enactments and behaviour that verges on autism there is a growing capacity to talk like two adults who can think about what happens to her – like a therapist with a neurotic patient. I always find these talks amazingly enlightening – like a beam of clear light in the ocean of darkness. Actually, this is what "the Writing Caroline" is like. I am left perplexed as to why she cannot be more like this when we are together.

A vignette

It is worth noting that Caroline always makes use of accidental outside events to let me know something important.
   Place: the clinic in my home.
   Event in reality: there are noises from upstairs in my house, sounding as though someone has perhaps dropped a plate.

c: Things are being broken.

I'm not sure what the noises are about, but share with her the information that I have a new cleaner and that I will later check and let her know if she, in fact, broke something. Caroline then reminds me of the time about ten years ago when I had *not believed her* about a detail in my car that she had pointed out to me: it had returned from the garage after a slight accident and she had told me that the licence plates had been changed. *I hadn't believed her* because they were the same number. As it turned out – she had been right and new licence plates, with the same numbers, had been fixed to the car without my being aware of it. Her attention to details, her vigilant perception of what, to me, were insignificant details shocked me. At the time I apologized for not believing her. From this memory of our common history I can now say the following:

T: Now I understand why (then) it was so important and upsetting if I didn't believe you about something you were sure about. In the past trauma – when you saw something buried, they then said you were mistaken, you were making it up. It was an attack on your capacity to think and you must be sure it doesn't happen again here with me. (Caroline eagerly nods in agreement.)

That's why it's so difficult for you to just "be", to ruminate, express thoughts freely, never mentioning feelings. Feelings change and can't be proven so you only allow yourself to talk about facts.

C: That's partly where the *constriction* comes from ... because everything gets contracted to things you can know and ... that includes thinking itself ... We never talked about the licence plates ... because you said I was mistaken ... there wasn't any way to talk about it ... So I couldn't say anything.

We have a history

1   The length of time spent feeling safe has enabled a much more coherent sense of self to develop. This allows for thinking about her experiences and not just experience overwhelming stimulation. Now she is able to tell me *about* her experience and not remain only in the realm of speechless experiencing. The disappointments and hurt she suffered in the past by my actions, or non-actions, she is now able to share with me without the fear of retaliation or disavowal.
2   I also realize how absolutely vitally important it was for her that I be open, honest and willing to share my thoughts with her. This honest sharing enables the development of trust, which in turn enhances her willingness and ability to think.

A growing awareness of her dissociated identity

A new memory of a stomach illness in childhood that she has not remembered ever before leads to the following conversation.

C: There are two people! With two histories. I don't even know the other history. Most of the time it isn't real because I have no contact with it.
T: Two people in one body, separated. (I describe to her how I felt when Violet first entered – as though she was someone else in Caroline's body.)
C: If I have two histories – the other history is real as well. Violet is like Emma[1] – they both got split off. The splitting was real!
T: You're only now understanding something we've often talked about because you are experiencing it.
C: But that's fragile. That gets lost. (whispering almost inaudibly) that's how fragile it is ... you met her? (yes). But I haven't.

T: But you know about her – and that's already a shift from when you didn't and thought I was playing tricks on your mind or making her up.
C: She doesn't want to talk to me or I don't want to talk to her? It's taken a long time to accept that she exists.
T: It involves an acknowledgement of her history that *you've needed not to know about for a long time*.
C: That need to make that split – comes from very traumatic experiences? … It doesn't happen … without a good reason?

At the door she asks me if we won't go crazy.

Danger on the way to therapy

Shortly after this session the bike accident happens. In bits and pieces Caroline recollects the chain of events: in our session she "sensed" the presence of someone from the past that "is being smothered". The next day, on the way to therapy she lost consciousness for a few seconds while approaching an intersection and flew off her bike. After the fall, she says that she thinks that the accident was a way to put a stop what was happening in the therapy.

For the first time in our history together Caroline asks me if perhaps we should stop the therapy. I am left pondering the dilemma: by continuing the analysis, is it helpful for Caroline or are we endangering her life?

Yet, before I even have time to give this dilemma enough thought a "flashback" occurs. Caroline tells me, in her own voice, that just before falling off her bike she saw what she describes as: "Like falling off the side of a *grave* …" I ask her if this reminds her of anything. Before my eyes she is transformed into Violet, covers her ears and in a pleading voice says: "I won't say anything. You have to go away … Please! Don't stay!"

After this session Caroline decides to do something that will lead to traumatizing both of us. She decides to write to her youngest sibling, the only one she trusts, about her bike accident and her thoughts that it has to do with the past, without giving any details. The next day she comes in very pale. I realize that her sister has *ignored* her email. This has no precedence. She has always been very kind and accepting of Caroline, although reporting no knowledge in her mind of abuse in the family. I suddenly feel panic in my stomach. I think: her sister must have been involved in some way. Maybe she, too, was one of the abused or the abusers and not to be trusted. I realize that Caroline has had the same thought. And on leaving the clinic, with panic in my heart, and paranoid thoughts beginning to overwhelm me, I too have a small car accident. I am on my way to my own analysis, late because of the accident and express a fear that perhaps her siblings belong to some paedophile cult, still active in their distant country and who knows – perhaps now that we are discovering their horrific activities, they will send someone to shut us up: she, me, my analyst – anyone with cause to suspect them.

A few days later she receives an email from this sister, in total disregard of Caroline's previous email to her, as though it had not been written. A few days after this Caroline has a dream.

The cult dream

> I had a dream … In a huge building and being hung upside down in the middle … like an exorcism … but it didn't work. They were talking about being able to see dark things … deep underneath. I don't know if that was inside or outside … they let me go … I had to try and escape from the building. When I woke up … it made me think of … a cult.

And after a few moments Caroline adds, "Can dreams be real?"

Two days later

Caroline seems unable to shake off this nightmare, continuing in the next session to describe the physical sensation of being swung around violently "Everything is spinning around so fast … your head is about to burst … you need to get off … can't stand straight … can't make it stop."

I think how she is describing a concrete experience of having the ground taken from under her feet. The next day Caroline has another dissociative experience outside the clinic: on leaving therapy she takes the *wrong* bus home and does not know where to get off. This has never happened before. Winnicott (1963a) describes disorientation in space as being part of a catastrophic event. Caroline has never gotten lost, been late, come to the wrong clinic. It seemed extremely significant and obviously related to the terror aroused by the cult dream that we both suspected might be representing a memory of some real experience from the past. I knew how important for Caroline was the stability of Place. I recalled something she had said many years earlier when much of the therapy was under the table: "I can't know who I am if I don't know where I am." Then, she had needed to feel the solid ground under her body by lying on the floor in order to feel safe. But it had been years since she had come out from under the coffee table.

I think of how I myself dissociated when I had the car accident. I feel myself getting dizzy thinking about her question "Can dreams be real?" and I share with her my thought that it is hard for her to know if her dream was: "only a dream" or a dream representing Caroline's experience in the past. I wonder to myself if it is not time that we both "get off" this rollercoaster and stop this analysis, which is becoming dangerous – not only to her physically but to my mental balance as well. Often, I feel myself taken over by this intensive involvement. I feel so grateful that I have my own analysis to go to – a place to rest, to help differentiate inside from outside, a place of safety and acceptance.

I come in contact with a deep appreciation that I can know the difference between daydreaming, dreaming and being awake. I have never been strung up on a rope and sent spinning until I don't know if it's me or the world around me that is going crazy. And I think – but what about Caroline? Because for her, analysis itself is becoming an unsafe place.

But Caroline is still determined to continue – to share with me what she is going through. As always, it is she who takes responsibility for the continuation of the therapy, and I try to let myself be used as an object, in the Winnicott sense, to the best of my ability.

Violence destroys language

A vignette

After an especially long silence,

C: If it's real it can't be talked about – it's too much. ... If it's not real ... it also can't be talked about ... So it can't be talked about either way ... but it can't be ignored either.
T: Maybe we can relate to it as: putting it aside in a potential space; not to be decided about now, yet not buried, as you did in the past.
C: It makes it worse because ... the moment I start talking about it ... something ... wipes out the whole issue ... It's like all the work that we did get to ... is gone. It's wiped out and ... it just goes up in smoke.
T: So there is a violent force inside you that the minute we speak about *it* starts to work against us, against our work and you want to save us.

Caroline nods in agreement.

(I think to myself: for her if the only important thing is "our work" and that is being destroyed by her mind, what is left? Our relationship, my caring and wanting for her to suffer less. But does she know this? Does it matter to her?)

T: I do believe that you and I together can be stronger than this violence inside you, and we'll find a way to beat it. We have gone through so much, so many dead ends we've come out of, I believe we'll find a way.

And the next day

C: So there is violence!

I relate to the violence as being in response to my vacation, which must feel to her like a violent act on my behalf. Last time she fell off the bike – she inflicted physical violence on herself; this time the violence against her mind includes annihilating me and our mutual work.

C: I need you to know that violence is real ... and I need you to know that it really is violent ... I need you to know that the danger is so serious ... I need you to really know that ... But then if it's here (in the room) like that ... it's too much.
T: Something feels too much – too much to communicate. That's when the violence destroys the language. You know Caroline, I can never experience and know violence like what you went through. Or like in that hospital dream where there was a boy who did not speak – just like you – but you knew he had experienced the same as you did.

On hearing this, Caroline cries and cries and I wonder if I should share with her how at times, vicariously I experience through my tears, helplessness and occasional dissociation a tiny part of her suffering.

C: And she didn't stay ... I didn't want it to hurt her. She went away ... she left me on my own ... and I made her go.
T: You made her go and then you were left *all alone*. That's punishment enough isn't it? A life sentence ...

***

The unbearable guilt from cruelty

As always, I learn a lot through my own countertransference experience. Here, in reverie I realize that I am feeling hate and resentment at her for making me feel so bad. She has just told me on my return from holiday how she has not been able to stop the spinning experience in her head the whole time I was away and has now returned to sitting on the floor. I feel so guilty for leaving her. It takes me a while to accept that yes, when I leave her, she is left alone with all this unbearable pain and it is cruel to her. I think: to feel cruel to another human being is very painful. I don't want to feel this. I'd rather blame her for causing *my* suffering. Then I think about the kind of suffering she had to endure. She couldn't contain the suffering if she had been made to kill someone! The pain of *unbearable guilt* created by cruelty of this degree to another human being.

At this point, I have my own "flashback" of a time, not so long ago, when there was a question of unclarity of memory as to who had written "fuck" all over that poor little doll. And that I had repressed that it was *I* who had done it, at her command. And I tell her how even memory can be affected when one feels extreme guilt about something one "by nature" does not want to do yet is forced to participate in. I repressed the memory of writing "fuck" all over the doll. I had not wanted to do it. I felt coerced. In a similar way but to a far more severe degree, she, Caroline, had needed to split her mind and create another person to contain the horrors. I recall a conversation we once had about Primo Levi – wondering what had caused his suicide. I think how I have often wondered if the suicide of many Holocaust survivors, years after the event, was not caused by such guilt – being made to be inhuman.

Then came the time when I needed to, again, cancel two sessions, but pre-planned. I find that Caroline's response to my absence, always having been very difficult, has now become even more severe. Both in the session before I leave and the session after my return, the deadness of Caroline's silence is far more than a reproof – it feels like a violent attack on me. I do not experience it as something soft like a puff of smoke but as an "active deadening". It feels unbearable and infuriating. I fear that my rage could threaten my ability to be empathic to her and I realize that she is creating a chasm between us. I already know from experience that this is a defence she uses before something more terrible will be acted out. When I say something to try and arouse her to some response she eventually says accusingly: "You can just walk away from something like that."

She repeats this sentence. "You can just walk away from something like that."

Over the course of time, I have come to learn that if she repeats a sentence it is a sign that she is letting me know something very important. No word is ever wasted in her speech. And then I have a visual picture of her leaving a dead thing in my lap and walking away. I recall how she had thrown that abused doll so cruelly into the wastepaper basket those many years ago and walked out on us. I "realize" that she wants me to know that in her past – not only had she been abandoned but *she* had walked away from some poor victim. I say something of this to her and then she remarkably "solves" that long lost mystery (see Chapter 2 for the full description of this) from years ago when she had left her blue paper clip in Auschwitz and had returned to therapy with a red one. She now tells me that she had to leave something *there* from here – *from our therapy*.

C: I didn't just walk away. I left my paper clips ... they were the one thing I didn't want to lose. They were from *here*.

I realize she is letting me know how precious therapy has been for her, as it was already then. I knew this from her telling me that she had bought the owl to embroider with the commencement of therapy. But these moments of actually sharing this with me were so rare. Her need to be able to tell me about *her* Holocaust was so strong from the beginning but then she had no way. She could only use physical space by the act of placing of an object: moving a thing from here to there. And to hope that I would notice and know. It had taken her 20 years to find the words with which to tell me. I understand now that the violent deadness I had been made to experience was the only way she had of communicating to me that atmosphere of violence and death to which she had been subjected.

A captive within a closed circle

I am about to take a week's vacation and Caroline gives me a book to read, *Room* (a 2010 novel by Irish–Canadian author Emma Donoghue, which in 2015 was made into an Oscar winning movie). The book is about an adolescent girl who was abducted and held prisoner in a closed room for many years by her abductor, a perverted man. He rapes her. She gives birth to a boy whom she brings up, the best way she can, in this closed room until he is five. She then manages to escape. Much of the story is told from the perspective of this boy. The first part of the book describes how the boy's whole understanding of reality is dependent on his mother, being closed off from the external world. She often makes up stories about reality so as to make life more optimistic and interesting for him. It is obvious in the book that the mother is a caring, heroic figure.

When I ask Caroline what was specifically significant in the book that was relevant for us here Caroline replies, "The boy believed the mother because he had no way of knowing what was real on the outside. *And she lied to him.*"

What I understand from her conclusion is that Caroline is telling me how precarious a child's grasp on reality can be and how dependent he is on his caretakers. More specifically, she is speaking to me of her dependence on me in the present, and that she experiences me as unreliable. After interpreting this to her Caroline lets me know how difficult it is for her to disagree with me but she knows she does not want to pretend to agree, as she had with her mother. The "disagreement" is about whether it is safe to continue with the therapy where she may discover truths too dangerous for her to know. Within myself, I also cannot be certain that this process will not be dangerous. She then reminds me of the first time I took her to see a psychiatrist; it was ten years previously, and he had prescribed medication for depression.

C: Are blackouts (when Caroline fell off her bike) more severe than getting depressed?
T: Yes.
C: So next time might get worse?
T: The blackout made you fall off your bike. You could have been killed by another car or the fall itself.

Within myself, I am feeling desperate – I have no idea what to do. Should I tell Caroline to stop therapy or not? She, in response to my helplessness, suggests we make an appointment with the psychiatrist and I agree, promising to arrange this for next time. But then I have second thoughts about the wisdom of doing this, doubting that increasing medication, nor anything from the *outside* can really provide the solution.

The following is Caroline's report of what happened next, in her own written words. For a moment, Caroline's writing self has returned to relate to the pressing question of whether we should pursue looking for Violet – pursue with the therapy. It seems in this critical time of uncertainty the Writing Caroline has "been mobilized" to take charge in some way.

> ~Tova suggested that, in contrast to physiotherapy, where there are precise exercises to get, say, a frozen shoulder moving again,[2] psychotherapy has no such rules. I asked her if Dr. T would know how to help and she agreed to ask him if we could make an appointment. The following day she said she had found herself wondering what it was she was going to tell him – the reason for seeing him now. I said that if it was fear that stopped me getting close to the inside, then he could help with the medication and that while I'm not sure what it signifies, he's associated with the hospital.[3]
>
> Tova said that it was as though I felt that we (she and I) were in a bubble, the two of us inside a locked circle, and that I needed someone outside to know that we weren't making things up – that the whole therapy wasn't just some fantasy I'd fabricated. Like in *Room*, it was like living in a closed un-reality.
>
> That made a whole lot of sense to me: we're locked inside a bubble of not knowing if the past is real (what actually happened); Tova's locked outside of me; I'm locked outside inside myself; inside myself is locked so firmly that I don't even know if it exists. I might be making up the whole thing – including the existence of an inside. If nothing happened in the past, then I'm not missing an inside – I'm looking for something which doesn't exist.
>
> I need Tova to be with the emptiness/being locked out of the inside/not knowing if it exists. At least I know what that is, know that that's real, can identify it as a feeling.~

The piercing clarity and insight and the depth of perception in this text is overwhelming for me. I find it the clearest description both of Caroline's genius and closeness to the danger of becoming insane.

Notes

1 Emma was the dissociated abused little girl in the book *Me & Emma*.
2 Caroline was at this time receiving physiotherapy for the shoulder injury from the bike fall.
3 Many years earlier, it had been Dr T. who had agreed to hospitalize her in his psychiatric unit in a large hospital when I went away for a long vacation.

Chapter 18

Alice in Horrorland

Timeline: the last two years in therapy

A change in imagery

There has been a change in Caroline's internal world. I can "see" it in the change of imagery she uses. If in the past to describe her experiences kinaesthetic imagery dominated: falling, fading, spinning ... I now notice that the imagery is becoming more visual: a shadow, a balloon, the book *Room*, circles containing circles. I think to myself that *internal space* is developing and this is allowing for and making room for an internal mental life. Caroline's nascent internal mental life might have a chance of surviving the attacks even if they too are from within. Hopefully, we are on the way for memory to have a Place to be in – an internal home.

Caroline is becoming more curious. She wants to understand why she had the blackout that led to her dangerous falling off her bike. She knows that she herself caused it. But having no answers is part of the experience of the emptiness of her inside. I say something about knowing that she has always tried to keep the inside and the outside completely separate and I think this is because on the inside it gets so confusing. The word "confusing" was exact for her.

A vignette

C: Separating the inside from outside ... comes from ... the need to have control
T: You need to control to feel safe; you need there to be no changes, no surprises.
C: Because if it's not safe ... I don't know what's inside and what's outside ... I don't know when something actually happened on the ... outside.
T: I believe extreme anxiety disrupts your ability to know and then you are unable to think.

C: So control allows for thinking?
T: For you – yes. But one often does not have much control over what happens on the outside – external noises for instance.

Researching the origin of emptiness

The next day Caroline comes in looking like someone on a serious mission – she is trying to learn about the origin of thinking. She wants us to continue, but very slowly.

C: (very slowly but clearly): The emptiness comes from not knowing, and that comes from not being able to think?
T: Yes, that's true ...
C: But change ... the lack of control is precisely because things change, *people change*. You think you know what they are but you don't, because one minute they are one thing and the next ... the change is precisely what causes the confusion. It's not just because anxiety stops the thinking but because things change as well. You can't think straight when things don't stay the same ... It's also the things that are not meant to change. It's scary because they are not meant to change ... Do you understand?

(I understand that she is telling me that if the outside is overwhelming and unpredictable, no wonder there is internal anxiety. And I wonder if she experienced her parents as suddenly changing their identity.)

T: Yes. When people around you change suddenly, unexpectedly, in a way you weren't prepared for, it is very frightening.
C: So control ... is a way ... to survive? If that's the case, then ... trying to get closer to the emptiness ... to be inside ... can interfere with the functioning ... or the survival?

I am at a loss for words.

***

After the weekend continuation is maintained. She wants to know if there might be other reasons for having difficulty in thinking – perhaps being born with a mental impairment – being stupid for instance?

T: (I am reluctant to agree): You got through school, several university degrees and graduated. That's from the past. Here in present time – in your writing you show you have an ability for excellent thinking, also here with me.

C: We need to cover all possibilities of where the not thinking comes from. No? There's the idea that I'm stupid like the idea of being crazy. They're both easier than the alternative.

And the next day:

C: So the blackout was an extreme form of anxiety?
T: I think so. A shutdown so as not to know.
C: Not being able to think is a symptom of PTSD?
T: Sometimes.
C: So emptiness comes from not being able to think?
T: Not only. You often *are* able to think here. I know that. It's not being able to hold onto what you do think and know that creates the emptiness. It evaporates and you are left empty on the inside. We have seen that many times here.
C: You said the other day that I have known you for a long time. But it's not on the inside. I can tell you things that have happened here and everything that you have said – but it's on a screen. So where does that come from?

As Caroline says this, I think to myself – it's like a balloon, having no centre. I have been holding onto the string (by functioning as her memory and holding on to the continuation) to prevent the balloon from flying off into infinite space, but what is the point if she cannot find an inner sense of having her own centre? I recall her saying many years ago that she wanted to be a spectator of life.[1] So this is what she meant! If she keeps me locked out, distanced as an unreal TV figure on her screen (as in the book *Room*) without allowing me any entry, this will not change. Internalization does not seem to be occurring. All I say is that I think this is to do with her relationship with her mother.

The next day, Caroline arrives in an emotional tumult. She does not want us to talk about her mother. It is a taboo. But she wants to continue researching the source of the emptiness. I tell her we are in a vicious cycle since the two are connected. Hesitantly, but with intent and curiosity, she allows me to relate my thoughts of this link to her.

I create a narrative of Caroline's past. In it I describe her early relationship with her mother, mainly relating to the narcissistic mother who is so self-involved with her own pains that she is completely insensitive to her daughter's needs. She needs her daughter to be *her* listener. The little girl Caroline develops a pretending mode of being mother's good little helper, yet feeling false and guilty about her insincerity. I am very careful not to describe the horrors that came up in the enactments, such as the imprisoned children, the rope, the possibility of a cult. It's as though I fear overwhelming her with such accusations about her mother. I also give a transference interpretation saying that often I am seen like a mother figure who Caroline fears might be dangerous, so my words are not taken in. And if they are they are quickly evacuated in some way, disappearing and leaving her empty. I am left on an external screen, like in the photo of the two of us she keeps as a screensaver on her computer.

I have been speaking very softly, like a good mother telling her child a bedtime story, hoping not to arouse anxiety.

While I speak, Caroline is very attentive, staring and quiet, and I think that perhaps she is "taking me in". I am left wondering how this will affect her. It is the first time I have "dared" make a generative interpretation. She has "let me in" after checking with me if it's safe. Will she get lost in my words, experience them as violent, lose her self? I think something made me feel she was able to hear it now. It is her curiosity about her inside self that is new. Until now her curiosity was mainly suspiciousness oriented outwards. As I write this I am reminded of the years where it was taboo to mention the word *want* in our relationship.

The next day I am greeted with Caroline in her paranoid mode, accusing me: "Why are you messing with my head? What are you trying to do?"

Then I notice that she has had her head shaven. She is back to wanting to physically be rid of what is stirring in her mind. But before leaving, slightly calmed she says: "It was helpful to talk about the emptiness, to know where it comes from. It makes sense. But this isn't helpful." And she tells me that she now feels just like she did just before the bike accident. (Nine months have passed since then.) We cannot talk about her mother and we cannot ignore her either. Another deadlock.

Alice in Horrorland

I open the session by saying how sorry I am that what I had said about her mother had been so disturbing for her.

C: What happened when Alice fell down the hole? She didn't understand anything.

I am a bit taken by surprise, and it takes me a minute to catch on that she is referring to *Alice in Wonderland*. I first relate to her in a somewhat "playful" way, saying something about her curiosity and that this is more hopeful than the Humpty Dumpty ending. But I quickly understand I am off track.

C: The hole is full of confusion and violence. Alice doesn't know where she is. Doesn't know what size she is. She keeps frightening everybody off by talking about a cat. Nearly drowns them all because she cries so much. And then she has to face the violence. The queen wants her head off. Everyone attacks the duchess and the baby. She falls down this long hole.

That's what she finds. That's where she ends up. So why are we doing this?

T: Alice woke up from her experience and she knew she awoke. Here we are trying to find a way to help you *know* – not that it was a dream – but that it comes from the past, is separate from the present. That helps you know that it's safe now. Maybe the long black hole of not knowing all the violence that preceded the fall – the queen being so violent, the duchess and the baby being so dependent on her – maybe all this is too much to know.

Here Caroline nods in agreement, letting me know in this way that I am on the right track. I experience both relief and fear. Relief that I have been able to find her again and fear of the unknown. What will happen to us when I accompany her in her fall – into the world of the Mad Hatter. After all, we are not playing at telling a children's story.

The following day I forget to adjust the lighting the way she is used to it and the room is quite dark. The minute we enter I realize this and quickly turn on the lights. But soon I realize that in the slight gap of darkness, Caroline has "disappeared" and so my interchange is with a frightened Violet and the session really does sound like straight out of the Mad Hatter's tea party – too mad to repeat here.

In retrospect, I wonder if my unconscious is not aware, better than "me" that we can go a little faster and I should not be so afraid. And perhaps it is my own unconscious that has thus "tricked" me into forgetting to put the lights on. It is from this little "accident" that I am witness to an impressive developmental step in Caroline's mental functioning. I shall give the vignette in full:

A vignette: a developing sense of self

Two hours after the above session Caroline sends me an email titled:

Hole

> So it's not just not knowing because of not being able to think (because everything disappears) that causes the emptiness – it's also because *I'm not there*. I don't know things not just because they disappear but because *I* disappear. *I* fall into the hole. *I'm* not inside myself.

I open the hour by commenting that I see her email as indicating something encouraging since it means there is *awareness of herself as disappearing*. This is very different from Violet appearing without Caroline being aware of it and needing me to tell her about it.

C: Like putting things together so that I can know that they are separate?
T: Yes.

(I am not sure I quite understand the paradox she is telling me about but feeling sure that she is right.)

C: To find a way to be inside, but to stop the inside from being the hole.
T: That's what we are trying to do.
C: Can you explain the paradox again?

I try to describe it, with some difficulty, and I say that that is the problem with paradoxes:

T: If there is a whole person, an "*I*", then you can know that you have holes even though you may not know what's in the holes. You can know that past and present are separate. If there is no "*I*" there is no one there to do the separating. So when the past comes it takes over the present and becomes the present. Paradoxes are so difficult to explain, aren't they!.
C: But the fact that it's difficult to explain doesn't mean that it doesn't make sense?
T: No. It's a critical difference isn't it? A difference between deep understanding and being mad.
C: Do you find it difficult to understand?
T: Not the experience. What's difficult is putting the understanding / intuitive knowing, into words that communicate. That's the difficulty.

Caroline nods in agreement. After a while she says: So it's a *sense of self* that makes the knowing possible? We're not talking about something that's simple or easy ... but we can work on understanding it ... yeh?

T: I think we've been doing that all this time. It just couldn't be formulated earlier.
C: And if it gets lost it'll come back?
T: It will, because for one: you're not alone here. I'm here to hold it together with you. And two, if you *know* you fall down a hole, *that's knowing a lot*.

Caroline agrees, looking a bit amazed. At the door she thanks me over and over. I am moved by the whole experience we have just been through and respond by saying: "Caroline – this is a joint venture so I thank you for giving me an opportunity to be part of this."

***

Thoughts about *Alice in Wonderland*

In retrospect, I think Caroline used Alice to show me how mad she was feeling. I think the reason for her despair was that she had experienced me, with my very moderate narrative depleted of the violence, as being similar to her parents denying that the violence she knew really happened. To hear her therapist resembling the deceptive parents must have aroused terror. I have thought about why I did not include the violence in this narrative. After all, I had done so in the past. I think that for me, too, really accepting that her mother was involved in the atrocities was too difficult to say out loud.

Note

1 See Chapter 1 of this book: "I don't want to participate in living. I want to be a spectator of life."

Chapter 19

The mysterious garden

> I am in a scenario where I know nothing of the text, yet I act it out perfectly.
> Françoise Davoine, *The Character of Madness in the Talking Cure* (2007)

Timeline: a year before the end of therapy

Caroline enters excited and announces:

> Something happened yesterday which has never happened before. Anne was watching TV in another room and I heard someone say, *"We'll just put it in a bag"*. And it took me back to the *garden* but not to *then*, to when I went to see it lately.

Caroline is not the only one to feel excited. I find myself experiencing something close to elation. Never before has she brought in a mental thought – a report of an association she has had the previous day. Until now, only facts – the most tangible, concrete thoughts – which have been aroused in real time, present time, or words in written form have been our material. This is evidence of the loosening up of the rigid organization of her dissociated mind. Links can be made and even remembered!

We both experience her observation as somewhat "mind-blowing". We find ourselves "researching" the meaning of this thought and more importantly – trying to find out what has made the birth of this first associative thinking possible.

Over a few sessions it becomes possible to summarize the conditions that led to Caroline being able to "sustain a thought" and tell it to me. The understanding came about slowly by her obsessively trying to comprehend what exactly happened that led to her thoughts. She wanted the steps summarized – so as to validate what had happened before all would once again be lost. The following summary is the step by step outcome of our combined effort:

T: You knew you didn't imagine it. (Anne was there as a witness.)

C: It (the TV comment) wasn't for long, and it wasn't frontal. It wasn't direct. I just heard it.
C: There was space to think about it.
T: You knew you would be believed so you retained the memory of it long enough to tell me the next day.

I understand that my sense of elation comes from having experienced a "meeting of minds" after so much struggling. It is the feeling, even if just fleetingly, that together there is a life force that has a chance of overcoming the overwhelming sense of death and destruction in this long analysis. A "small thought" arousing a great feeling.

The comment heard on the TV linked up in her mind to the persecutory statement spoken by her mother in her humiliating attitude towards her. She recalled the way her mother answered "Go put it in the bath" to her naive questions in childhood: "Where shall I put it?" (see Chapter 1). There was a story behind it that now was unravelling. The words on TV, "We'll just put it in a bag", linking up with this memory led her back to the memory of her recent visit to her home town where she had gone to look at the garden of her childhood home, to see if there were any signs that something (someone) had been buried there.

To both of us this associative link was clear as to its implications. Nothing needed to be said more specifically. But since the words from the TV related to Mom – the destructive force, the attack on linking (Bion, 1959) literally, was soon to come. But before the darkness was to descend on us (as it invariably did) – there was an opening – a space illuminated that revealed some important mother–daughter experiences. They developed from an integration between our understanding as to how thinking is made possible and the understanding that was becoming more clear, that for Caroline, being in her mother's presence paralyzed her capacity to think.

Here is how it happened:

I had summarized the conditions that reinforced associative thinking:

T: I think the conditions here have helped you know that what you have experienced is real. Sharing your experiences and knowing that I would believe you, have helped to establish a place for memory. And the memory could now be available to bring here the next day. If you had not told me, and if it had stayed as a thought in the closed space of your mind, after a while it may have turned into a doubt if it had happened or not.

As I say this I know that Caroline can hear me talking also to the little girl of the past who had no one to tell and with time, stopped thinking so as to avoid facing the continual doubting of the validity of her experiences.

Caroline nods in agreement and says, "So the therapy can become a transitional space. Most of the time it's not." (We had often looked for "a transitional space" when the concrete was overwhelming. Caroline, as mentioned, was knowledgeable of Winnicott's writings.)

I find myself speculating if what she is expressing in this way is that because of her awareness of my separateness from her, and thus being deprived of the omnipotent control, arouses her alert diligence and sense of fear that she may be attacked, criticized or humiliated by the "other". This emotional state prevents having an inner space for more relaxed associative thinking when she is in the presence of an other. Hearing the comment on TV when alone in an adjacent room enabled her to have the freedom to think. Fortunately, I have become an internalized good object that she knows she can now share her association with. And I say:

T: When you heard those words on TV you had conditions that weren't threatening and you wanted to share your thoughts with me.
C: Does it go with what you said about Mom and the pain?

I am a little surprised at what Caroline had just said. I thought talking about Mom was taboo. But if she is inviting me to do so, then I must trust her judgment. I narrate what is already familiar – how she wanted to help Mom out by listening to her, because Mom suffered from Dad's uncommunicativeness. Caroline wanted to be a good little girl and was all attentive to Mom when she talked endlessly about her physical ailments.

C: And that blocked out all other things. All the things that got said that I wasn't supposed to remember.
T: Yes. And I remember how, when I had expressed the thought that because you were very dependent on your mum and needed her, it was very difficult to contain the feelings that her talking upset you. You would become very angry at me and say, "How can you say such things about her!" Then we couldn't talk about it anymore.

Here, as I speak, *this gets re-enacted again.* Caroline starts to cringe, puts her head in agony into the cushion she is holding and then starts scratching herself.

T: Right now there is again a feeling of no space. You wanted to hear me, hoping it would not be so frontal, so direct and now it feels like an attack and you are afraid.

While I say those words Caroline continues to gesticulate with her arm movements of "fight or flight". Her hands are fisted, up in the air, turned against herself, as though she is about to attack herself.

But she suddenly pulls herself together, struggling to continue and sends words out to me from under the couch – words for me to record, live, to be a witness to her experiences from the past that are now threatening to drag her into the pit of oblivion. I feel she is fighting for her sanity and I offer my writing pen as the only protection that I have to offer. She dictates, slowly – in agony:

C: *Her* pain taking over everything ... *She* was the one hurting ... and that took everything else away ... Like the black hole that sucks in everything else, ... blanks everything else out ... all the other things that hurt ... before they get sucked into ... a void ... that's on the outside. You can see ... you can see she can't walk or do things ... and that swallows up all ... everything else that happened ... I'd sit and ... mask it.
T: Your pain would be swallowed up by her talking about her pain – a pain that could be seen because of her arthritis.
C: And then the inside is empty – just because ... everything gets sucked into the black ...

By the following day this whole session has been *obliterated* from her mind. She turns on me with bristling hostility:

C: What (the hell) are you trying to do?
T: I'm trying to *connect* with yesterday – but it doesn't sound like you are with me. It sounds like you are seeing me as attacking you. Maybe you've fallen into the black hole again where you can't make sense of anything.

Caroline nods in agreement.

T: Yesterday you could talk *about it*, the black hole. Today you are *back inside it*.

***

The next week all is lost again. Nothing makes sense. Caroline even cancels a session because of an emergency eye problem and a doctor's appointment. This reminds me of her last cancelation – almost a year ago, when she called from the emergency ward after having fallen off her bike and injured herself. On both occasions, her roommate, Anne, had gone overseas to visit her family and she was left alone, with only me for company. I think how strong is the psychotic transference from the mother "drowning her in words" to my "talking cure". She fears being alone with me when there is no third person close by in outside reality. When she was young she had her father to go to for refuge from this overwhelming mother, but that refuge held other dangers.

Anne returns and with her return Caroline "returns" to therapy. She now seems determined to reveal and to discover more. Again – this happens through enactment. When she does not knock on the door I look for her and she is not in her usual "hiding place" in the corner of the corridor. Rather, she seems to be going towards the garden, wanting me to follow. This is new. But I insist she enters the therapy room. She enters reluctantly, sits on the floor, but with her back towards me, hiding her face.

T: Today is especially difficult for you. Caroline starts to suddenly undo her shoelaces and I become strict about not allowing her to do this, knowing it means undressing.
T: Why are you undressing?
C: (accusingly) Why are you acting as thought you don't know?
T: You want to give them your body to stop them killing you. You saw someone killed and you're afraid. I won't let them kill you.
C: How can you do that?

Caroline is now transformed into Violet of the past and we find ourselves enacting a horrific scene where I am in the role of a mother being helped by her daughter *to bury* the remains of .... someone in a *grave* made in the *garden*. In this role I threaten her that nothing should be said and that if she behaves like mummy's good little girl, all will be well; she will not be hurt anymore, nor killed like the others. The session ends with my saying – still in the role of the mother: "I'll protect you. I'll be a good mummy. You just be a good little girl and forget everything."

VIOLET: (obediently): Nothing happened?
T: (as Mom): Nothing the recent flash back of falling into a grave just before her bike accident happened.

She leaves, head down, looking desolate and after her exit I notice that she has not taken the monthly receipt that I had left for her on the table. She has never left it behind. I am a little panicked – did she not return into her adult self before leaving?

***

After this enactment I feel quite traumatized. How had I been transformed to the extent where here I was re-enacting the part of a cruel, murderess mother so easily. My tone had even played the part to perfection. I am so distraught that I turn to a colleague who has experience with PTSD and DID patients and tell him what had happened. He is not sure it had been wise of me to have taken on the part of the *abuser* in the enactment. I understood then how much I had acted out of intuition in a trance-like state that I was drawn into. How wise this was was yet to be known.

It is only after my colleague applies some relaxation techniques that I am able to return to myself. And then I try to analyze what happened to me. I realize I had been "activated" after I had forbidden her to undress in the session (something she had not tried to do for a very long time) and in response to my asking: "Why are you undressing?" She had responded angrily. "Why are you acting as though you don't know?"

This sentence was like a catalyst – it encouraged me to *dare* "put the pieces together" for her. For over ten years she had been dropping clues about sordid things to do with the *garden*: from wanting to bury the hanging doll in the garden of my clinic, then insisting I had killed my dog and buried him in my garden, the flashback she recalled having just before the blackout that led to her fall off the bike. And the most recent association to the T.V comment had been to her search for a grave in the garden of her childhood. And today she had, on the outside, wanted me to follow her to the back garden of the clinic.

I realize now, as I have many times before, that Caroline cannot be the one who actually says out loud the words about the killing. She can only give me the clues but it is I who have to say them.

Is it the result of a deep ingrained fear resulting from real or imagined threats, that if she told she would be killed? Probably. She has often dissociated after having revealed scraps of information as Violet, saying, "I didn't say anything" or when she at times realized she had been "absent" in a session she would ask if she had said anything, acting fearful for her life. I was beginning to realize that these dissociations were always after something to do with her mother's involvement had been revealed.

These cumulative experiences had led me to act out the role of the threatening parent who imposes secrecy and forgetting on her mind. It was as though all the bits and pieces had fallen into place. Humpty Dumpty was coming together again, at least in my mind. And it was my task to share this knowledge with her. Or at least, so I believed.

Part III

From inside to outside: choosing life

Part III

From inside to outside: choosing life

Chapter 20

Thou shalt not tell

> As long as I play dead I don't have to worry about being killed. But if I'm not dead I can be killed.
>
> Caroline to her therapist

Timeline: the last year

It is becoming clear that in her internal world there is a growing development of Caroline's self-awareness that she shifts between different self states (Van der Hart et al., 2006) and while she is in the persona mode in the therapy room with me, her adult self of the present disappears. However, if this movement had been mostly confined and contained in the safety of the transitional space of the therapy, now there began to be a "spilling over" into the outside world. Her first bicycle accident, and then the disorientation that led her to get on the wrong bus were signs of real danger to her physical survival.

The next two chapters will describe some of the process that eventually will lead to the decision to end the therapy so as to prevent her real death.

***

For a brief moment, after two years of "disappearance", Caroline is able to write again. She brings me a description of her inner experience of being dissociated:

> ~I can know *about* things but don't know them. I can tell Tova things but don't know where they come from because that's when Violet was there in the past. I'd understood them somehow (not seen them, but heard about them in some way) but hadn't experienced them – only knew about them from/through a "replay".[1]~

Reading this, it seems as though there *is* communication between the dissociated parts of herself that Caroline is aware of at some strata of consciousness. But this still leaves her with the disturbing feeling of de-realization. On the other hand, I find that *I* experience very intense feelings most of the time while with her. *There is a split between us* in the way present reality is experienced: she experiences life as "a replay on a screen" and I am the one with strong, alive feelings.

From such intense feelings of mine a new insight is sometimes born.

A vignette: a split: I know and you don't

Caroline sits silently, looking at me in pain. I say something that isn't particularly helpful. Eventually, after 20 minutes, as though "throwing me a bone" so I will stop being irritated by her silence, she says something that seems unrelated to anything.

c: Why do you want a dog?

I am at a loss and say so, expressing my helplessness at her choosing to join the "forces of silence, the forces of death" after having been a partner to trying to put the pieces together.

c: It's just the opposite. That's the only way that maybe it's possible to survive. If the threat was: *death* if I said anything, told anyone – then not saying, not telling anything – is the way *to stay alive.*

She cries and at the same time looks into my eyes imploring me to find a way to help her come out of this overwhelming stalemate.

T: It's so difficult. For over 30 years you have lived away from your country yet you still feel the danger and it's threatening from the inside but feels like the threat is on the outside.
c: (begging for reassurance) You're trying to help … to stop that happening?

***

Two days later I find myself again so exasperated – there have been more understandings – but it as though I am talking to myself. I even feel clever at times about the creative links I make for her and then I realize that I am the only one making links, although she is the one who subtly gave me hints enabling me to do this. This realization and her looking at me as though she has no idea what I'm talking about, leads me to say:

T: You need *me* to be able to connect, make sense of things, but it seems I am not to expect *you* to make sense. There is a division here, a split: *I* know and *you* don't.

Caroline assents.

I understand today, suddenly with clear insight, that this is the set-up: when I hold the meaning, I am the one who understands, knows things, then she is the one who knows nothing – is mad or simple-minded. This is her dissociated state.

Yet, in spite of my exasperation or perhaps because of it, her pain reaches me. I know that she really does want my help, that I must not give up on her. So after telling her that her *knowing* that she splits reality is in itself an accomplishment, I add, resorting to the language of fairy tale:

> Hansel and Gretel left a trail to make a path in the woods so that they could find the way back home after their parents tried to be rid of them. At first they failed, using breadcrumbs which the birds ate, but later they learnt better ways, like leaving a trail of pebbles so they could find the way back home.

I know that Caroline understands the metaphor as a way that describes my belief that with time, practice and motivation she, too, will be able to hold onto the different parts of her mind. I want her to know that I am using her trail of pebbles to try and find her in the dense forest of madness in order to bring her home to sanity. But as often in this unprecedented therapeutic encounter, what I believe and what actually happens did not necessarily coincide.

(An afternote: only much later do I realize that I have distorted the original fairytail and reversed the order of breadcrumbs and pebbles. It seems in my unconscious I needed to feel optimistic and perhaps not have a" bad witch" constantly threatening the happy end that I needed to believe in.[2])

***

We are in a different psychological place now. We both know from the "evidence" gathered slowly and meticulously over the years, that Caroline's mother not only knew about the atrocities **but was an active participant**. The enactment of the burial in the garden seemed to have been the final piece needed to put Humpty Dumpty together again. But this knowledge, no longer deniable, no longer hidden from her, becomes unbearable. It becomes a threat to her very existence. This soon gets acted out in two very dramatic ways, both extremely frightening.

1. Caroline starts having more frequent bicycle accidents and is physically injured.
2. She becomes, *in vivo*, in front of my eyes, a very frightening and threatening *man*. She turns into her father who forbids the mother's exposure!

And I am a witness.

A vignette: a barking dog

My dog has been barking and she shows visible annoyance. I say that this is the only way that my new dog can let me know about her fear at a stranger passing because she has no words.

C: Does Violet have words?
T: Yes. When she felt safe she could tell me … but she is afraid of you – that she doesn't have your permission to tell.
C: So she needs to talk?
T: She can only do that if she knows you won't hurt her or hate her.
C: But she knocks me out. She makes me not be here!
T: Yes, because she fears you. You're bigger – more powerful – so she "puts you to sleep" so you won't hurt her. We have to find a peaceful way to let her speak.

Caroline here is telling me of some recognition of her dissociated state. The "knocked out" experience is when her experiencing self is contained in the Violet persona and Caroline cannot connect with her. For her (Caroline) she (Violet) is experienced as a separate person rather than as a part of herself.

I then need to reprimand my dog quite assertively in an attempt to stop her barking. Caroline becomes frightened. My potential anger is a threat. For her, any anger becomes a fear of death. I share with her my memory that she thought I had killed and buried my last dog in my garden. She goes blank, suddenly understanding nothing I am saying. She has fallen down the hole again. I have lost her. Just mentioning anger has turned it into a demolishing force.

In the next session she says her head is spinning and she can't remember the previous session. I say that the spinning is a way to be able *not* to think.

C: It's not just not being able to think – it has an image that goes with it: it's spinning because something is wrong – someone is being swung …have you ever seen children swinging a cat around by its tail? (becoming frightened) … but I can't talk about it.

Caroline becomes Violet, blocking her ears, rocking then "comes to" and looking bewildered asks me: "Where did you go?" then accusingly "What are you trying to do?" I ask her if she was ever strung up and spun around on a rope. She crawls under the couch to hide from me and I speak softly:

> Poor Violet – she was strung up and spun around as punishment because she wanted to tell. Those people did terrible things to you. But you've been let down now, let off the rope. No one is going to hurt you here.

***

Soon after this session – a new "character" arrives. It is two years since the first persona Violet (first as LGC) had made her first appearance. This is how it happened:

Because she now knew that she dissociated and was distraught by this discovery about herself, she asks that I summarize for her where we are in the therapy – what we know, relying on *my* memory and the notes I take when we are together.

So, summarizing, I say this:

> What we have here are three voices. There is the Adult Caroline who comes to therapy to integrate things – who wants to know her history and to take ownership over her experiences. The second one is Violet, who wants to tell what she knows. Both of these voices are on the same side now. And there *is a third voice* who identifies with the parents who made you swear not to tell; threatens punishment if you tell. This "voice" cannot be heard on the outside. Only its silencing effect is seen. It forbids you to tell me anything.

Caroline seems genuinely shocked: "So there's not only Violet?"

Then she covers her ears, clutches her fists and before my very eyes, she *becomes* Violet:

> Who is speaking? ... I don't know where she comes from ... I said I can't talk about that ... I told you that ... there are things you never talk about ... but you want to know things ... you shouldn't do that.

Something in what I just said must have frightened her immensely. And suddenly, most dramatically, and again in front of my eyes, she changes again. Now her voice becomes very stern and threatening and masculine while her face changes to a frightening face that I have never seen before. **A man's voice is coming from Caroline's body.**

MAN: There's no asking questions ... why would you want to ask questions?
TOVA: I'm someone trying to save the children (I intuitively answer from her past) Who am I talking to?
MAN: (in a threatening voice): No asking questions! (When "he" speaks like this, I feel a chill of terror in my spine.) Coming here isn't good. Not a good thing to do.
T: (not quite finding my way ... hesitantly): You're very forbidding, disapproving. Are you warning me?
MAN: You don't mess with that!
T: You're telling me this is serious, that I should take your warning seriously. What will happen if one would not take this seriously?
MAN: (making a distorted face that I find impossible to describe) You get killed!

T: That's very frightening. Now I understand why no one is talking ...
MAN: Not something to play around with.

At this point, I become so afraid that I ask "him" to call Adult Caroline "who is the one in charge". I feel I need her help. To my relief, Caroline returns.

She asks me innocently: "Why are we ending early?" I realize *she* knows *nothing* about this monster that just came out of her. Or at least, so it seems.

T: You were absent. That's why you feel there is time unaccounted for. Another part of you was here. It's a part you don't yet know about. When you're ready I can tell you about it.

The next day Caroline is very bewildered, asking what happened. I tell her about a new persona who had been here; a persona who is the "forbidden to tell" voice.

C: Someone else! It's not going crazy?
T: I don't think so – it's bringing the craziness to therapy so that we can work on it – rather than having it run havoc inside of you and leaving you alone with it.

***

A new era begins with the entry of this threatening male persona into the therapeutic space. I think of it as: The Era of Terror. At my request she gives him a name: the Minister.

I soon find myself acting quite insanely whenever he appears. I am aroused to protect Caroline/Violet. I try to get rid of him in every possible way – even using threats that I will call "the authorities". When this has no impact I try to outsmart him, seduce him with promises of getting help for him. If anyone would have observed me at these times they would have wondered who was the mad one in the room

Frightening enactments occur where "he" and I threaten each other –"he" threatens to kill me if I continue to be curious about him. "He" demands that I stop taking notes. "He" warns me the police will have evidence and "the children" will be accused of murder. I defend the children, saying the police are welcome and they will know the children are not to blame. When I think I have outsmarted "him", like a genie being pushed back into its bottle, "he" suddenly turns up unexpectedly. Caroline later tells me that this is a trick of his:

> One of the things he does is to make me think that he doesn't exist. If he doesn't exist – he can't do anything. If he can't do anything – there's no reason to fight him. So then he does what he wants!
> I think to myself, the genius of madness!

How is one to think about this "setup"? A psychiatrist could easily label it a paranoid hallucination. Yet, my experience with Caroline was, that *"he"* is experienced as a separate entity – a real person living inside her that she has no control over because "he" is autonomous; "he" is separate from her. A "dibuk". This must be how people suffering from DID feel. It is very hard for outsiders to believe, unless they also see it. She needed "to become him" so that I could know in the deepest way how it was in her experience. "Seeing is believing" again feels most apt but this time no photo could be taken.

One of the descriptions that came close to resembling my experience of the Minister's autonomous existence in Caroline's body was to be found in Judith Herman's classic book *Trauma and Recovery* (1992). In a chapter devoted to the therapist's ordeal with dealing with what she calls "Traumatic Transference" she writes: "… the transference…does not reflect a simple dyadic relationship, but rather a triad." And quoting the psychiatrist Eric Lister she adds:

> The terror is as though the patient and therapist convene in the presence of yet another person. The third image is that of the one who inflicts the damage, who can be called the "victimiser", who … demanded silence and whose command was now being broken.
>
> (pp. 137–138)

***

When I am able to think – I am faced with difficult questions: Whom do I represent? As long as I see "him" as the enemy what does it mean? *"He"* is also a part of her so why does *she* not "let go of him?" What benefit does she derive, what gain is there in her mental makeup that makes her hold on to him in spite of all my efforts and her own endeavours to "overcome" him?

I understand that by having "him" externalized in this way she is letting me know more about her abuser and hoping that I will be able to deal with him because she cannot.

"All that interests him is violence and sex" she warns me so that I shall be careful and also that I will be able to seek him out, hiding behind the acts of violence.

The violence takes two forms: the attack on her mind by deleting all memory of "him" in our sessions. At times like this, because of her "clue" that he is hiding, I would ask: "Is 'he' telling you to say you know nothing?" And she would silently confirm.

The other aspect of the violence was the physical violence outside the therapy room: the accidents she has by falling off her bike with consequent serious injuries.

***

Our therapy has become a stage where a battle between the forces of Good and Evil is being waged in a most archaic way. Everything feels so real that I often have to remind myself that this male persona is a part of *her* and not a concrete enemy invading my clinic. I remember her hospital dream, how the abuser–father entered our space and demolished all sense of safety. Was it a prophetic dream? I feel we were living in her nightmare without knowing how or if we will wake up into a safe world.

At times the Minister frightened me so much that on the days we met in my home-clinic I would on occasion ask my husband to stay home in case I felt real danger to myself or her. With the increase of accidents caused by the male persona Caroline starts to seriously express the concern that the time has come to end therapy in order to save her life. But she leaves the actual decision with me. As always, for her to actually *make* a decision was no simple feat. The choice now is between saving her mind or saving her body! It seems we have run out of time to find that middle ground of saving both.

Notes

1 Caroline, recently, in trying to describe the experience of "replay" had described it as the difference between watching a tennis match in real time and a replay of it a moment after. I had responded that it was an excellent example.
2 Credit is due to the staff at the Tel Hashomer Hospital Psychiatric Unit who pointed this out in a seminar I taught.

Chapter 21

From pregnancy to birth

> One cannot overcome an enemy who is absent or not within range.
> Freud (1914, p. 151)

Timeline: the last nine months of therapy

The nine months leading up to the last session with Caroline were traumatic for both of us. It is well known that in transference–countertransference work with traumatized patients there is a revival, to a lesser extent of course, of the original traumatic feelings in the therapist. I found the confrontation with the unexpected new persona to be such unusual and rare therapeutic events that I thought it important to share these encounters with others. Perhaps my experience can be of some benefit to others who find themselves with this DID phenomena. In addition to this educational aim, I do know that the need to have my difficult experiences witnessed by this sharing mode, is a part of the motivation for this writing.

An example: through the "Minister" Caroline reveals much of her past relationship with her father. I had asked something about him, and instead of her answering me, "he" appears:

MINISTER: Why don't you mind your own business!
T: Because I want to help Caroline be free of you.
MINISTER: But she belongs to me. I'm the one who controls her. Nobody else!
T: What do you want with her?
MINISTER: She's my plaything!
T: You like to play with her? Do you care about her in any way?

Caroline returns to her adult self. She looks bewildered.

C: But we were talking about stopping.
T: I don't think it's a good idea to stop now out of fear. You'll be running away from yourself and you'll be alone. Here I am with you to help find a way together.

***

I spend a long time thinking about whether it would be better for Caroline to leave therapy or to remain so that we can find a way to deal with the threats introduced by the appearance of this threatening Minister. I recalled how she had searched out therapy after a man appeared at her work place and she had run away and had an emotional breakdown.

If I decide to go along with her thoughts of ending, she voices the concern that we are abandoning the little girl. I find myself having no clear-cut answers. To go on might endanger her, whereas to stop will make her feel like she is betraying another self. This too may lead to self injury. I feel imprisoned with her in a closed circle with no way out to safety. There is no one on the outside that can show us the way out and when I search inside I am not sure what is best. After extensive soul-searching, I come to the conclusion that there is no right answer as to what is better. I feel her dilemma in the depths of my soul. I feel at this time that it is not for me to make the choice about stopping the therapy.

***

In the last year of this long analysis, a struggle ensues between us. It is about ending the therapy and it will continue for almost a year. It is characterized by Caroline creating a split between us: if I represent hope – she represents helplessness; if I am the representative of integration, appealing to her commitment to Violet, her right to live – the Minister "prohibitor" suddenly turns up to sabotage "our" efforts with a death threat. An example:

T: It is a complex question (in response to Caroline's question about whether we should stop now). The answer may depend on how much *you*, the adult Caroline can deal with whatever comes up from the past.
C: (in desperation) So how can I make a decision – to know if to stop or not, if you say that? If we can't go on and we can't stop – then what?
T: We need time – to look for a way that feels safest.

How will time be used? Just saying that time will help may not be enough. My dealing with the Minister inside Caroline has not been very successful. Her suggestions to end therapy leaves me helpless as well, wanting to do the best for her and yet not knowing what is right for her. As long as she keeps coming to therapy – does this not represent her hope that we will find a way? Is her hope unreasonable? In the wish to believe she will be able to come to a decision I tell myself that after all, she does not need my permission to leave therapy. She is not my prisoner and I even tell her so. But she continues to come. It feels like we are in a deadlock.

***

One day, in desperation, Caroline asks me, "If you don't understand how can you help? And if I can't tell you – how are you going to understand?"

Hearing her despair, and having experienced myself the impossibility of knowing what is best for her I search for something that might lead us out of this deadlock.

Finally I ask her:

T: Caroline, do you think that if I were to understand that we need to stop meeting, that would feel like help to you?
C: Yes, because then you'd understand that it's too dangerous.

So I agree. And then I suggest that we now plan the ending of the therapy. Although in my head I know it was in the past she had experienced real danger to her life, I also know that she is experiencing this danger as *existing in the present* and I am not finding a way to change that.

As though to prove the point, the next week she comes with her arm in a plaster cast. She has had yet another accident! She fell off her bike, without losing consciousness this time, but she had lost control of her bike when a car suddenly braked in front of her. I know that she is taking this as a sign of the malicious workings of the Minister, who has by now been accepted by her as someone present in our work, in her life.

***

Throughout the therapy I had been helped by supervision. At the time of our debate about ending the therapy, I was having Skype supervision with a supervisor whose expertise included analysis with psychotic patients. When Caroline continued to endanger herself, he suggested I get extra counselling with a colleague of his who worked with DID patients. He connected me with Valerie Sinason,[1] and by email communication she generously gave me extremely valuable advice from her extensive experience. Here is a quote from Sinason which shows some of the complexities involved:

> In other areas you get a bonus when you understand more but with DID the better the work you do, the more bad memories! It is a sign of progress that others are coming forward but since they were needed to keep her alive and spare her from terrible memory the becoming aware of them leads to the fear of fragmentation again. *No-one in a system is a baddie.* Everyone has a reason for the position they are in and is trying to keep the system safe and alive. The system is finding its own ways of trying to neutralize the new disclosure and agreeing with how important it is to be slow and careful can also help.

***

I thought that one way to try and be *slow and careful* was by trying to give Caroline more active control. After Caroline had stood a whole session in the middle of the room as a way to prevent "him" from coming, I suggested she now try and return to sitting on a chair, rather than on the floor, while trying to keep her eyes open so as not to fall back into the past. This lasted for less than two weeks. Then she entered, telling me that she again had had an experience of losing time while riding her bike. Luckily, this time she was not injured. While passing my old clinic she had a memory of a time in therapy there, ten years earlier, when she had seen *a cockroach* there and had been terrorized, saying then: "Why do you let others into the room?"

While recounting this to me *now* she re-experiences the terror of her childhood and says that this is the *first time* she can link the terror to her parents! I saw that she had seated herself in the corner on the floor again. The chair was no longer helpful. She needed to go back into her past again. While covering her ears so as not to hear herself, she says: "The not wanting to know ... and being able to know ... most of that is because of the threat of telling."

Caroline, for a brief moment, is able to tell me directly about the effect of extreme fear on her whole way of being. The therapy, by enabling the strengthening of her ability to think, to remember and to know what is real, is now arousing overwhelming terror because of threats from the past were she to tell what she knew.

It is only now, while writing this book, that I am suddenly aware that the word Caroline used, and her terror at it, "cockroach", contains the word "cock". She was using it to let me know how her parents prostituted her. In my mind this memory connects to the dream she had just before first coming to my home clinic, about being prostituted. (See Chapter 13.)

***

Caroline was not the only one to have accidents. One day, on the way to meeting her in my town clinic I drive into an intersection and hit a car that was in the midst of making a U-turn on my left. I had not seen him because I was looking in the other direction to see if the road was clear. I am a very experienced driver, but in my "absent mindedness" resulting from the "traumatic countertransference" (Herman, 1992) I did not see the oncoming car because of a "blind spot". Luckily no one was injured, except my car. In trying later to analyze my "blind spot" – I realized that I had subconsciously known for a long time that she had been involved in killings. She had let me know in many ways what I did not want "to see".

It was too frightening for me.

What exactly was I afraid of? On that particular day I had woken up early after a restless night. The previous session had been around her question of what would happen if she *did* "meet" Violet but would not believe what she had to say. After some thinking I had replied that on the contrary, it might be too difficult if she *does believe* her. After the session I realized that I was truly concerned that if Caroline was to know what she had done as a child she might kill herself. I was not able to come to any decision or idea as to what I could do to prevent this. Nor could my supervisors reassure me in that this would not happen.

After much reflection bearing the above in mind I came to the conclusion that if I left things as they were and brought the therapy to an end, that would amount to a psychological death. What would become of her? Would she turn catatonic or need hospitalization for paranoia? All these years she had been coming to therapy to find out the truth about her past and now, when we seemed so close to knowing, her very life, physical as well as psychic life, was in danger. The ruthless and brutal killer from her past together with the brutal killer-self from within her seemed to join together and cause not-so accidental accidents in the present. At this time, less than a year before this analysis would come to an end, I had no clear idea if or how this "nightmare" would end.

I resorted to taking Caroline's lead and at the same time, if she insisted upon continuing to search for her lost memories, I would try and develop in her a way to be able to forgive herself. I thought that deep down, it was unbearable guilt that she suffered from and that punishment by death was now a real and present danger.

***

Sinason's perception that "no one in the system is a baddie" opened my thinking about the Minister. I tried to come to terms with the fact that I would not be able to be rid of him forcibly. That I also would not be able to outsmart him. I went back and re-read Caroline's writings about her relationship with her father. Again, I was struck by its complexity. He had been both husband and lover and the only person she had had any intimacy with.

I change my tactics. The next time the Minister appears in our session and she says in a frightened tone, "I'm not going to talk about him" I say: "You must care for him. You want to protect him. You're afraid something may happen to him if you talk about him. I also tend to think you felt cared for by him at times. It wasn't all bad." (She covers her ears.)

I continue,

T: I think it's very confusing for you to have so many different feelings for the same person: care and fear. For children it's terribly confusing if the same person can change: be kind and cruel, good, then bad – and they don't know who to believe."

Caroline falls in slow motion from the chair to the floor.

T: It is so painful – you want to protect him from your angry thoughts at him for hurting you so much.

She is lying on the floor sobbing her heart out. The room fills with her pool of tears. I try to empathize with her need for him when she felt so unloved and lonely. I tell her that today, in such great contrast from the past, she is not alone. She has Anne and myself and maybe this will help her let go of him with time.

***

Yet, soon we are back to the deadlock – going around in circles. I still think the choice of ending must be left to her. Even though she seems to want me to decide, I suspect it is her way, in the enactment in the transference, to make me be responsible for "the death of Violet". If she participated in killing a little girl in the past *I would be just like her* – "*a child killer*". I won't do it. I interpret that she wants me to take responsibility, but she came to therapy to be able to be the one who takes responsibility for *her* decisions. I'm not even sure if my thoughts make good sense. Since I won't actively initiate the end she stays. But soon I notice that her presence has a different quality. She seems dead – robot-like. This is different from the "living–dead" presence of the past. I am reminded of the chronic schizophrenics I knew from my internship. She seems to lose her curiosity and shows no interest in looking for her past. She becomes passive – not only silent, but passive. I suspect the "Minister" is behind this – inside her, commanding silent obedience. But whereas in the past while obeying him she encouraged me to not give up, now it felt as though she has given in completely to "his" command.

Eight more years to go

One day in our last few months of therapy, as though out of the blue, she says: "Only eight more years to go!" She tells me that in eight years she will be 60 and then her life will come to an end. It is a fact she has always known. "It means not having to worry about what happens" she explains … "It can't go on forever. At least you can say it will end then."

I feel we are now starting a countdown – to what? Her death by suicide? For a minute I wonder if she has been brainwashed – has had a command implanted in her to stop life at 60! I feel overwhelmed by a sense of helplessness, which suddenly turns to fury. I am furious at her determination not to let therapy be helpful to her in any way. This anger I expressed in one of the next sessions when I had to make an unexpected cancellation from one day to the next, something that rarely happened. It was a Tuesday and I needed to cancel our midday Wednesday session. So I offered her a choice between an alternative early morning Wednesday session I could offer or a cancelation of the next day's session. The following is our interaction that ensued in response to my offering her this choice:

C: (accusingly): Why would you ... if you're going to do something then do it ... don't make me part of it.
T: By saying that it means you feel you are a passive recipient of my action – so if I offer you the choice between coming tomorrow earlier or cancelling, it feels to you that I am sadistic – as though I'm making you decide if to participate in a sadistic act or not.
C: If you make me *choose* you make me an *active participant* ... (cringing as though in great pain) ... If it happens ... it happens ... don't make *me* responsible.
T: (angrily): It's as though you're relating to the therapy here as abuse. Is that how you see it? Is this therapy here abusive?!

She then lets me know that she cannot decide because it would be an expression of her *desire* to come if she chooses to take up my offer for the alternative hour.

T: You are interpreting my offer as an invitation to an abusive situation. *That's our biggest problem!* What makes you stick to that interpretation?

I express my indignation. I "accuse" her of sitting here for 25 years – going through the motions of being in therapy and in eight years, when "it's all over" she'll be able to say to herself: *I've been a good patient, I've stuck to therapy all these years and it didn't help, and I was faithful to Dad, and nothing will have happened!*

It's the end of the hour and I tell her rather sharply that she can let me know by tonight by email if she will be coming the next morning. At least I can decide that she will decide.

That evening I receive an email titled: I'LL SEE YOU TOMORROW (nothing more but nothing less).

In retrospect, I think how anxious and threatened I felt by her time-to-live deadline. I could only act out my anger and fear by being concrete, critical and challenging. I had no inner space to allow for the re-enactment of her wanting to not be held responsible for actions imposed on her and for her daring to say so out loud.

***

The next morning there is no knock on the door. But I open it on time, knowing she is never late. She is standing there. I am no longer angry. I see her suffering. She enters.

T: I think you are trying to tell me something about the guilt you feel about having been a participant in things in the past ... (Caroline covers her ears with her cushion) ... and for some reason the guilt is with you all the time. You can't let go of it. The way you are trying to deal with it is by living a life that says: *I don't want anything, so I'm not responsible for anything, so I'm not guilty.* I'm glad you've decided to come this morning.

C: I can't talk about what I don't know.

T: But perhaps you can talk about what you think, hypothesize, speculate.

C: That's being crazy ... that's ... inventing things ... I can't do that! Why would you want to do that?

T: By relating to it like that – it's as though you are in a court of law where you fear every word you say will be treated as evidence that can be held against you if you can't prove it. As though you will be accused of making things up. But this is not a court of law. Therapy is a place to think. If you had the freedom to think, we could make sense of some of this behaviour. It's almost as though you've made a pledge: *I'll never let a word out of my mouth that can't be proven.* So there is almost total silence – because almost nothing can be proven about the past.

C: But maybe I don't know because Violet is the only one who knows.

T: Maybe – but lately you're not looking for her. She lives inside you. Do you *want* to meet her? Maybe it's safe for her to let you know about the past. To allow that, you have to take responsibility for wanting her to talk; and not to judge her.

C: I thought maybe that the silence ... was a way of avoiding the Minister ... but is he a danger to her as well?

T: I think the Minister has to hear that he's not in danger. No one is going to kill him or put him in jail. Maybe in the past that might have happened. (Caroline folds over and covers her ears.) It's as though you don't want to hear that. It's hard for you because you're also attached to him. To continue therapy is to continuing to give life to Little Girl Caroline, to Violet.

***

I feel that in this session I have fought perhaps my last battle over Violet. From now I hope I will let Caroline decide to what extent she wants her memories exposed and acknowledged. My anger. which was sparked by my wish for life for her, seems to have touched Caroline. In the next session it is noticeable that she has struggled to find a solution and she has come up with something that seems quite ingenious.

A new pregnancy?

"I can't talk about things I don't know but you say that ... *you* know what Violet says and have written it down... so... *even if I don't know* ... that's not making things up. Yeh?"

Caroline has bought us time. She has found a way to bypass "his" command and threat lest she tell anything.It seems Violet was created to fulfil this function. In response to her suggestion I agree to look over my notes from the last three years and collect all of Violet's words in preparation to show her. Unbeknown to me at the time – this happens exactly nine months before the analysis ends!

At the end of this session I feel some relief. Caroline seems to have "saved the day" when I myself was lost for a way out of the closed space in which she had imprisoned us. Life energy returns to our work.

I can now understand something she had said a few sessions earlier: "*I need to know what's happening without knowing what's happening.*" Creating Violet allows precisely this.

***

Future time

The next day:

C: So what now?
T: In the meantime ... until I have all the pages of Violet's words collected?

As I speak, and see she has no suggestions as to how we are going to "get through this waiting period" while I read over three years of notes, I suddenly have an idea: that we let a new element, "Time", become an active participant. After all, she has introduced "eight years" into our thinking – future time, or the end of time. I can play with time too. I suggest that since we both know how slow things move in the therapy, let's relate to time in a fast-forward way, as though in a week I'll have Violet's words ready. While I know it will take me some months to go through three years of notes, we could now start preparing for that day, so that it will not only be theoretical as it is now, but be with the potential of being practical, real. We can prepare for the day when she will be ready to read and take in the words and experiences of Violet as part of her own narrative.

C: Like a pregnancy?
T: (taken aback) That's an interesting association. Something that takes time to develop ... a joint endeavour, at the end of which a new creation is born, one that can develop, and not be aborted or killed.

(Caroline nods in assent and I feel a sense of hope, even excitement, for the first time in so long. This suggestion, coming from her, is allowing for two minds to come together, in a life giving way. There is a future birth to look forward to.)

C: But is that a good idea?
T: If you're asking – then you must have some questions.
C: What if I'm not good for her, to her?

T: Well – since there's time until she's "born" – you can bring all your worries here – and after she's born, you won't be alone. Here you'll have "joint parenting" to help you help her grow, That's what this therapy is about.
CAROLINE: But you don't work with babies.

(An important note here to the reader: I know that to someone reading this it may sound that she is psychotic and that I am encouraging her to stay stuck in her psychosis, but I know that we both know that it is not a "real live baby" we are talking about – but a future life for the "Caroline baby" who is to be reborn, and to have a chance for a future once she can own her past narrative.)

T: To ensure the baby's well-being one needs "a good enough mother".

At this point it goes through my mind, with fervent hope, that if I have been a good enough mother to her perhaps she will be able to mother herself now.

C: (starting to cry) But I can't be that!
T: I think you've been preparing for the last 25 years to be that.
C: Why would you say that?
T: I know. because you needed to make it very safe here before you could let me know about her. You tested and you checked me out, and once you knew it was safe you realized that it was not good for her to stay hidden in the womb – an enclosed space – safe, but eventually stifling – so now you're preparing to give birth to her. It's natural to have fears about how it will feel to become a real person and to have Violet as an alive part of you. You will learn to deal with that.
C: Are we talking about nine months?
T: I hope much less. But I do want to say: it's *not a concrete* pregnancy, so no harm done if I finish much earlier.

I am aware of this sudden need on my part to reassure us – worrying that she may take it too literally. I also realize that I have been treading that fine line between sanity and madness and though I tend to believe that when I join her in the madness it helps pull her over to the other side, I am not always sure that this will happen.

***

From our session the following day:

C: It can be painful?

I understand she is referring to this whole process of preparing to know her past traumas – a painful birth. I am silent.

C: It feels like … having been raped … and not wanting to have anything to do with it … (She curls over in anguish.)
T: Not wanting to have anything to do with a pregnancy and baby born out of rape, that's very understandable – a normal response for a pregnancy out of rape.

(I am relating to the level of the past – the real foetus – the outcome of rape and incest. I am unable here to consciously think that perhaps she is relating to the new project of my writing her past via Violet's words and she is having second thoughts – letting me know she wants nothing to do with having been raped into agreeing to stay in the prison therapy to please me. I am still happy about her wanting to continue in the direction that I think will lead to healing: integration. I thought that she was also pleased.)

C: And if it becomes too much … to stop this too before it's too late.
T: I think you know that you're a free person and can stop or continue any time. I do believe, even if it does get painful, we'll find a way to help you deal with the pain. You want to have her taken out from the inside to the outside.
C: You understand that? … It would have to be very slow. You can't kill it by going too slowly?

I am left perplexed. While still pondering over her comment, she adds:

C: You don't have babies at 60!

So she is letting me know that time is pressing. The countdown has started and something must happen here to stop her ending her life at 60. It sounds as though she believes that the psychological birth of "Violet" through "her" words with the help of my midwifery will allow Caroline to continue to live.

***

But a few days later she recants. "I can't do this" she tells me and then she reminds us of her Hospital Dream six years previously: "…it was safe inside until they let Dad in and then, if the Minister had been let in …."
I recall how in that dream she had equated the hospital to therapy. And truly we cannot ignore the facts – that with the entry of the "Minister" the bike accidents are impinging dangerously both inside and outside the therapeutic space. The obsessive separation between inside and outside that she had managed to maintain for so many years has no longer been possible to maintain. I feel at a loss as to how to make this therapy a safe place for her again.

***

It will take *another seven months* before we separate. But something happens at this time that retrospectively, could have been turned into the moment of ending.

On entering, Caroline opens accusingly, "What happened to the picture?"

At first I am bewildered: I haven't the faintest idea what she's talking about and then realize that on entering the town clinic, she noticed, and I didn't, that one of the pictures that always hung on the corridor wall, was absent. (This was a clinic I shared in town and there was no cause for my colleagues to inform me that they had decided to take away one of their pictures.)

T: The things that happen when I'm not here that I don't know about!

Caroline is staring at me in an odd way. I continue.

T: I know you can think – is this how it was with Mom? Did she really not know. Or was it convenient for her to not know what was going on?
C: What *would* you notice!
T: You feel I don't notice what you need me to notice when you need me to notice without you telling me.

Suddenly, Caroline *coughs*. This is outstandingly rare for her, so unusual that I am shocked and before I recover she coughs again!

T: You can cough! You can make that sound! You do have a voice!
C: (silently crying as I talk and after a few minutes …): You were saying … that she didn't know … and I couldn't let that go … It's not that she didn't know … and I had to hide it from her … No … *She knew*! She was involved … (in agony) … I didn't know … if I should stop you saying that … so I coughed it … the cough stopped it.
T: (after recovering) It's good that you stopped me because I wasn't getting the truth. The coughing stopped me – but by *telling* me the reason for the cough I now know.
C: But that means *that I know!*
T: Yes. I hope you won't fragment this by our next session.

***

To my relief Caroline continues with where we were in the next session. Continuity has been maintained over the weekend.

C: I had to cough … I tried not to … you were saying that Mom didn't know … and I thought that if I'd done that … it must mean that… (doubling over in pain) I know… that she knew … Does that make sense? … How?

T: You coughed, so unusual for you, though you know how to restrain a cough. You even wrote me about it once. Your body spoke. Your body doesn't lie. Your *language can be ruined* [2] but your body language is always true.
C: I didn't know ... what to do ... and ... then something ... took over.
T: I think the coughing came because we were again getting nowhere. And continuing to make yourself mad was "no place to be".

Caroline had recently told me that "No Place to Be" was also a place. The coughing was to allow for a new place where the truth can be known. Perhaps it would have been appropriate to say that this cough, this body language that she could now give words to, was an indication that therapy was getting "somewhere".

C: Did you write that down? Caroline leaves, turning to thank me at the door.

***

A few days after this most dramatic event Caroline brings me what will be her last written page. Many months have passed without any sign of the Writing Caroline. Only long after the therapy ends will I realize the significance of what she writes here. For this reason I will quote this text in length.

> ~Tova was talking about Mom as though she hadn't known what was going on. Then I had to fight off an urge to cough. I couldn't stop it and had to let it out. I don't cough in the sessions. But evidently it was a way of saying that I had to stop Tova. It literally interrupted the session – knowing I don't cough. Tova remarked on it. So the cough was a way of stopping her. I was then able to tell her what had happened – and that the coughing meant that I (my body) knew what had happened – that Mom was involved. I couldn't let her say things which weren't true. So on some level at least, I know something.
>
> Since then most of the sessions have been about the need to stop therapy – although it was there before as well. Yesterday I told Tova that if I don't feel too bad when she's away (in the next breaks)[3] that would be an indication that it's alright to stop. She asked why the feeling of not being able to go on had come up now – what had happened to make me feel that, after so many years of looking after Violet. I said that it wasn't that something had happened – before I felt I could go on; now I can't do it any longer. Tova said that she would feel irresponsible if she only listened to me – and ignored the other personae. It's as though I'm in a story and am listening to the author's version of it. But there are other people in the plot – and outside it (Tova) – and so there are other versions.

I asked her if she was saying that the feeling that I can't go on any longer is complicated by something else. She said yes. I think what she means is that my need to stop isn't just my feeling – like people feeling that they've got all they can out of therapy and so concluding it. The feeling is being influenced by something else. She keeps saying that it's not good to stop therapy if that's a way of running away from something frightening.

Tova suggested that if I could write this up it would be a good idea.~

***

This document was the last one written by Caroline and the analysis would continue for another six months. These last months were experienced by both of us as probably the most difficult of all. While being inside the process I could not "see", nor was I aware of my own blindness. Only in retrospect would I be able to understand Caroline's words: *"It's as though I'm in a story and am listening to the author's version of it. But there are other people in the plot – and outside it (Tova) – and so there are other versions."*

What I, the person outside the plot, saw was the different personae fighting over Caroline. All this time, I believed I was her "objective" therapist who knew what she needed: to integrate the different personae by being able to accept the different parts of herself and thus take ownership over her history so as to be able to let go of it. I was not aware of the extent of the rigidity in my thinking processes that saw the necessity of integration as an "absolute truth" about what is mental health.

Writing this today, almost five years after this therapy ended, I wonder at how close to becoming mad I was (Searles, 1959). It seems, if I relate seriously to the Writing Caroline, one could think that I myself was playing a part in a plot of my own: where I was playing the part of a therapist who thought she was doing good work with her patient Caroline but didn't realize that the *real* Caroline was not the one in the room with me but acting from behind the scenes! The "real one" seemed to be the Writer. It seems the split had an impact on me so strong that I too, at times would relate to the part as though it was a whole. Reflecting upon this today – I think that the Writer was the "Observing Ego Caroline" who knew, but needed at all costs to also maintain the capacity *not to know*, not to take that knowledge in, so as to be able to live. The Caroline I *met* physically represented this aspect. To **really know**, to have stared unflinchingly at what had happened in that house of madness would have led to madness or suicide.

Back to the clinic. The battle became ruthless. To show me how cruel the Minister could be, and the extent of the danger she felt we were in, Caroline brought me the last book she would ever bring: *No Country for Old Men.*[4] It is a story about the epitome of cruelty where an indifferent, inhuman evil man, sadistically and capriciously, destroys anything and everything in his way. The story is totally fatalistic where Evil overcomes Good; there is no remorse, no mercy and no capacity for any dialogue. The sheriff in the story who had tried in vain to capture the serial killer eventually retires with the following words, (lightly underlined in pencil by Caroline, as in the previous books she had given me to read):

> (Sheriff to his wife Loretta:) "Loretta, I can do it no more." And she smiled and said: "You aim to quit while you're ahead?" And I said "No, Mam, I just aim to quit. I ain't ahead by a damn sight. I never will be."
> (p. 296)

Caroline's last underlining was the sheriff telling a colleague about this decision: "... you have come upon something that you may very well not be equal to ...."

When I read these lines aloud to Caroline – I was at a loss as to what she expected of me. Should I resign like the sheriff and just call it quits. Let the power of evil win her soul? Surely, she knew me better than that! Or was it really that Caroline desperately wanted me to continue my relentless search for her hidden past and not give up on her just because "he" – the Evil one was trying to scare us both away.

Somehow, I had not taken in that line in her writing which related to her as being the author of this drama who wanted to end therapy. I was still under the influence of the personae in her plot, thinking they represented the fragmented parts of her which I was trying to assemble in order to enable her to put herself together. At that time, having been subjected to so many contradictory forces represented by the different personae, I could not yet conceptualize that Caroline had reached a certain level of integration, in her way, who felt she had discovered enough and *needed to know no more*. I see that I was much more in the role of an expectant "grandmother-to-be" wanting to help prepare my maturing "daughter" Caroline, for the birth of "our" Little Girl Violet!

But I did suggest we plan a gradual process towards ending. I ask her if she could think how it might be for her without therapy. Her response: "I don't think anything!" and then she burst out, "I don't see how it can be worse than this!"

That day, I wrote in my notes: *I feel that if I don't allow her to go she experiences me as her jailer in a psychotic transference, and if I do let her go, it would be "casting her out" to a death- like existence. I feel stuck. There is no space. With no space to move in I too am in a mental jail.* And the next day, when I try to ask what made her say this, wondering if it's the Minister talking from within her, she responds with **"You can't ignore him. You can't pretend he doesn't exist!"**

Again I am left baffled. What does "he" represent that she cannot let go of?

And the next day, when I suggest he represents in enactment the prohibiting voice that does not want her to face that her mother was involved, she says very loud and clear: "You can tell me about the re-enactment. I can understand what you're saying. It's just not an experience. It's not mine, not attached to anything. It's floating in the air." And a few days later: "Nothing is real ... no evidence of danger in the past ... It's not that I think we've been making things up. It's just that *I don't know* if we have."

We should have ended on this note. But Caroline continues to come. She comes for more sessions that become too painful to bear for both of us. She begins to repeatedly say, "I can't do this" yet continuing to come without being able to have any dialogue. And then on one occasion she stayed standing immobile the whole session in the middle of the room repeating these four words over and over. I see her determination in her strong stand while sounding her voice, loud and clear. This she could not do in the presence of her father but she feels safe enough here with me to insist. I felt I had to find a way to free us. I said that if she felt the same way the next day I would understand that she really meant it and that would be our last session.

And so it was. When I say that I understand that this is to be our last session she asks if I understand. I say that I'm not sure that I do but I do understand she cannot stay. Gently, she says: "We did the best we could." It is a moment of kindness.

I then ask her what she would like to do with the things in her box. She will take them with her. I put them into a plastic bag: the diaries from her childhood, the doll with "fuck" written all over her, the remnants of her blue hair, the photographs of the bleeding hanged doll. I am left only with my notes and the cushion into which she has shed an ocean of tears. At the door she asks me if I will keep my promise to write up her story and I promise that I will.

And I remember that the first book she brought to me almost 26 years earlier had been *The Promise*.[5]

Notes

1 Valerie Sinason, Director of the Clinic for Dissociative Studies in the UK and an editor of several books including *Attachment, Trauma and Multiplicity* (Routledge, 2nd edition 2011).
2 I use this word knowing it will echo the line from Auden's poem "... ruined languages" that she had brought to me often.
3 It is June now. The next vacation I will take is in August and then again at the Jewish High Holidays in September.
4 Cornac McCarthy, *No Country for Old Men* (Vintage 2005). It was made into a thriller movie in 2007 by the Coen brothers, winning many awards.
5 By Chaim Potok, alluded to in Chapter 2.

Epilogue

Polonius: [Aside] Though this be madness, yet there is a method in't.
W. Shakespeare Hamlet Act 2, scene 2

The understanding of the dissociated mind has been a challenge in the history of mankind even before the time of Freud (Eigen 1993). In this book I do not go into the controversies of different theoretical schools of thought and their ensuing terminology concerning this complex phenomenon. Many books have been written and are still being written on the subject. I have intentionally decided to focus on my clinical experience with one such patient over a very long period of time. The main reason for this was that over the many years of working with Caroline I found myself needing to be open to anything that I found useful and useable and to be committed to one theory would have been limiting at times even incapacitating. Although this often left me uneasy in terms of being able to defend theoretically what I had done clinically it was of some comfort for me when one of my supervisors[1] directed my attention to the wise words of the nineteenth-century writer George Meredith: "There is nothing like a theory for blinding the wise." Bion's advice of the importance of listening with an open mind: with no memory, no desire and no theory, was always a guide and Winnicott's influence on me, with his emphasis on awareness of the lived experiencing in the patient-therapist unit is paramount.

In this epilogue I will share some of my understandings arrived at after some distance in time has been taken from this very intense involvement with Caroline.

What creates a safe place?

As noted, it took Caroline a very long time to feel she was in a safe place and only once this sense of safety was established was it possible for part of her traumatic history to be revealed.

What contributed to the creation of a safe place for Caroline?

Firstly, safety came from the **reliability of the setting**. This contributed, as in all therapies, to a sense of reliability and continuity in time and space. I want to emphasize here that the existence of a safe *physical space* was of utmost importance in a very concrete way for Caroline. As described, the slightest change in the physical surroundings was experienced as disrupting, be it a piece of furniture or even a change in the intensity of lighting. A move to a new physical locality demanded months of preparation and Caroline's stalking of me for years was her way of ensuring I was the same person outside our common space as I was inside it. She needed the total stability physically so as not to disintegrate psychically. I believe the reliability of the *outside* physical space made available to her and adapted to her needs in the transitional space of therapy provided the overlap needed for the slow but systematic development of a sense of Being in the felt sense of "I exist", which gradually allowed for *internal space* to develop within her.

What did "adapting to her needs" involve? One important element was my allowing Caroline to have as much *control* as she needed in the therapy, over me and the therapeutic environment, within the boundaries and limitations of my ability. I found myself setting boundaries when I felt that her actions were harmful to herself, and equally so when I felt that her control was on the verge of suffocating my sense of freedom. There was an attempt to balance between being with her as a real separate person, while simultaneously trying to allow an environment where the illusion of her omnipotent control would be experienced to the extent that she needed. For example, I allowed her to sit for several years under a table while I sat next to her on the floor. This was a physical bodily accommodation not approved of by some peers and supervisors. Yet, I felt this was a necessity for her. (I must admit that it was also of no difficulty for me since I happen to practise yoga and am quite flexible physically.) Only many years later, when Caroline already had words to describe some of these experiences, did I learn that this act contributed to a growth in a sense of body self. Caroline needed to feel the solid ground under her in order to feel her body as solid. In her words: "I can't know who I am ... if I don't know *where* I am. It will wear me out ... if I can't be ... I'm not inside myself." Winnicott might call this an "in-dwelling" that developed from an attitude of "primary maternal preoccupation" (Winnicott, 1956).

This example is perhaps a good one to illustrate the fact that I first acted and only later understood the reason for the actions. These were "now moments" in the language of Stern, which allowed for the enactments (Stern et al., 1998) Part of this was an outcome of necessity. There seemed no other option. If I refused to "adjust" to how she seemed to need me we would be stuck in "freeze" state. I think this adjustment on my part was possible because most of the time I did not feel her demands as coming from some sadistic or manipulative motivation, but rather out of a need that she had no way to put into words. In that respect one could say that intuitively I trusted Caroline's guidance and myself to keep us both safe. But I could not have done this if I myself did not have a safe place to which to bring my anguish and confusion. Throughout the years I had supervision and the supervisors I chose were those that I knew would create a place where there was freedom to think and an overall emotional atmosphere of mutual respect.

This brings me to the next point of what contributed to Caroline's sense of safety. It was that I **believed** her. This was never demanded as a condition. On the contrary – Caroline often tried to challenge and at times even dissuade me from believing her, trying to arouse doubt in me, requiring of me proof as to what enabled me to believe her. Not only did I believe her needs to be real and legitimate but I always believed that Caroline was telling me the truth, or, more specifically, she was being honest with me. This is a strange statement, since at the same time there was an ongoing sense of feeling that she was often hiding things from me or that there was even contradictory evidence in what she said. For example, denying she had said something I knew she *had* said. But I experienced this as puzzling rather than as lying This puzzle would only be deciphered once the DID was exposed, yet the sense of believing her to be honest was a predominant experience. It is also one difficult to describe how it comes about. This issue or inner attitude of mine is particularly relevant especially since Caroline's predominant way of being in the world was expressed, once she had found words, in the following: "If *I* can't be sure if anything happened why should anyone believe me?"

The devastating effect of being lied to by her parents, who had a vested interest in hiding the truth from her as well as denying the reality of her perceptions and experiences led to her suspiciousness and paranoia. Trusting the other, as well as trusting her own mind was the last thing she knew. By my allowing her as much control as I was able to survive I hoped to help her develop trust from an intersubjective experience that might become a source of reparation of what she had known. Fonagy (2002) in describing how the mentalization of the child develops, quotes Hegel (1807): "It is only through getting to know the mind of the other that the child develops full appreciation of the nature of mental states" and Fonagy continues: "The process is intersubjective, the child gets to know the caregiver's mind as the caregiver endeavours to understand and contain the mental state of the child" (p. 27).

As Caroline slowly developed a sense of being in a safe place, she increasingly dared to ask me questions such as: "How did you get there?" or "Can I ask you something?" Her curiosity was aroused by some comment that I made that she found meaningful or true. I shared my thinking processes with her. Describing how I came to my understandings helped her know I was real and thus that she was real. As she wrote in one of her texts: she learnt that there was an alternative real world outside herself through me.

The sense of trust and believing was two directional. But I found out through experience with her, that it was not only *what* I said that was important, it was also *what I thought*. I often felt that Caroline could "read my mind", as it were, and if I were to hide something or not be truthful in any way, she would sense this and it would be devastating. Thus, I found myself constantly needing to analyse my countertransference. Symington

(1983) in discussing Bion's work, notes that psychotic patients can discern the inner state of the analyst – that is why it is not the words in themselves or the interpretations but the analyst's inner state that makes the difference. In a similar vein Ghent (1990) notes that the analyst's *beliefs* play an important role in psychoanalysis.

I believe

Since this issue seems so very important, I need to make a statement here of a belief that grew within me as this analysis progressed. I want to say clearly that **I believe** that my patient Caroline really did experience the events described in this book. I believe she had incest with her father, got pregnant by him and gave birth, either to a live baby or to an aborted baby that did not live. I also believe that she witnessed at least one real killing when she was a child. I believe this to be true just as I believe that the Holocaust is a true historic event. But in contrast to the Holocaust, which we know about because of the concrete evidence available through witnesses and extensive documentation as well as physical evidence of the buried remains of the murdered, Caroline had no access to objective truth – no historical documentation, no evidence of concrete buried bodies and no reliable witnesses. She had nothing outside her own mind to help her know if this happened or not. I also believe that her mind being manipulated in such a way, resulted in her not being able to trust it. This led to an obsessive need for absolute control. If there is no inner self to rely on then the outside must be subjugated to tyrannical control

It is not easy to explain what makes one believe another. The processes involved are both conscious and unconscious and much can be explained only through "intuition". It was not that I made a conscious decision to believe her. It happened slowly, but surely as the analysis proceeded. I believe that the way Caroline was so careful in the way she spoke with me contributed to this feeling of never doubting that she was telling me the truth. She never took anything for granted and her concreteness was part of this need to be sure of everything she said, never making non-provable assumptions in her desperate need to be believed. Perhaps her often denying that what I believed really happened was paradoxically a strong contributing factor – as though I knew her negation came from a truth too terrible to know. (Freud, 1925).

Another contributing factor to my believing her was her use of *body enactments* when words were too meagre to transmit an experience. One of the most dramatic examples of this was manifested in her strange way of dressing: for years I could make no sense of why Caroline insisted on wearing her sleeves rolled up to the elbows in all weather. The day that changed was after the enactment of the "burial in the garden" session where I came away traumatized at having taken on the role of the murderous mother. Seeing her dressed "normally", sleeves covering her arms appropriately from the next day on suddenly gave sense to her years of coming with exposed arms: *this was her way of letting me know that she had blood on her hands.* Once I knew and believed that, as she felt in my ability to enact this macabre Lady Macbeth scene, there was no longer a need for her body to shout this out.

An external concrete bodily sign, through the active witnessing by the therapist and the understanding of its meaning, was transformed into an internal mental element. There was no longer a need for this bizarre behaviour expressed in her outer form of dressing. Years earlier when she had enacted the Hanged Doll scene, she had spread red paint all over her bared arms, but then I thought, and perhaps so did she, that this represented "only" the blood from the abortion. The fact that it did not change her dress at the time is now understandable.

Another important source influencing my believing her was the clarity of descriptions in her writing. The Cult dream which had the convincing quality of a memory was yet another convincing source. The outside world also had some impact on my belief system. News items and books being written on DID as being a common phenomenon in victims of Satanic cults, reinforced my worst suspicions. And I knew that Caroline came from a family of devout Christian faith and in her country of origin many such cults exist until this day. I could not be oblivious to the impact of the real outside world on my consciousness. Nor did I think that I should be. The important task therapeutically was for me to be aware as much as possible of the origin of the sources of influence on my mind.

Making sense of the different personae

The second phase of this analysis was characterized by much drama, through enactments and the dramatic entry of seemingly "separate personae." Simultaneously with the enactments of her traumatic past, Caroline introduced her own written pages into therapy. However, this writing stopped immediately with the entrance of the personae into the therapy.

The personae were separate in that in what they represented was not her *memories about* her experiences. Rather, what they said or felt was experienced by her as separate identities, fragmented from her ego, but living in her body. This was a "not me/not mine" experience. As a therapist, experiencing this DID phenomena for the first time was a very dramatic event and quite mind blowing. DID is the ultimate personification of non-integration. In this book I have tried to describe how this felt in as close an experience-near way as language available to me permitted.

The dramatic entry of each persona was timed in a very meaningful moment psychologically. Understanding the timing helps understand Caroline. It also raises many questions about the defensive function of the mind and brain in protecting the traumatized person from total fragmentation.

***

For the sake of clarity, the adult Caroline who came to therapy I will at times call here the Adult Caroline.

The little girl persona, Violet, arrived when I insisted Caroline stop her obsessive use of other people's written texts as a means of looking for her past. Violet appeared and started *telling* her past from the voice and time regression of a little girl. We first called her Little Girl Caroline so that I could tell Adult Caroline about "her". Dramatization of events implying incest, prostitution and eventually "the revealing" of hangings in cult rituals had the impact of convincing me about the reality of her experiences. By giving her a name, Caroline was, in fact, accepting, through my mediating function, that Violet was a representative of *her own* childhood experiences, even though she herself did not remember them. Caroline had put this clearly in her words even before Violet had arrived. It was when relating, in her writing, to the book *Me & Emma*: "…Cathy externalized Emma so that she became an 'outside reality' as it were. That way she could 'know' what she didn't know."

This is a very complex state of mental affairs yet in need of deeper understanding and conceptualization.

But to continue with the narrative: at a specific moment, when the Adult Caroline realized that her mother was involved and that she, Caroline, really *knew* this to be true, the persecutor male persona arrived.

"*His*" function was quite complex and multifaceted. The following are some of my understandings:

His appearance represented just how violent, frightening and seductive Caroline experienced her father. The little girl had experienced him as the "unfaithful lover" who chose to protect his wife rather than his daughter. This created great confusion and guilt as to who was the "other woman", who the transgressor and who the victim. Underlying these painful questions was the unspoken question about her mother's identity. By becoming the ruthless aggressor who made Violet–Caroline stop revealing more about her past no more could be know about her mother. This had a life-saving function for Caroline.**I do not know what I do not know**. I cannot know what horrific events Caroline did not reveal to us that would earn the description of being inhuman. But I believe it was for her own good that no more atrocities were revealed. Psychoanalysis has learnt much from Sophocles' tragic drama of *Oedipus*: One of the lessons is that to know all the unbearable truth can end in psychosis (as expressed in Oedipus's physical dismembering of his own body) or suicide (Jacosta). Caroline's taking action on her body by the act of sterilization many years earlier had been a psychotic episode. I believe if we had not ended the analysis when we did, at her insistence, suicide might have been the result.

Paradoxically, the dangerous father-persona was also the one who "protected" her from knowing the unbearable. In her childhood her father, being the desired and desiring object enabled a partial separation from the enveloping symbiotic merger with an engulfing mother. But this father failed in his protective function (Bollas, 1987) and caused great psychological damage by subjugating his daughter to an incestuous relationship where she was left psychologically orphaned – a foundling. To avoid the feeling of absolute desolation and emptiness on leaving home after the abortion, Caroline created her unique solution. As she wrote, "...took her father with her – inside her." In this way she was left at least with *something*. In her words: "Something (some-thing) is at least better than nothing (no-thing.)"

Anne Alvarez (1992, 152–153), from her extensive experience and understanding of traumatized children writes:

> ...many of the chronically sexually abused children arrive in therapists' hands long after the event. Their condition may require rather different kind of treatment ... I am suggesting almost a theory of forgetting, as opposed to a theory of remembering, although I am aware that this is a gross and indeed false over-simplification.

In adults suffering such severe early traumatization, often enactments are as far as the trauma can be experienced. Winnicott, also implies that there can be a danger to remembering. In his article "The Psychology of Madness" (1965a), he advocates on the one hand that:

> ... madness that has to be remembered can only be remembered in the reliving of it ... the aim of the patient is to reach the madness i.e. to be mad in the analytic setting, the nearest the patient can ever do to remembering.
>
> (p. 125)

Yet, on the other hand, he speaks of danger: "...the anxiety at this level is unthinkable. It's intensity ... beyond description and new defences are organized immediately so that in fact madness was not experienced. Yet on the other hand madness was potentially a fact" (p. 127).

As seen, Caroline was to end therapy without integration of the violent part into her identity. It was maintained as a "not me" part living inside her. And in her experience, "he" really lived inside her. This explained a lot of her silence that baffled me for years. From her inside he could *hear* her, yet not *see* her. That is why she could only affirm something by a visual head nod, without *saying* anything aloud. In a way, this can be seen as representing the continuation of her experience of the way her father was with her: physically penetrating her but never *seeing* her needs as a separate person: as a daughter. As she so brilliantly described in her writing – this word was lacking in her vocabulary.

***

On the importance of writing

Although Caroline's outward behaviour *in my presence* did not change over all the years, a most dramatic internal development and growth was evidenced. She functioned well in outside reality (work and her relationship with Anne) but the most dramatic development was evidenced in Caroline's writing capacity. From her psychotic poetry of the first years, Caroline left therapy as a lucid, coherent writer capable of contributing to any psychology textbook on the topic of the impact of early childhood incest and terror on the mind and the person of a young child.

Although I never met this writer Caroline, in person, I felt I knew her well. She also knew me well because she wrote about us in her pages. In fact, she often guided me in her writings about how to assist her in the analysis. There in the writing, she could tell me all the things she could not speak to me about when we met. Without her written input I would never have known that the therapy was helping her. She, in fact, quite often was my co-therapist. We were a team. She was the Caroline that we both admired and liked. This writing-self was not the same self that curled up under my table in the clinic. Could "the writer" be seen as a partially autonomous self whose seeds were awakened in that very bright Little Girl Caroline who at an early age needed to be very alert to survive? Long before she came to therapy, as an adolescent she diligently copied into a diary from books she read pieces that were meaningful to her. Books seemed to function as a protective shell – providing an outer cover while enabling intellectual nourishment on the inside. Her curiosity and hunger to understand herself and her chaotic experiences led her to a ceaseless search in books of all fields. Once she felt some safety in my presence she presented me with texts of immense value. The development of this autonomous self went through developmental stages – first a more passive searching (devouring of books in hunger to find meaning) then through more active ambivalent expression (as expressed in her early writings using my name). Then, with the continued nurturance in the therapeutic environment she was able to identify with her psychoanalyst–mother and produce her own deep psychological observations. An observing ego was evolving.

Most importantly, I believe that her writing developed because she now had a *someone* to write to and, of special importance – a someone that believed her. A someone that validated her experiences and allowed for the development of a sense of feeling real. Knowing she was no longer alone in the world and that I was committed, interested and curious reinforced her belief that there was someone who wanted her to live. In her words – I took her seriously. She was not my "plaything".

With the evolution of the capacity to write she was able to put this experience into (written) words:

~It [the writing] seems to be helping Caroline to make sense of the chaos of her life ... the pages also seem to form a bridge for communication between "her world" and "the world".~

And with time there emerged a hope that I would be able to write a book about her saying, in a way that touched my heart: "If you can ... write about her ... it won't be so lonely."

With time she was able to elucidate her wish for me to write her story. Shortly after her mother's death she wrote:

~A lot of the original problem in my case arose from the fact that there was no one in my childhood to act as a "mediator". Both Mum and Dad had a vested interest in making sure things weren't open, logical or honest. The whole incest situation was, in that respect, designed to create confusion – to make sure that things weren't clear or understandable.

Therapy can function as a replacement for the lack of a "good enough mothering" in childhood. What we've been doing all along is trying to make sense of things – not just of what happened but of helping me know how to know. More specifically with regard to the writing, Tova may be able to help me mediate my experiences – which are so difficult to convey because communication is a problem in and of itself – through explaining her perspective on therapy. Her language/thought will be familiar and intelligible to ordinary readers – and hopefully help explain what is incoherent to most people.~

And on another occasion:

~Her (Tova's) writing is a way of confirming my experiences: someone understanding them sufficiently to be able to explain them; be sufficiently invested to want to try and make sense of them to others, because she feels that they're (I am?) sufficiently important. Writing in this sense is a way of feeling more normal, because even if I'm never actually going to get there, if other people can understand the experiences I've come some way to being understood. And if I can be understood, I can't be so not-normal as to be totally unintelligible.~

The end of writing

And then, seemingly suddenly, the writing stopped and was substituted by the personae. These, in contrast to the writer, were a "not me" manifestation. With her growing ego strengths Caroline realized that her writing meant that she knew that what she wrote about was real. And as we entered the realm of revealing the atrocities of the past, she could no longer allow herself to know in any direct way (see her understanding of Freud's "The Uncanny"). To stop writing was to prevent integration. And the atrocities presented to my eyes through the enactments of the personae were documented only by myself, in *my* notebook only. In this way she could maintain the Not Knowing state, or, as she put it so aptly into the language of transitional phenomena just before leaving therapy: "It's not that I think we've been making things up. It's just that *I don't know* if we have."

However, her last request was that I write this book. It seems, having been a witness to her life, she wanted the outside to know through my mediation. The following is the reason she gave when she first thought of this idea, at the time still "hiding" in my voice:

> ~… I feel that the writing is important because it is creative … We agreed that the writing together could perhaps serve as a way of breaking this pattern of "incestuousness" as well as function as a way of creating something good, not something to be ashamed of or hidden away in secret. If there had to be an abortion … then to "compensate", the writing could possibly produce a live "child" in the form of a "book". "Creative" in this sense also means "creating": the writing enables Caroline to find a way of expressing her real self, which means that it has a place to "be" and to "become".~

***

After our 26-year journey together much had changed in Caroline, yet integration had not occurred. The split between the still seemingly petrified Caroline I met in the clinic and the bright, flowing creative writer was maintained in some form to the end. After 26 years Caroline left analysis neither needing nor wanting to resolve this. I tend to believe that her inability to feel free in my presence was evidence that, at least in her case, the long-term exposure to the trauma of terror within her relationship with her primary caretakers left her scarred to the extent that I was to remain always a trigger and a reminder of that unbearable emotional suffering. I think the traumatization was neurologically embedded in her.

With that in mind I like to think that Caroline's freedom to walk away from therapy in the way she did, in spite of my wanting her to stay a little longer, was her act of freedom as well as an expression of what in the Book of Genesis is so strongly advised to Lot's wife when leaving Sodom and Gomorrah[2]: *not* to look back lest she become a pillar of salt. The Caroline who had come to therapy as "a stone" feeling no pain, left knowing she was capable of feeling human anguish and with this experiencial knowledge move froward into the living of her life.

***

An afternote

I have not seen Caroline since that last meeting. However, we have had some communication by email. I know she has gone on with her life. When I let her know the book was ready for publication and needed her written consent for it, she immediately gave it. When I asked her if she would like to meet before I sent it to the publisher she replied in her concise way: "No, but thank you for the offer, the update and – for doing it."

Her response came as a relief to me. I was not at all sure that to read what we had uncovered would be for her benefit. I understood her response as a confirmation that **she needed to leave her past behind with me and not look back.** Yet, it was of great significance for her that I had remembered her and made a record of her life. I also know from outside sources that today, five years later, she is actively engaged in life. Her psychiatrist, whom she meets annually, speaks of her as a changed person – being warm, easy to converse with and even having a delicate sense of humour.

Notes

1 Neville Symington.
2 Genesis XIX 26.

Bibliography

Alvarez, A. (1992). Child sexual abuse: the need to remember and the need to forget. In: *Live Company: Psychoanalytic Psychotherapy with Autistic, Borderline, Deprived and Abused Children*. London: Routledge.
Amir, D. (2010). The split between voice and meaning: the dual function of psychotic syntax. *International Forum of Psychoanalysis*, 19: 34–42.
Balint, M. (1968). *The Basic Fault: The Therapeutic Aspects of Regression*. London: Tavistock.
Bion, W. R. (1956). Development of schizophrenic thought. *International Journal of Psychoanalysis*, 37: 4–5.
Bion, W. R. (1957). Differentiation of the psychotic from the non-psychotic personalities. *International Journal of Psycho-Analysis*, 38: 266–275.
Bion, W. R. (1959). Attacks on linking. *International Journal of Psycho-Analysis*, 40 (5–6): 344–346.
Bion, W. R. (1962a). A theory of thinking. In: W. R. Bion (1967) *Second Thoughts: Selected Papers on Psychoanalysis*. London: Heinman.
Bion, W. R. (1962b). *Learning from Experience*. London: Marsesfield.
Bion, W. R. (1970). *Attention and Interpretation*. London: Tavistock.
Bion, W. R. (1976). Evidence. In: W.R. Bion (1987) *Clinical Seminars and Other Works*. London: Karnac.
Bion, W. R. (1991). *A Memoir of the Future*. London: Karnac.
Bollas, C. (1987). *The Shadow of the Object: Psychoanalysis of the Unthought Known*. New York: Columbia Univ. Press.
Bollas, C. (1989). The trauma of incest. In *Forces of Destiny: Psychoanalysis and Human Idiom*. London: Free Association Press.
Brenman, E. (2006). *Recovery of the Lost Good Object*. London: Routledge.
Brenner, I. (2014). *Dark Matters – Exploring the Realm of Psychic Devastation*. London: Karnac.
Bromberg, P. M. (2003). One need not be a house to be haunted: on enactment, dissociation, and the dread of 'not-me' – a case study. *Psychoanalytic Dialogues*, 13: 689–709.
Davies, J. M. & Fawley, M. G. (1994). *Treating the Adult Survivors of Childhood Sexual Abuse – A Psychoanalytic Perspective*. New York: Basic Books.
Davoine, F. (2007). The character of madness in the talking cure. *Psychoanalytic Dialogues*, 17: 627–638.

Eigen, M. (1993). *The Psychotic Core*. NJ: Jason Aronson. (Reprinted in 2004, 2005) London: Karnac.
Eigen, M. (2010). Madness and murder. In: *Eigen in Seoul (Volume 1)*. London: Karnac.
Eigen, M. (2016). Graduation speech given in September 2016 at NPAP: "Where are we going?"
Enriquez, M. (1990). The memory envelope and its holes. In: D. Anzier (Ed.), *Psychic Envelopes*. London: Karnac.
Felman, S. & Laub, D. (1992). *Testimony: Crisis of Witnessing in Literature, Psychoanalysis and History*. London: Taylor & Francis.
Ferenczi, S. (1932). Confusion of tongues between adults and the child. *International Journal of Psychoanalysis*, 30: 225.
Fonagy, P. (1991). Thinking about thinking: some clinical and theoretical considerations in the treatment of a borderline patient. *International Journal of Psychoanalysis*, 72: 639–656.
Fonagy, P. (2002). Multiple voices versus meta-cognition. An attachment theory perspective. In: V. Sinason (Ed.), *Attachment, Trauma and Multiplicity: Working with DID*. New York: Routledge.
Freud, S. (1914). Remembering, repeating and working through (further recommendations on the technique of psycho-analysis II), *S.E.* 12. London: Hogarth.
Freud, S. (1917). Fixation to trauma – the unconscious. In *Introductory Lectures on Psychoanalysis. Volume 1. S.E.* 15. London: Hogarth.
Freud, S. (1919). The "Uncanny". *S.E.* 17: 217–256. London: Hogarth.
Freud, S. (1920). Beyond the Pleasure Principle. *S.E.* 18: 1–64. London: Hogarth.
Freud, S. (1925). Negation. *S.E.* 19: 235–239. London: Hogarth.
Freud, S. (1937). Constructions in analysis. *S.E.* 23: 255–269.
Ghent, E. (1990). Masochism, submission, surrender: masochism as a perversion of surrender. *Contemporary Psychoanalysis*, 26: 108–136.
Green, A. (1986). The dead mother. In: *On Private Madness*. London: Hogarth.
Gurevich, H. (2008). The language of absence. *International Journal of Psychoanalysis*, 89: 561–578.
Herman, J. (1992). *Trauma and Recovery*. New York: Basic Books.
Joseph, B. (1985). Transference: the total situation. *International Journal of Psycho-Analysis*, 66: 447–454.
Khan, M. (1963). The concept of cumulative trauma. *Psychoanalytic Study of the Child*, 18: 286–306.
Khan, M. (1989). None can speak her/his folly. In: *Hidden Selves*. London: Maresfield Library.
Little, M. (1958). On delusional transference (transference psychosis). *International Journal of Psychoanalysis*, 39: 134–138.
Laub, D. (1992). An event without a witness: truth, testimony and survival. In: S. Felman & D. Laub (Eds.). *Testimony: Crisis of Witnessing in Literature, Psychoanalysis and History*. London: Routledge.
Levin, P. A. (1997). *Waking the Tiger. Healing Trauma*. Berkeley, CA: North Atlantic Books.
McCarthy, C. (2005). *No Country for Old Men*. Vintage.
McDougall, J. (1974). The psychosoma and the psychoanalytic process. *International Review of Psychoanalysis*, 1: 437–459.

Molon, P. (2002). Dark dimensions of multiple personality. In: V. Sinason (Ed.), (2002). *Attachment, Trauma and Multiplicity. Working with Dissociative Identity Disorder*. New York: Routledge.
Morrison, T. (1990). *The Bluest Eye*. Picador
Ogden, T. H. (1995). Analysing forms of aliveness and deadness of the transference-countertransference. *International Journal of Psycho-Analysis*, 76: 695–709.
Ogden, T. H. (2004a). On holding and containing, being and dreaming. *International Journal of Psycho-Analysis*, 85: 1349–1364.
Ogden, T. H. (2004b). The analytic third: implication for psychoanalytic theory and technique. *Psychoanalytic Quarterly*, 73: 167–195.
Ogden, T. H. (2016). Destruction reconceived: on Winnicott's "the use of an object and relating through identifications". *International Journal of Psycho-Analysis*, 97: 1243–1262.
Phillips, A. (1988). *Winnicott*. Cambridge: Harvard University Press.
Rosenfeld, H. (1987). *Impasse and Interpretation*. London: Routledge.
Sartre, J. P. (1952). The melodious child in me long before the ax chops off my head. In: *St Genet: Actor and Martyr*. Paris: Libraire Gallimard.
Searles, H. F. (1959). The effort to drive the other person crazy – an element in the aetiology and psychotherapy of schizophrenia. In: H. F. Searles (Ed.), *Collected Papers on Schizophrenia and Related Subjects*. New York: International University Press, 1965.
Segal, H. (1957) Notes on symbol formation. In: H. Segal (Ed.), *The Work of Hanna Segal*, Northvale, NJ: Jason Aronson, 1981.
Seligman, Z. & Z. Solomon (Eds.) (2004). *Critical and Clinical Perspectives on Incest*. Tel Aviv: Hakibbutz Hameuchad (in Hebrew).
Shengold, L. L. (2000). Soul murder reconsidered: did it really happen? *Canadian Journal of Psychoanalysis*, 8(1): 1–18.
Sinason, V. (2002). *Attachment, Trauma and Multiplicity. Working with Dissociative Identity Disorder*. New York: Routledge.
Steele, H. (2002). Multiplicity revealed in the adult attachment interview: when integration and coherence means death. In: V. Sinason (Ed.), *Attachment, Trauma and Multiplicity. Working with Dissociative Identity Disorder*. New York: Routledge.
Stern, D. N. (1985). *The Interpersonal World of the Infant*. New York: Basic Books Inc.
Stern, D. N., Sander, L. W., Nahum, J. P., Harrison, A. M., Lyons-Ruth, K., Morgan, A. C., Bruschweilerstern, N. & Tronick, E. Z. (1998). Non-interpretive mechanisms in psychoanalytic psychotherapy. *International Journal of Psychoanalysis*, 79: 903–921.
Symington, N. (1983). The analyst's act of freedom as an agent of therapeutic change. *International Journal of Psychoanalysis*, 10: 288–290.
Symington, N. (2007). *Becoming a Person through Psychoanalysis*. London: Karnac.
Symington, N. (2002). *A Pattern of Madness*. London: Karnac.
Tustin, F. (1980). Autistic objects. *Int. Review of Psycho-Analysis*, 7: 27–39.
Van der Hart, O., Nijenhuis, E., & Steele, K. (2006). *The Haunted Self. Structural Dissociation and the Treatment of Chronic Traumatization*. New York: W. W. Norton.
Wiesel, E. (1958). *Night* (translated 2006). New York: Hill and Wang.

Winnicott, D. W. (1949). Mind and its relation to the psycho-soma. In: D. W. Winnicott (1958), *Collected Papers: Through Pediatrics to Psycho-Analysis*. London: Tavistock.
Winnicott, D. W. (1951). Transitional objects and transitional phenomena. In: D. W. Winnicott (1958), *Collected Papers: Through Pediatrics to Psycho-Analysis*. London: Tavistock.
Winnicott, D. W. (1952). Psychosis and child care. In: D. W. Winnicott, *Collected Papers: Through Pediatrics to Psycho-Analysis*. London: Tavistock, 1958.
Winnicott, D. W. (1955). Clinical varieties of transference. In: D. W. Winnicott, *Collected Papers: Through Pediatrics to Psycho-Analysis*. London: Tavistock, 1958.
Winnicott, D. W. (1956). Primary maternal preoccupation. In: D. W. Winnicott, *Collected Papers: Through Pediatrics to Psycho-Analysis*. London: Tavistock, 1958.
Winnicott, D. W. (1960s). A note on the mother-foetus relationship. In: D. W. Winnicott, *Psychoanalytic Explorations*. Edited by: Winnicott, C., Shepherd, R., & Davis, M.London: Karnac, 1989.
Winnicott, D. W. (1960a). Ego distortion in terms of true and false self. In: D. W. Winnicott, *The Maturational Process and the Facilitating Environment*. London: Karnac, 1965.
Winnicott, D. W. (1963a). Fear of breakdown. In: D. W. Winnicott, *Psychoanalytic Explorations*. Edited by: Winnicott, C., Shepherd, R., & Davis, M.London: Karnac, 1989.
Winnicott, D. W. (1963b). On communicating and not communicating leading to a study of certain opposites. In D. W. Winnicott, *The Maturational Processes and the Facilitating Environment*. London: Karnac, 1965.
Winnicott, D. W. (1965a). The psychology of madness: a contribution from psychoanalysis. In: D. W. Winnicott, *Psychoanalytic Exploration*. Edited by: Winnicott, C., Shepherd, R., & Davis, M.London: Karnac, 1989.
Winnicott, D. W. (1965b). The concept of trauma in relation to the development of the individual within the family. In: D. W. Winnicott, *Psychoanalytic Explorations*. Edited by: Winnicott, C., Shepherd, R., & Davis, M.London: Karnac, 1989.
Winnicott, D. W. (1971). *Playing and Reality*. London: Tavistock.
Winnicott, D. W. (1977). *The Piggle. An Account of the Psychoanalytic Treatment of a Little Girl*. New York: Penguin.

Index

abortion: countertransference in sterilization 51; enacted 38–9; identification with 41, 42, 43; immobility 48, 59–60; interpretations of 63–4, 66, 93, 102; reality of 54–5; of therapy 105, 106, 107
absence, sense of 115–16
acting out *see* enactment
Alice in Wonderland 199–200, 201–2
Alvarez, A. 241
anger: danger of 113; and decision making 113–14, 115; enactment of rejection in transference 133–5; and real person 135–6; and safety 145
annihilation, fear of 28–9
anorexia and incest 102–3
Asperger's syndrome 67–8, 83–4, 116
Auden, W. H.: "Hymn to St Cecilia" 181–2

badness, feeling of 11, 13, 14, 33, 37, 63; taking out 34, 41–2, 46–7
Barry, S.: *A Long Long Way* 59–60
beginning therapy: appearance 7; background 1–4, 8–11; choosing therapy as choosing life 12–13; decision 8; keeping secrets 11–12; movement/non-movement 17–18; speech and silences 15–17; therapeutic relationship 13–14
believing 2–3, 8, 29–30, 40, 87–8, 237–9
bike accidents 184, 189–90, 213, 217, 221; and blackouts 143, 194, 196, 198, 207, 208
Bion, W. 15, 22, 26, 30, 59, 64, 98, 107, 204, 235, 238
Blake, W.: "The Sick Rose" 56
Bloch, D.: *So the Witch Won't Eat Me* 13, 66

body enactments 238–9
body language 41, 43, 128; as alternative communication 23; cough 230–1; rocking 169–71; *see also* immobility
boss (Mr D. and work contract) 113–14, 114, 116, 119

certainty, sense of 109–12
childhood sexual abuse *see* incest
closed circuits 81–2, 194–5
"cockroach", fear of 222
contamination, fear of 33, 89, 90
conviction, sense of 39, 99–100, 104–5
cough 147, 230–1
countertransference 15, 16–17, 39–40, 152–3, 192–3; and believing 237–8; in sterilization 49–51
cruelty, unbearable guilt from 192–3
cult dream 190–1, 239

Damasio, A.: *Descartes' Error* 114–15
Davies, J. M. and Fawley, M. G. 160–1, 166–7, 171–2
decisions: feelings allow for 113–15; to start therapy 8
desire to live, danger in 105–6
dictionary 24–6, 33, 47; father 75–6; hiding 82; object 33; table 47
dissociation 57–9, 186; in dreams 161–4; *in vivo* 116–17; and incest 42–3, 117–18; inner experience 211–12; rocking 169–71
Dissociative Identity Disorder (DID) 2, 3, 62–3, 150, 151, 162; complexities of 221; end of therapy and contact 244–5; growing awareness of 188–9; importance and end of writing 242–4; making sense of different personae 239–41; safe place and belief 235–9

doll: assault 34–6; as baby 41, 42, 46; burial 53–4, 176–7; enacting abortion 38–9; enactment of four-letter word 34, 52–3, 168, 192; hanged 51–2, 56, 75, 161, 162, 176, 177–8, 239; response to separation 43–4, 45
Donoghue, E.: *Room* 194, 195, 196, 198
dreams/nightmares: of animal attack 171; of being called four-letter word 33, 34, 35; as blank slate 28; cult 190–1, 239; dissociation in 161–4; hospital 120–3; of pimps and prostitution 141–2; therapist's 36, 127–8

Eigen, M. 64, 130, 235
emptiness, origins of 197–9
enactments: as alternative communication 23, 241; body 238–9; decoding 103–4; instead of memory 157–74; *Oedipus Rex* (Sophocles) 102; of rejection in transference 133–5; therapist's perspective 154, 173–4; in unsafe place 182–4; of violence 164–8; *see also* doll
experience and re-experience 43
eye test and therapy, comparison 109–12

faith in therapy 130
false memories 30
father 9–10, 45, 69, 72; boss as 113–14, 119; death of 131–8, 139–41; end of life 124; holding onto 73–5; hospital dream 122, 124, 229; as Minister 214–18, 219–20, 223–4, 226–7, 229, 232–4, 240–1; as pimp 141; splitting 136; therapist as 35, 36–7, 70, 77; use of term 75–6; *see also* incest/childhood sexual abuse
Flock, E.: *Me & Emma* 57–9, 240
foetal position 18, 34, 51, 55, 64, 144
Fonagy, P. 237
formlessness and void (*tohu vevohu*) 95–6, 98, 141
"freeze" state 17, 70, 105, 112, 128, 236
Freud, S. 219, 238; "The Uncanny" 128–9, 243
friends/colleagues 8, 10–11, 29, 55, 112, 203, 206, 224

Gaslight (Hitchcock) 117
Genesis, Book of 95, 96, 113, 244
Genet, J. 62, 65, 80–1, 129

gifts 83–4, 89–90
guilt 80–3, 102, 179–80, 192–3, 225–6

Haddon, M.: *The Curious Incident of the Dog in the Night-Time* 23, 83, 175–6
hanged doll 51–2, 56, 75, 161, 162, 176, 239
hanging enactment 177–8, 185–7
head banging incidents 165–6, 172–3
Herman, J.: *Trauma and Recovery* 38, 175, 217, 222
"hiding" 18, 19–20, 24, 25, 26; dictionary term 82; from neighbour 116–17
Hitchcock, A.: *Gaslight* 117
Holocaust 2–3, 19, 38, 177–8, 192–3, 238
honesty 12, 13–14, 22, 44
hope 106–7, 123
"Humpty Dumpty" metaphor 40
hypnosis 30–2
hysterectomy 34, 41–2

immobility 36–7; as dead aborted baby 48, 59–60; foetal position 18, 34, 51, 55, 64, 144; "freeze" state 17, 70, 105, 112, 128, 236; mother's death wish 48; movement and 17–18, 120, 121
incest/childhood sexual abuse: and anorexia 102–3; decoding nonverbal signals 103–4; and dissociation 42–3; fictional account 57–9; honesty in therapeutic relationship 44; importance of being believed 40, 87–8; and kindness 100–1; leaves no place to be 90–2; omnipotence fantasy 14; poetry 20–2; and psychosis 106–7; reality of 86–7; remembering vs forgetting 241; resistance to knowing 113–14, 117–18; search for proof of 70–1; sense of responsibility for 12, 102; siblings and parental "impingement" 68–9; as sort of marriage 92–5; space for the soul 91; supressed memory and feelings 108–18; therapist's reflection on 96–7; *tohu vevohu* 95–6, 98; wise owl gift 89–90; written material on 91–5; *see also* father; mother
inhuman, threat of becoming 125–7
insight 138
internal world: change in 196; experience of dissociation 211–12; and outer

reality 119–21; separating inside from outside 19–32, 196–7
Israel 9–10, 12, 91, 145

kindness and incest 100–1

Laing, R. D.: *Self and Others* 65
language: alternative communication 23–4; "playing among the ruined languages" 181–2; speech and silences 15–17, 187–8; therapist's 47, 184; violence destroys 191–2
Laub, D. 2–3
Lister, E. 217
Little Girl Caroline (LGC) 145–9, 150, 151–2, 157–61, 179, 180; and Adult Caroline 162–4, 168–9; dissociation in dreams 161–2; enactments of violence 164–9; *see also* Violet
lived experience 40
loneliness 132–3, 136–8
love, starved for 37

masturbation and self-injury enactments 164–7
memory 23, 29, 43; and deletion 79; enactments instead of 157–74; and hypnosis 30–2; and insight 138; "physical memories" 86, 87; and reality 79–88; remembering vs forgetting 241; and sense of identity 69–70; suppressed 108–18; therapist's amnesia 52–3
Menninger, K. 14
Meredith, G. 235
Minister 215–18, 219–20, 223–4, 226–7, 229, 232–4, 240–1
Morley, J. D.: *The Case of Thomas N.* 81, 82–3, 142–3
Morrison, T.: *The Bluest Eye* 90–1
mother 9–10, 58, 66; abuse by 50; cough 230–2; death of 55–7, 73, 104–5, 119, 132, 243; death wish 48; fear of 104–5, 132; involvement in violence and burial 178–9, 180–1, 203–8, 213; transference 198–9, 206–8, 238–9
movement *see* immobility

neonatal unit, donation to 55–6
neurological diagnosis, advantages of 116
nightmares *see* dreams
No Country for Old Men 232–3

non-integration 70–1
non-verbal communication *see* body language; enactments

object constancy 77
Oedipus Rex (Sophocles) 102
omnipotence fantasy 14, 36
oral sex 85–6
"other" personae: as alternative communication 23; making sense of 239–41; *see also* Little Girl Caroline (LGC); Minister; Violet

paper clip 17, 19, 177, 193
photographs 55, 56, 164, 176, 177, 178; witnessing through 51, 52, 53
"physical memories" 86, 87
pimps and prostitution dream 141–2
pleasure, different meanings of 109–12
poetry 20–2
Potok, C.: *The Promise* 22, 122–3, 234
pregnancy to birth 219–34
Projective Identification 26, 30, 39–40
psychosis: distortion of reality 99; and incest 106–7

real person: feeling anger as 135–6; vs imaginary person 57–9
real space, therapy as 54–5
reality: of abuse 86–7; development of emotional thinking and sense of 40–3; and memory 79–88; possible perception and loss 98–100
recovery, definition of 1
religion 9, 11, 12, 239; space for the soul 91
responsibility: for abuse 12, 102; taking 112, 186, 191
rocking 169–71

Sachs, O.: *The Last Hippie* 23
safe place, therapy as 26–7, 32, 40–3, 47, 129, 188
safety and anger 145
Sartre, J. P. 62, 65, 80–1
secrets, keeping 11–12
self: dead 153–4; developing sense of 200–1
self-injury enactments, masturbation and 164–7
Seligman, Z. and Solomon, Z. 150–1, 153, 157

separating inside from outside 19–32, 196–7
Shakespeare, W.: *Hamlet* 1, 2, 3, 185, 235
Shengold, L. L. 22, 101, 102
silence 84–5, 124–30; hospital dream 120, 122–3, 125, 129; in hypnosis 31–2; poem 181–2; speech and 15–17, 187–8; and staring 27–8, 89–90, 112, 113
Sinason, V. 221, 223
Sophocles: *Oedipus Rex* 102
"soul murder" 22, 97
speech and silences 15–17, 187–8
splitting 136, 212–13
stalking 36, 127–8
sterilization 46–7, 49–51
Stern, D. N. 236
suicidal thoughts 60, 125; and medication 178–80
supervision 14, 64, 221, 235, 236–7

taping sessions 82–3
therapeutic relationship: history of 188; honesty 12, 13–14, 22, 44; trust 27, 84, 89, 109, 129–30, 188, 237–8
therapist: amnesia 52–3; borrowed voice 25–6, 67–70, 71; as father 35, 36–7, 70, 77; meeting with parents 9–10; as mother 198–9, 206–8, 238–9; nightmares 36, 127–8; reflection on incest 96–7; supervision 14, 64, 221, 235, 236–7; tasks in enactments 173–4; vacation 28–9, 43–5; *see also* countertransference; transference
tohu vevohu state 95–6, 98, 141
touch and contamination fear 33
transference 11, 27, 70, 103–4, 219, 224; enactment of rejection in 133–5; mother role 198–9, 206–8, 238–9;

sterilization 47; traumatic 217, 222; *see also* countertransference
transitional objects 108–9
transitional space 41, 122, 123, 181–2, 204–5, 236
trust: in hypnosis 31; in therapeutic relationship 27, 84, 89, 109, 129–30, 188, 237–8
"The Uncanny" (Freud) 128–9, 243

undressing 171–3, 207–8

violence 139, 140, 141; destroys language 191–2; enactments of 164–8; mother's involvement in 178–9, 180–1, 203–8, 213; prelude to 142–5
Violet 181–4, 186, 188–9, 200, 207, 208, 222–3, 233, 240; and Minister 214–18, 220, 223–4, 226–7, 229

Wiesel, E: *Night* 76
Williams, D.: *Somebody Somewhere* 67–8
Winnicott, D. W. 27, 29, 40, 63–4, 69, 71, 79, 84, 87, 99, 190; "Fear of Breakdown" 42–3, 104; *The Piggle* 63; *Playing and Reality* 79, 108–9; "primary maternal preoccupation" 236; "Psychology of Madness" 241
Winston, R. 120
witnessing 87, 150–4, 239; through photographs 51, 52, 53
words for unspeakable trauma 37–8
writing 62–78; as alternative communication 23; end of 243–4; importance of 153–4, 242–3; on incest 91–5; therapist's voice 25–6, 67–9, 69–70, 71; "Writing Caroline" 59, 136–7, 138, 187, 195, 231–2

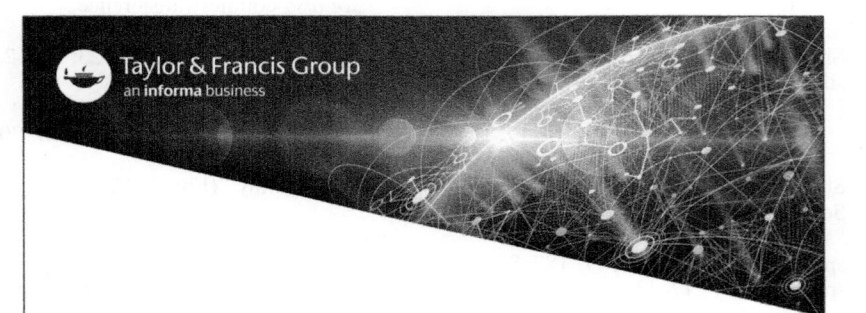

Taylor & Francis eBooks

www.taylorfrancis.com

A single destination for eBooks from Taylor & Francis with increased functionality and an improved user experience to meet the needs of our customers.

90,000+ eBooks of award-winning academic content in Humanities, Social Science, Science, Technology, Engineering, and Medical written by a global network of editors and authors.

TAYLOR & FRANCIS EBOOKS OFFERS:

- A streamlined experience for our library customers
- A single point of discovery for all of our eBook content
- Improved search and discovery of content at both book and chapter level

REQUEST A FREE TRIAL
support@taylorfrancis.com